OLD TESTAMENT MESSAGE

A Biblical-Theological Commentary

Carroll Stuhlmueller, C.P. and Martin McNamara, M.S.C.

EDITORS

Old Testament Message, Volume 22

PSALMS 2

(Psalms 73-150)

Carroll Stuhlmueller, C.P.

Michael Glazier, Inc.
Wilmington, Delaware

First published in 1983 by MICHAEL GLAZIER, INC. 1723 Delaware Avenue, Wilmington, Delaware 19806
Distributed outside U.S., Canada & Philippines by: GILL & MACMILLAN, LTD., Goldenbridge, Inchicore, Dublin 8 Ireland

Library of Congress Catalog Card Number: 82-83728
International Standard Book Number
   Old Testament Message series: 0-89453-235-9
   PSALMS 2
      0-89453-257-X (Michael Glazier, Inc.)
      7171-1185-6 (Gill & MacMillan, Ltd.)

Cover design by Lillian Brulc

Typography by Susan Pickett
Cartography by Lucille Dragovan
Printed in the United States of America

CONTENTS

Editors' Preface

Old Testament Message brings into our life and religion today the ancient word of God to Israel. This word, according to the book of the prophet Isaiah, had soaked the earth like "rain and snow coming gently down from heaven" and had returned to God fruitfully in all forms of human life (Isa 55:10). The authors of this series remain true to this ancient Israelite heritage and draw us into the home, the temple and the marketplace of God's chosen people. Although they rely upon the tools of modern scholarship to uncover the distant places and culture of the biblical world, yet they also refocus these insights in a language clear and understandable for any interested reader today. They enable us, even if this be our first acquaintance with the Old Testament, to become sister and brother, or at least good neighbor, to our religious ancestors. In this way we begin to hear God's word ever more forcefully in our own times and across our world, within our prayer and worship, in our secular needs and perplexing problems.

Because life is complex and our world includes, at times in a single large city, vastly different styles of living, we have much to learn from the Israelite Scriptures. The Old Testament spans forty-six biblical books and almost nineteen hundred years of life. It extends through desert, agricultural and urban ways of human existence. The literary style embraces a world of literature and human emotions. Its history began with Moses and the birth-pangs of a new people, it came of age politically and economically under David and Solomon, it reeled under the fiery threats of prophets like Amos and Jeremiah. The people despaired and yet were re-created with new hope during the Babylonian exile. Later reconstruction in the homeland and then the trauma of apocalyptic movements prepared for the revelation of "the mystery hidden for ages in God who created all things" (Eph 3:9).

While the Old Testament telescopes twelve to nineteen hundred years of human existence within the small country of Israel, any single moment of time today witnesses to the reenactment of this entire history across the wide expanse of planet earth. Each verse of the Old Testament is being relived somewhere in our world today. We need, therefore, the *entire* Old Testament and all twenty-three volumes of this new set, in order to be totally a "Bible person" within today's widely diverse society.

The subtitle of this series—"A Biblical-Theological Commentary"—clarifies what these twenty-three volumes intend to do.

Their *purpose* is theological: to feel the pulse of God's word for its *religious* impact and direction.

Their *method* is biblical: to establish the scriptural word firmly within the life and culture of ancient Israel.

Their *style* is commentary: not to explain verse by verse but to follow a presentation of the message that is easily understandable to any serious reader, even if this person is untrained in ancient history and biblical languages.

Old Testament Message—like its predecessor, *New Testament Message*—is aimed at the entire English-speaking world and so is a collaborative effort of an international team. The twenty-one contributors are women and men drawn from North America, Ireland, Britain and Australia. They are scholars who have published in scientific journals, but they have been chosen equally as well for their proven ability to communicate on a popular level. This twenty-three book set comes from Roman Catholic writers, yet, like the Bible itself, it reaches beyond interpretations restricted to an individual church and so enables men and women rooted in biblical faith to unite and so to appreciate their own traditions more fully and more adequately.

Most of all, through the word of God, we seek the blessedness and joy of those
who walk in the law of the Lord!...
who seek God with their whole heart (Ps. 119:1-2).

Carroll Stuhlmueller, C.P.   *Martin McNamara, M.S.C.*

Method and Style of This Commentary

Each psalm is studied according to four stages of its presence in Israel and in the Christian community:

(I) According to the *origin* of the psalm in the socio-religious background of ancient Israel and the *absorption of later modifications* from the life and worship of Israel;

(II) According to the psalm's *literary form and structure*;

(III) According to *key words or phrases* and other important or difficult items within the psalm;

(IV) According to the *impact of the psalm today* in public worship, private devotion or social-moral questions.

Method Recommended for Using This Commentary

1st) Always read the text of the psalm before studying the commentary.

2nd) After reading Sections I & II of the commentary, re-read the text of the psalm in order to become more deeply appreciative of the word of God in the Bible and in the context of its origin.

3rd) After studying Section III of the commentary of each psalm, reread the psalm in the light of its key words and phrases. Also, check the biblical references cited, so as to see how the psalm and its key phrases are enriched by the larger patterns of biblical theology.

4th) After reflecting on Section IV and on the relevance of the psalm to our world today, it is crucial to see how the psalm applies to your own needs and inspirations. Then read the psalm carefully and prayerfully again.

BOOK III
(PSALMS 73-89)

Almost all the psalms in Book III are attributed to levitical groups: Pss 73-83 to Asaph (also Ps 50 in Book II); Pss 84-88 to Korah (also Pss 42-49 in Book II), with the exception of the single Psalm of David (Ps 86); the final Ps 89 is attributed to Ethan. Overlapping with Books II and III is the so-called "Elohistic Psalter," Pss 42-83 which generally avoid the divine name Yahweh and use the more general title for God, *Elohim*, perhaps for recitation outside the sanctuary, perhaps in foreign countries.

The Psalms of Asaph are difficult to describe: they can include such mystical insights as in Ps 73, violent images of a warrior God *shouting because of wine* (Ps 78:65), an extended allegory for Israel as that of the vine (Ps 80).

Psalm 73
A Psalm Of Asaph.

I

¹Truly God is good to the upright,
   to those who are pure in heart.
²But as for me, my feet had almost stumbled,
   my steps had well nigh slipped.

[3] For I was envious of the arrogant,
when I saw the prosperity of the wicked.

II
[4] For they have no pangs;
their bodies are sound and sleek.

III
[8] They scoff and speak with malice;
loftily they threaten oppression.
[9] They set their mouths against the heavens,
and their tongue struts through the earth.

IV
[13] All in vain have I kept my heart clean
and washed my hands in innocence.

[16] But when I thought how to understand this,
it seemed to me a wearisome task,
[17] until I went into the sanctuary of God;

V
[21] When my soul was embittered,
when I was pricked in heart,
[22] I was stupid and ignorant,
I was like a beast toward thee.
[23] Nevertheless I am continually with thee;
thou dost hold my right hand.
[24] Thou dost guide me with thy counsel,
and afterward thou wilt receive me to glory.

VI
[25] Whom have I in heaven but thee?
And there is nothing upon earth
that I desire besides thee.
[26] My flesh and my heart may fail,
but God is the strength of my heart
and my portion for ever.

[28] But for me it is good to be near God;
I have made the Lord God my refuge,
that I may tell of all thy works.

(I) As in Pss 37 and 49, the question of reward and punishment is discussed. Ps 37 resolutely holds a middle course, closely in accord with sapiential literature generally, that the virtuous are rewarded and the wicked are punished. A prophetic impact is also discernible (*cf.,* Jer 2; Ezek 18). Ps 49 manifests some disdain for material goods and therefore avoids the full impact of the question. Ps 73, however, faces the difficulties more openly and then perceives, at least with flashing insight, that nothing in heaven or upon earth can compare with God. Unusual for sapiential literature, Ps 73 steps hesitantly on the threshold of belief in personal immortality. It is led here more by personal, private piety than by any clear, doctrinal development. Ps 73 willingly admits life's injustices and puts the question squarely before God, as did other great leaders: Moses (Num 11:4); Habakkuk (Hab 1:5); or Jeremiah (Jer 12:1). Combining an unflinching faith (the psalm begins with the clear statement, *Truly God is good*) with total honesty (v. 3, *I was envious of the arrogant*), Ps 73 will slip beyond the borders of clear exposition and find its peace ultimately in mystical perceptions. The psalmist, although a member of temple singers (see Ps 50), speaks here as a private person, immediately in God's presence. Ps 73 seems too profoundly personal, even individualistic, to have been composed for temple worship, particularly that of the preexilic age.

(II) This sapiential psalm shows a simple enough structure:

vv. 1-3, Introduction of the two main themes: God's goodness and the problem of evil people who seem to survive unscathed;
vv. 4-7 and 8-12, two stanzas about the wicked;
vv. 13-17a, one stanza about the psalmist;
vv. 17b-20, one stanza about the wicked; vv. 21-24 and 25-28, two stanzas about the psalmist's desire for God.

(III) Vv. 1-3, Introduction. The psalm opens with a common enough refrain: *God is good* (Pss 106:1; 107:1; 118:1; 135:3; 136:1). Therefore, the psalmist is not doubting God nor the faith of Israel; this faith, however, did not seem clearly enough manifest across the lives of God's people. And so *I was envious of the arrogant* for the harmony and self-confidence that mark their lives; these qualities rightly belonged to the virtuous and sincere! *Prosperity* translates the Hebrew word *shalom*, an integral wholeness and right blending of life's ingredients.

Vv. 4-7, 8-12, the prosperity and scandal of the wicked. Their life flowed so smoothly that it must be the correct way! All the while, we suspect the genuineness of their peace and happiness, for they appear sleek, pampered, easily angered, sarcastic. V. 10 is caught in textual problems; perhaps, later scribes scrambled what had been blasphemously spoken by *their tongue* [*that*] *struts through the earth* (v. 9).

Vv. 13-17a, psalmist's puzzled reaction. To have *kept my heart clean* aligned the psalmist with the prophet Jeremiah in the first of his agonizing confessions (Jer 12:3) where the prophet experienced God's probing presence ever more deeply within his dark and questioning heart. The psalmist refers to sanctuary worship — the ritual of washing hands (Ps 26:6; Deut 21:6; Matt 27:24) and entering God's presence, such a stark contrast with God's absence elsewhere through the land.

Vv. 17b-20, a final stanza about the wicked who disappear quickly, caught in their own deceit.

Vv. 21-24, 25-28, the psalmist's reach towards God. By comparison with the wily and arrogant, the psalmist feels *stupid and ignorant*, yet the psalmist does not judge himself according to this norm. In a dramatic way, the grammar of v. 23 states clearly: "Yes, I am that one, continually with you," enjoying the favored place at the *right hand* (Ps 110:1), and like the levite in Ps 16, looking to God as "my strength and my portion for ever" (v. 26). In a moment of ecstatic vision, heaven and earth seem to melt away, *nothing . . . I desire besides thee*. This peaceful strength and exalted joy are not reached by comparisons but by the commitment of faith, *it is good to be near God* (v. 28). The final line, *tell of all thy works,* may have been adapted and added from Ps 9:15; it anticipates what God will achieve through this new intimate union with the psalmist. It also seems anticlimactic to speak about results after the psalmist has reached an exalted, really selfless and pure experience of God's presence. "Works" then are best understood as God's wondrous, redemptive deeds for the people Israel. Ps 73 takes its rightful place among those achievements.

(IV) As in the case of the confessions of the prophet Jeremiah (Jer 12:1-5; 15:10-31; etc.), God does not directly answer the questions but addresses the underlying faith of his servant. The questions are necessary, not so much for reaching an answer, but for purifying the motives of the prophet or psalmist. The psalmist does not arrive by steps and carefully formulated reasons, but suddenly and abruptly, as we see in the transition from vv. 21-22, *my soul was embittered . . . stupid and ignorant,* to vv. 23-26, "Yes, I am that one, continually with you." Faith is responsible for these leaps of love and intuition. With motivation stronger than what any reason can provide, we then confess: *for me it is good to be near God.* The full force of the psalmist's statement is realized in Paul's magnificent confession: "I am sure that neither death, nor life, nor angels, nor principalities, nor things present, nor things to come, nor powers, nor height, nor depth, nor anything else in all creation, will be able to separate us from the love of God in Christ Jesus our Lord" (Rom 8:38-39).

Psalm 74
A Maskil Of Asaph

I

¹O God, why dost thou cast us off for ever?
　Why does thy anger smoke against
　the sheep of thy pasture?
²Remember thy congregation, which
　thou hast gotten of old,
　which thou hast redeemed to be the

tribe of thy heritage!
Remember Mount Zion, where thou hast dwelt.

II

³Direct thy steps to the perpetual ruins;
the enemy has destroyed everything in the sanctuary!
⁴Thy foes have roared in the midst of thy holy place;
they set up their own signs for signs.
⁵At the upper entrance they hacked the wooden trellis
with axes.
⁶And then all its carved wood
they broke down with hatchets and hammers.
⁷They set thy sanctuary on fire;
to the ground they desecrated the
dwelling place of thy name.
⁸They said to themselves, "We will
utterly subdue them";
they burned all the meeting places
of God in the land.

III

⁹We do not see our signs;
there is no longer any prophet,
and there is none among us who knows how long.
¹⁰How long, O God, is the foe to scoff?
Is the enemy to revile thy name for ever?
¹¹Why dost thou hold back thy hand,
why dost thou keep thy right hand in thy bosom?

IV

¹²Yet God my King is from of old,
working salvation in the midst of the earth.
¹³Thou didst divide the sea by thy might;
thou didst break the heads of the dragons on the waters,
¹⁴Thou didst crush the heads of Leviathan,
thou didst give him as food for the
creatures of the wilderness.
¹⁵Thou didst cleave open springs and brooks;
thou didst dry up ever-flowing streams.

16Thine is the day, thine also the night;
    thou hast established the luminaries and the sun.
17Thou hast fixed all the bounds of the earth;
    thou hast made summer and winter.

V

18Remember this, O Lord, how the enemy scoffs,
    and an impious people reviles thy name.
19Do not deliver the soul of thy dove to the wild beasts;
    do not forget the life of thy poor for ever.

20Have regard for thy covenant;
    for the dark places of the land are
      full of the habitations of violence.
21Let not the downtrodden be put to shame;
    let the poor and needy praise thy name.

VI

22Arise, O God, plead thy cause;
    remember how the impious scoff at
      thee all the day!
23Do not forget the clamor of thy foes,
    the uproar of thy adversaries which
      goes up continually!

(I-II) A community lament over the destruction of the Jerusalem temple, Ps 74 is almost as significant for what it does not say as for what it says! Nothing is mentioned of Israel's sins that provoked the leveling of the temple and the Holy City; there are no prayers asking for forgiveness. The psalm is silent about exile, the other tragic side of Jerusalem's devastation. The immediacy of the shock, the hopelessness of any quick remedy, the harrowing memory of the final assault — all these factors within the psalm make us think of the people left behind in Palestine after the larger number had been dragged into Babylonian exile. The former still came to the ruined site of the temple for worship (*cf.*, Jer 41:4-5). Typical of the Asaph psalm, this one is vigorous and blunt, but shows little creativity; it repeats well-known phrases. Yet how can one be innovative amid tragic ruins?

The psalm can be read according to the following structure:

vv. 1-2,   Introductory lament;   vv. 12-17, Hymn to Yahweh
vv. 3-8,   Exposition of the   Creator;
            tragic events;   vv. 18-21, Prayer for help;
vv. 9-11,   Cry of anguish;   vv. 22-23, Conclusion.

(III) Vv. 1-2, Lament. The opening word, *Why?* has been heard in other laments: Pss 10:1; 22:1; 44:24; 79:10; etc. *Sheep of thy pasture:* the phrase implies helplessness, tenderness, special property: *cf.,* Ps 95:7, "For he is our God, and we are the people of his pasture, and the sheep of his hand." In v. 2, the word, redeem — *ga'al* — implies a close bond, usually of blood, an idea that continues in the phrase, *tribe of thy heritage:* Jer 10:16; 51:19. The opening lines seem to recall the initial great redemptive act of bringing Israel out of Egypt.

Vv. 3-8, the tragic events are vividly recalled. In v. 4, the enemy with a maddening roar breaks through the walls of the city and temple (Lam 2:7; Josh 6:5, 16, 20) and sets up military standards in the holy place; in vv. 5-6, they pillage and hack apart; in v. 7, out of hatred they burn everything to the ground (1 Kgs 25:9; Lam 2:2-3).

Vv. 9-11. Cry of anguish. The desolation of *no longer any prophet* not only reflects the terrifying silence of God (*cf.,* Lam 2:9, "her prophets obtain no vision from the Lord"), but also a decline of respect for prophecy, many of whose members had prostituted their art for personal ambition and gain (Hos 4:5; Mic 3:5-7).

Vv. 12-17, a typical hymn, effectively calling to "You, God!" with the presence of the 2nd singular pronoun at the beginning of each line, vv. 13-17. The first part of the hymn convulses with the battle of primeval sea monsters (vv. 12-14); while the second part reveals God's masterful control of earth, its seasons and fertility (vv. 15-17). Because the temple and royalty were considered the center of world stability and full life, the destruction of these two institutions would unleash chaotic forces. This happened at the death of a king and is featured in the initial part of the coronation of a new king (*cf.*, Ps 2:1-6; 89:9-18). The imagery was drawn from Canaanite mythology, who in turn took it from the winter storms that lashed the coastland from the angry western sea, till Baal, the god of fertility, overcame the sea monsters and summoned the peaceful spirit of spring and new life.

Vv. 18-21, a prayer for help, in which Israel is again compared to a *dove* (*cf.*, Ps 68:13). Vv. 22-23, a desperate call for God to *Arise!* (*cf.*, Ps 44:23-26).

(IV) In the Jewish calendar the threefold destruction and profanation of Jerusalem, by the Babylonians (587 B.C.), by Antiochus IV Epiphanes (167 B.C.), and by the Romans (A.D. 70 and 135), were commemorated on the 9th Day of Ab (2 Kgs 25:8; Jer 52:12). Not only has the Book of Lamentations been chanted traditionally on this day, but a strong influence upon the day's prayers and liturgy was made by Pss 74 and 79. Looked at from a more general need of expressing grief, Ps 74 allows time for the human spirit to be sorrowful and to settle into the realism of loss and radical change. It is not healthy, even in the name of accepting God's will, to pass abruptly from tragedy to new life; sorrow too has its mysterious purpose.

Psalm 75

A blend of many moods and literary styles, Ps 75 was put together for "generic" use in the liturgy. It seems that gratitude controls the setting in vv. 1 and 9-10, lines that could have been sung by the entire congregation. In between an oracle is pronounced by a priest or temple prophet (vv. 2-5) and a type of commentary or response to it was sung by a small choir. The oracle is introduced in the style of a theophany or divine appearance (*cf.*, Exod 19:17-20; Ps 46:2-3); in the commentary, its effects are extended to the four corners of the universe. Blessings are summarized under the *name* of the Lord (v. 1), a practice emphasized by Deuteronomy (Deut 12:11; 21:5, "priests...to bless in the name of the Lord"), and ever more prominently present in the postexilic age. Curses or punishment are meted out by drinking from the *cup with foaming wine (cf.,* Isa 51:17-23, "cup of staggering, the bowl of my wrath," or Jer 25:15-28). These key themes of "name" and "cup" continue through the New Testament: Col 3:17, "Whatever you do, in word or in deed, do everything in the name of the Lord Jesus, giving thanks to God the Father through him"; and the well-known incident in the garden of Gethsemane when Jesus struggles to drink the cup of the Lord's will in his passion and death (Mark 13:46), the one from which his disciples too must drink (Mark 10:38-39).

Psalm 76
To The Choirmaster: With Stringed Instruments. A
Psalm Of Asaph. A Song.

I
¹In Judah God is known,
   his name is great in Israel.
²His abode has been established in Salem,
   his dwelling place in Zion.
³There he broke the flashing arrows,
   the shield, the sword, and the weapons of war. *Selah*

II
⁴Glorious art thou, more majestic
   than the everlasting mountains.
⁵The stouthearted were stripped of their spoil;
   they sank into sleep;
 all the men of war
   were unable to use their hands.
⁶At thy rebuke, O God of Jacob,
   both rider and horse lay stunned.

III

7But thou, terrible art thou!
Who can stand before thee
when once thy anger is roused?
8From the heavens thou didst utter judgment;
the earth feared and was still,
9when God arose to establish judgment
to save all the oppressed of the earth.   *Selah*

IV

11Make your vows to the Lord your
God, and perform them;
let all around him bring gifts
to him who is to be feared,
12who cuts off the spirit of princes,
who is terrible to the kings of the earth.

(I) This victory song among the Psalms of Asaph corresponds with Pss 46-48 among the Psalms of Korah. Along with Pss 2, 20-21 and 68, these psalms celebrate a moment of military splendor, achieved through God's presence at the Jerusalem temple and resulting in justice for the oppressed and needy. Ps 76 could be a song for many occasions: the coronation of a new king or a royal anniversary, a thanksgiving service for victory or again its anniversary, any Jerusalem festivity. The psalm seems to reflect the united monarchy, either under David and Solomon (1000-922 B.C.), a more probable position in our opinion, or under King Hezekiah (715-687 B.C.) after the departure of the Assyrians (as the title in the Greek Septuagint states) or under King Josiah (640-609 B.C.). If we follow E. Beaucamp and accept a date under the reign of King David, then we are dealing with one of the earliest psalms in the psalter. To support this early date, we also note that Ps 76 shows much less theological development than Pss 46-48; the style, moreover, is typical of those of Asaph: vigorous, rapid and down to earth.

(II) The structure is simple but also attractive in its variations:

vv. 1-3,   about God's dwelling at Zion and past victories;
vv. 4-6,   addressed to God, glorious in Israel's past victories;
vv. 7-9,   addressed to God, gracious and all powerful for
            future victories;
vv. 10-12, about God and the vows for future victories.

(III) Vv. 1-3, the opening stanza displays several stylistic flourishes, like the play on words: *his name* (*shemo*), *Salem* (or *shalem*), *there* (*shammah*), very effectively focusing attention upon the Holy City. Only here and in Gen 14:18 is *shalem* a proper name (presumably) for Jerusalem. *Great is his name:* reflects not only royal protocol, as in 2 Sam 7:9; 1 Kgs 8:42; Gen 12:2, but also the later Deuteronomistic thought that Jerusalem is "the place where the Lord your God will choose to make his name dwell" (Deut 12:5, 11, 21). Typical of Deuteronomy and Deuteronomic books like Joshua, God is the warrior who fights Israel's battles.

Vv. 4-6, a skillful contrast between Zion, where God dwells more glorious and stable than the everlasting mountains, and the humiliated, stunned enemy soldiers, stricken by the powerful word of God.

Vv. 7-9, we are frightened, in a wonderful way, by God's theophany of justice for *the oppressed of the earth* — principally with Israel in mind but not excluding a universal outreach.

Vv. 10-12, A final act of worship. The Hebrew text of v. 10 is somewhat disturbed and its meaning not altogether clear.

(IV) The military tone and purpose of this psalm may be embarrassing to some, but upon closer reading we see the norms that lead away from war toward true and lasting peace: a sense of God's continuous presence at Salem, a word that signifies peace in the Hebrew language; the word of God as the principal instrument for opposing the enemy, a word that is controlled principally by compassion and forgiveness; a main concern for *all the oppressed of the earth.* Here as frequently elsewhere, we intuit secret messages in the Scripture that not only reach beyond the clear meaning of the individual words but also circumvent and even challenge their explicit purpose, here of military victory.

Psalm 77

I

¹I cry aloud to God,
  aloud to God, that he may hear me.
²In the day of my trouble I seek the Lord;
  in the night my hand is stretched out without wearying;
  my soul refuses to be comforted.

⁵I consider the days of old,
  I remember the years long ago.
⁶I commune with my heart in the night;
  I meditate and search my spirit:

II

¹⁰And I say, "It is my grief
  that the right hand of the Most High has changed."

¹¹I will call to mind the deeds of the Lord;
  yea, I will remember thy wonders of old.
¹²I will meditate on all thy work,
  and muse on thy mighty deeds.

III

¹⁶When the waters saw thee, O God,
  when the waters saw thee, they were afraid,
  yea, the deep trembled.

¹⁹Thy way was through the sea,
  thy path though the great waters;
  yet thy footprints were unseen.

IV

²⁰Thou didst lead thy people like a flock
  by the hand of Moses and Aaron.

(I-II) If read privately, Ps 77 seems like two psalms, arbitrarily united; but if heard within a liturgical assembly, the sections follow in good order:

vv. 1-9,   An individual lament, of loneliness and separation even from God; night wraps the psalmist in silent darkness;

vv. 10-15,   A confession of faith that God's ways do not change; the psalmist will meditate on God's great redemptive acts towards Israel as communicated through the liturgy and its confessions of faith;

vv. 16-19,   A hymn, celebrating the new creation of Israel's world through the exodus;

v. 20,   Conclusion, God continues to lead his flock by the hand of Moses and Aaron, the founders and religious mediators of Israel.

This division respects the *selahs* or liturgical dividers as well as the metric variations in the lines: while most of the verses are two lines with 3 + 3 beat, vv. 16-19 are composed of three lines each, 3 + 3 + 3 beat. Two key motifs extend through the major part of the psalm: one of silence and isolation, the other of remembrance and meditation.

(III-IV) The lonely lament in vv. 1-9 extends a dark stillness over soul-searching questions and contemplative prayer. This contemplation did not turn inward into a form of psychological analysis but reached outward, through liturgical memory, to God's redemptive acts for the people of Israel. To be alone with God means to be reunited with the family of God's people. Liturgy, then, possessed the common sense setting of allowing people to live with their grief and loneliness (vv. 1-9); it even begins its new section of liturgical remembrance by the transitional line: *my grief that the right hand of the Most High has changed* (v. 10). The meditative mood continues in vv. 11-15, though preparing for the communal singing of an ancient hymn (vv. 16-19), where ancient creation motifs about the struggle of chaos and order, about dark roaring waters and God's strong, directive hand dominate the scene. Such creation themes centered particularly around the temple and its liturgy where God was enthroned, keeping the chaotic forces at a distance (Ps 29), and providing the people with life and fertility symbolically through the sacred stream of fresh water (Ps 46:4). The creation motifs are modulated and folded into Israel's creation to new life through the exodus (*cf.,* Isa 51:9-10). Finally, liturgical remembrance was not an empty solace but an active force of reliving anew what God is always achieving for his people. Such is the affirmation of God's steadfast, covenant love (v. 8), by which he redeems by a close bond of blood (v. 15) and leads the people to new life (v. 20).

Psalm 78
A Maskil Of Asaph

I
¹Give ear, O my people, to my teaching;
    incline your ears to the words of my mouth!
²I will open my mouth in a parable;
    I will utter dark sayings from of old,
³things that we have heard and known,
    that our fathers have told us.

II-a
¹²In the sight of their fathers he wrought marvels
    in the land of Egypt, in the fields of Zoan.
¹³He divided the sea and let them pass through it,
    and made the waters stand like a heap.
¹⁴In the daytime he led them with a cloud,
    and all the night with a fiery light.
¹⁵He cleft rocks in the wilderness,
    and gave them drink abundantly as from the deep.

¹⁷Yet they sinned still more against him,
    rebelling against the Most High in the desert.
¹⁸They tested God in their heart
    by demanding the food they craved.

²¹Therefore, when the Lord heard, he was full of wrath;
    a fire was kindled against Jacob,
    his anger mounted against Israel;

²⁴and he rained down upon them manna to eat,
and gave them food in abundance.

³⁰But before they had sated their craving,
while the food was still in their mouths,
³¹the anger of God rose against them
and he slew the strongest of them,
and laid low the picked men of Israel.

-b-
³⁴When he slew them, they sought for him;
they repented and sought God earnestly.

³⁸Yet he, being compassionate,
forgave their iniquity,
and did not destroy them;
he restrained his anger often,
and did not stir up all his wrath.
³⁹He remembered that they were but flesh,
a wind that passes and comes not again.

III-a
⁴⁰How often they rebelled against him in the wilderness
and grieved him in the desert!

⁴²They did not keep in mind his power,
or the day when he redeemed them from the foe;
⁴³when he wrought his signs in Egypt,
and his miracles in the fields of Zoan.
⁴⁴He turned their rivers to blood,
so that they could not drink of their streams.

⁴⁷He destroyed their vines with hail,
and their sycamores with frost.

⁵¹He smote all the first-born in Egypt,
the first issue of their strength in the tents of Ham.
⁵²Then he led forth his people like sheep,
and guided them in the wilderness like a flock.
⁵³He led them in safety, so that they were not afraid;
but the sea overwhelmed their enemies.
⁵⁴And he brought them to his holy land,
to the mountain which his right hand had won.

55He drove out nations before them;
he apportioned them for a possession
and settled the tribes of Israel in their tents.

56Yet they tested and rebelled against the Most High God,
and did not observe his testimonies,

58For they provoked him to anger with their high places;
they moved him to jealousy with their graven images.

60He forsook his dwelling at Shiloh,
the tent where he dwelt among men,

64Their priests fell by the sword,
and their widows made no lamentation.

-b-

65Then the Lord awoke as from sleep,
like a strong man shouting because of wine.
66And he put his adversaries to rout;
he put them to everlasting shame.

67He rejected the tent of Joseph,
he did not choose the tribe of Ephraim;
68but he chose the tribe of Judah,
Mount Zion, which he loves.

70He chose David his servant,
and took him from the sheepfolds;

(I) After Ps 119, this psalm is the longest in the psalter; unlike Ps 119 it is entirely preoccupied with Israel's history, from the exodus out of Egypt to the reunion of north and south in the days of King Hezekiah (715-687 B.C.) or King Josiah (640-609 B.C.). The "Asaph" author or editor of this epic-length poem energetically rearranged the historical sequence, dwelling on the wilderness episode first and then the exodus out of Egypt, also differing from any tradition known to us in the order of the plagues. The poet's ability and independence show up in each verse, chiseled into place as though it were a mini-statement by itself. The psalm has a litany-style in which each line of invocation possesses its own strength and message. This literary finesse is also manifested in the larger, structural arrangement.

The psalmist is a supreme interpreter of history, not an archivist to preserve its data. It is helpful to compare Ps 78 with other great historical poems: Ps 105 will scan Israel's history to emphasize Yahweh's fidelity; Ps 106, to point out the people's infidelity. Ps 78, for its part, is principally in accord with the Deuteronomic tradition whereby history imparts a serious lesson: fidelity to God brings blessings, sinfulness invites severe punishment, but God's mercy always prevails with a new beginning.

Because Ps 78 presumes the construction of the Jerusalem temple, its earliest possible date would be the reign of Solomon (961-922 B.C.). It presupposes a serious tension between the north and south, a fact that brings it at least towards the end of Solomon's reign (*cf.*, 1 Kgs 11:26-40, when Jeroboam, future first king of the north, was chosen by a prophet to rule the ten northern tribes). If the psalm also reflects an attempt to reunite north and south, then we find ourselves in the reign of King Hezekiah (715-687 B.C. — *cf.*, 2 Chron 30:1, "Hezekiah sent to all Israel and Judah, and wrote letters also to Ephraim and Manasseh, that they should come to the house of the Lord at Jerusalem, to keep the passover to the Lord, the God of Israel.") Hezekiah's reign seems a better choice than Josiah's (640-609 B.C.); the latter's reform was not popularly received because of its ruthless imposition (2 Kgs 22:15-20). Nor is the psalm in close accord with the preaching of Jeremiah, who invoked the destruction of the northern sanctuary of Shiloh as an example not for the choice of Jerusalem as in Ps 78, but just the opposite, for Jerusalem's possible destruction (Jer 7:12-15; 26:6).

(II) Ps 78, as an historical, didactic epic, can be arranged according to Richard J. Clifford's investigation:

Vv. 1-11, *Introduction in Deuteronomic style*
First Recital	*Second Recital*
Wilderness Events,	vv. 12-32 From Egypt to
	Canaan, vv. 40-64

God's gracious acts, vv. 12-16 God's gracious acts, vv. 40-55
Israel's rebellion,   vv. 17-20 Israel's rebellion, vv. 56-58
God's anger,   vv. 21-32 God's anger,   vv. 59-64
Meditative response, vv. 33-39 *Meditative response*, vv. 65-72

The entire psalm interprets history and the fate of peoples and nations in terms of Israel and eventually of the choice of Jerusalem-Zion as God's sanctuary and of David as king. God's gracious acts or angry reactions are seen from Israel's viewpoint; the plagues, therefore, manifest God's mercy towards Israel.

According to the rabbis (*Kiddusin*, 30a), Ps 78:38 is the middle verse of the entire psalter, halfway among its 5,896 verses or *pesuqin*. This shows that God's great redemptive acts in history are at the center of prayer and worship. Yet the center is such that we cannot stop there but must proceed onward to the end of the psalm in our reinterpretation and actualization of that history. This same verse (78:38), which speaks of compassion and restraining one's anger, was recited with Deut 28:58, 59, when a person was punished with 40 stripes less one (*cf.,* 2 Cor 11:24).

(III) Vv. 1-11. *Introduction.* The psalmist adopts the style of preacher, rebuking, exhorting, promising blessings, warning with curses, as we see in Deut 29:2—30:20. The style is close to Deut 32:1-3; the Deuteronomic spirit of this "Song of Moses" continues throughout the psalm. We see some parallels with the sapiential literature (Prov 3:1; 4:2; Ps 49:2-5). Deut 8:15 announced that "the Lord your God will raise up for you a prophet like me"; Ps 78 feels endowed with this Mosaic mantle. Because the psalm ultimately wants to unite all Israel around God at the Jerusalem sanctuary, the reference to Ephraimites (v. 9) is intended to be typical of infidelity among any of the people, north or south. The allusion to *dark sayings from of old* (v. 2) advises us that the psalmist will be dealing with divine mysteries and the wonderful ways of salvation within Israel's history.

Vv. 12-32, *the first recital: the wilderness events.* God's gracious acts towards Israel (vv. 12-16) are surrounded with wonder and excitement. The same verb, *baqaʿ* in Hebrew, used in v. 13 for dividing the sea (literally, to split it open, a very energetic word) occurs again in v. 15 for splitting the rock to provide water. This water which surges up *from the deep* (v. 15), the Hebrew, *tehom*, is associated with the primeval watery seas that surround the earth and occupy a prominent place in creation (*cf.*, Pss 42:7; 46:1-3). The next subsection, vv. 17-20, details Israel's rebelling against God. *They tested God* to see how far they could get with their selfish cravings (Exod 17:2, 7; Num 14:22). God responds with anger and punishment (vv. 21-32). The people are said to have no faith in God (v. 22). This statement is not to be understood speculatively; rather, the people had concluded that God was no longer concerned about his people and his promises to them. God, however, cannot tolerate this false charge against himself; he loves his people too much. The manna, therefore, which was the *bread of angels* (v. 25) — a difficult phrase in the Hebrew, indicating a source of super-human strength — was turned into a sign of divine wrath, like the quail in Num 11:31-35.

Vv. 33-39 close the first section in a meditative sequel. It relies upon the theological position, articulated in Judg 2:6-3:6, that sin always brings punishment (*cf.*, Pss 7; 50:16-21); this sorrow leads the people to cry out for help in a repentant way; God can be relied upon to pardon the sorrowful, God who is patient and loving. A rich vocabulary of atonement, uniquely different from Ps 51:1-2, adorns these lines: *seek God, repent, remember, compassionate, forgive, restrain anger.*

Vv. 40-64, *the second recital, from Egypt to Canaan.* The preceding section concluded with God's remembrance that Israel was weak flesh, as fragile as the air (v. 39). How true, for the people quickly fail to remember and so they grieve their God. Within this context the psalmist recalls God's great gracious acts for Israel (vv. 44-55), first in Egypt, where their enemy was punished by the plagues, to prepare for their departure from the land of bondage. The order of the plagues is different from Pentateuchal traditions;

further adaptation is seen in v. 47 where the hail strikes *vines* and *sycamores* (in Ps 105:33, it was vines and figs, in Exod 9:31, flax and barley). The psalm follows the order of the song of Moses, vv. 44-51 correspond with Exod 15:1-12, vv. 52-55 with Exod 15:13-18 and the procession to the holy mountain of Jerusalem-Zion. The final line, *he apportioned them for a possession* of the Promised Land, places the seal of divine approval upon Israel's long process of acquiring the country. After recounting God's merciful acts, the psalm details Israel's ingratitude and rebellious actions (vv. 56-58). This then gives way to God's anger (vv. 59-64), particularly with the destruction of Shiloh by the Philistines (1 Sam 4-5). Because the ark of the covenant had been enshrined here, the place should have been totally safe. Israel was not to put false trust in sacred objects and places. Divine punishment is called *fire* (v. 63), frequently a sign of God's anger, as in the oracles of Amos where God sends fire upon the house of Damascus (Amos 1:4), upon Gaza (v. 7), etc. There is *no lamentation* (v. 64), possibly because the people are too stunned by the horrendous scale of the disaster.

Vv. 65-72, a meditative sequel to close the second section and the psalm. The rejection of Shiloh did not mean the end, even if the ark had been captured by the Philistines. Writing straight with crooked lines, God prepares thereby for the choice of Jerusalem and David.

(IV) Ps 78 provides good norms for interpreting "salvation history." Historical details are remembered but also put to use for imparting a new sense of history in each, contemporary age. Typical especially of Deuteronomy, "today" always adds an essential ingredient to the presentation of history (*cf.,* Deut 5:1-5). The history of Moses, the wilderness and the occupation of the land are never ended; the Bible is waiting for us to become part of that history. The cycle that does repeat itself is that of the Deuteronomic preface to Judges: luxury and riches can bring selfishness and sin; sin always leads to punishment; this sorrow in turn urges God's people to call for mercy and compassion which God always gives (Judg 2:6-3:6). There is no definitive end to this history till the messianic era. True, we do not return to worship any more at Shiloh; even the ark has been destroyed and Jerusalem is understood by Christians symbolically wherever the church throughout the world bows in worship before its God. The typological interpretation prevents any end from being final; God's compassion brings a new fulfillment of older hopes, far greater than ever anticipated.

The history of Ps 78 was continued in the New Testament by its many citations. V. 2, cited by Jesus for speaking in parables (Matt 13:35) and seeking new meaning within the mysteries of the word; v. 3 was evoked by 1 John 1:1-4, to remind us of the divine wonder within each Word that is Jesus in our midst. 1 Cor 10:8 alludes to v. 18 in that we should not be putting God to the test. John 6:31 cites v. 24 according to the Greek, in a discourse about the bread of life which Jesus was to provide, more wondrous still than the manna in the desert. As in Ps 78, the manna was to lead to trials and to Someone beyond itself. Peter quotes v. 37 when he reprimands a certain Simon who wanted to purchase the power of bestowing the Holy Spirit (Acts 8:21). Finally, v. 44 reappears in Rev 16:4, as the angel pours the third bowl of wrath upon the earth. In the spirit of Ps 78 this angry moment will be followed by a manifestation of the new heavens and the new earth (Rev 21:1).

Psalm 79
A Psalm Of Asaph.

I

¹O God, the heathen have come into thy inheritance;
  they have defiled thy holy temple;
  they have laid Jerusalem in ruins.
²They have given the bodies of thy servants
  to the birds of the air for food,
  the flesh of thy saints to the beasts of the earth.
³They have poured out their blood like water
  round about Jerusalem,

and there was none to bury them.
4We have become a taunt to our neighbors,
   mocked and derided by those round about us.

II

5How long, O Lord? Wilt thou be angry for ever?
   Will thy jealous wrath burn like fire?
6Pour out thy anger on the nations
   that do not know thee,
  and on the kingdoms
   that do not call on thy name!
7For they have devoured Jacob,
   and laid waste his habitation.

III

8Do not remember against us the iniquities of
  of our forefathers;
   let thy compassion come speedily to meet us,
   for we are brought very low.
9Help us, O God of our salvation,
   for the glory of thy name;
   deliver us, and forgive our sins,
   for thy name's sake!

IV

10Why should the nations say,
   "Where is their God?"
  Let the avenging of the outpoured blood of thy servants
   be known among the nations before our eyes!e, the

flock of thy pasture,
   will give thanks to thee for ever;
   from generation to generation we
    will recount thy praise.

(I) The Asaph collection of psalms contains three which
deal with the nation Israel: Ps 79, a national lament; Ps 80,
the restoration of a broken and tragic-ridden people; Ps 81,
Israel's full return to God's service and worship. Ps 79

belongs as much to the entire psalter as it does to Asaph; it was composed in anthological style:

v. 1c—Jer 26:18, where the quotation is attributed to Micah

v. 4—Ps 44:13

v. 5—Ps 89:46

vv. 6-7—Jer 10:25

v. 8d—Ps 142:6, in 1st singular, "I"

v. 9d—Pss 23:3; 25:11; 31:3

v. 10a—Ps 115:2; Joel 2:17

v. 11—Ps 102:20

v. 12—Ps 89:50-51

v. 13a—Ps 100:3

vv. 2, 5, 13—Ps 74:19, 1.

Sometimes it is difficult to recognize the source: *i.e.,* who is quoting from whom? At other times, it is not a question but a phrase from the repertoire of Israel's laments.

The psalmist appeals to Yahweh from a wide variety of motives: defilement of the temple; sins of Israel, now or in the past; God's compassion; God's honor; the groans of the prisoners. Even though the city and temple have been leveled and the people's memories are haunted with multiple terrifying trauma, nonetheless, we sense throughout that this is not the end; there is hope. The psalmist is close enough to the tragedy to speak of it this poignantly, yet far enough away to draw upon the Scriptures for this national lament and cry of hope. The style is vigorous, a hallmark of the Psalms of Asaph. We place it sometime during the Babylonian exile (587-539 B.C.).

(II) The meter and strophic arrangement are not clear, due no doubt to the anthological style of the psalm's composition. We suggest:

vv. 1-4, description of ruin

vv. 5-7, prayer against enemy

vv. 8-9, prayer for Israel's pardon

vv. 10-12, revenge against enemy

v. 13, promise of thanksgiving.

(III) We comment on several verses. V. 2, for corpses to remain unburied was considered a supreme insult, an agony that will haunt the deceased into eternity, according to a pattern of popular thinking across the ancient Near East. With unbridled anger Jeremiah curses King Jehoiakim: "With the burial of an ass he shall be buried, dragged and cast forth beyond the gates of Jerusalem." The prophet Elijah heaped the same curse on Ahab and his wife Queen Jezebel (1 Kgs 21:19, 24). Liturgically, bones and corpses made a sanctuary thoroughly unclean and desecrated: *cf.,* 2 Kgs 23:16, "Josiah...took the bones out of the tombs, burned them upon the altar, and defiled it." V. 6, *nations that do not know thee;* it is clear that God uses the foreign nations in his plans for Israel, to punish a sinful people (even if some innocent people also perish as in v. 2, *bodies of thy servants*), but biblical theology at this point goes no further, except that the nations themselves will be punished for brutality, blasphemous taunts and interference with God's plans for Israel (Isa 10:5-16). Implied in this negative attitude towards the nations is a vague, far off possibility that God may eventually think of them in a positive way and include them in Israel's salvation. In any case, their salvation can be considered only in relation with Israel's, just as God's glory cannot be separated from Israel, a strong position throughout the psalter (Pss 23:3; 25:11; 31:3; 44:26). Vv. 10-12, if the revenge sought by the psalmist against the enemy is unashamedly cruel, who are we who have never experienced the horror of angry military invasion, to tell others how to respond! God too declared "vengeance... sevenfold" will be taken upon anyone who harms Cain (Gen 4:15).

(IV) Jewish people are accustomed to recite Ps 79 especially on late Friday afternoon at the Western [or wailing] Wall of Jerusalem, all that remains of the former temple. It is also chanted in the liturgy of 9 Ab, commemorating the destruction of Jerusalem under the Babylonians and Romans. V. 3, about pouring out blood, is quoted again in Rev 16:7, adding "thou has given them blood to drink"! V. 6 is repeated in 1 Thess 4:5, warning Christians not to live "in the passion of lust like heathen people who do not know God."

Psalm 80
To The Choirmaster: According To Lilies. A Testimony Of Asaph. A Psalm.

> ¹Give ear, O Shepherd of Israel,
>   thou who leadest Joseph like a flock!
> Thou who art enthroned upon the cherubim,
>   shine forth
> ² before Ephraim and Benjamin and Manasseh!
> Stir up thy might,
>   and come to save us!

> ³Restore us, O God;
>   let thy face shine, that we may be saved!

> ¹⁴Turn again, O God of hosts!
>   Look down from heaven, and see;
>   have regard for this vine,
> ¹⁵ the stock which thy right hand planted.

> ¹⁷But let thy hand be upon the man of thy right hand,
>   the son of man whom thou hast made strong for thyself!

(I) As a national lament, Ps 80 differs from the preceding one, not only because the emphasis is more upon God's restoration of the devastated country, but also because the impact of military invasion was not as total as in Ps 79. This psalm, probably because the Jerusalem temple and perhaps other shrines in the northern kingdom were still functioning as a house of worship, is more conscious of God's liturgical presence and of the power of prayer, addressed to God before the ark. The images of the shepherd and the vine extend a more tranquil atmosphere over the psalm; this tone is accentuated by such phrases as "bread of tears." For this last reason, this psalm of Asaph is closer in tone to Pss 42-43 of the Korah collection than to other Asaph psalms.

The date and place of origin are strenuously debated. The references to the northern tribes in v. 2, *Ephraim and Manasseh*, would favor a composition in the kingdom of Israel, sometime after the loss of the upper section of the kingdom, the tribal portions of Zebulun and Naphtali, under an Assyrian onslaught by Tiglath-pileser, 733/2 B.C. (*cf.,* 2 Kgs 15:29; Isa 9:1). Because there is no mention of any king, others feel that the entire northern kingdom has been destroyed, therefore after 722/1 B.C. (2 Kgs 17). In this latter case the poem would come from a sympathetic levite in the south at Jerusalem, perhaps during the attempt by Hezekiah (715-687 B.C.) or Josiah (640-609 B.C.) to win back the north (see Ps 78, part I).

(II) The psalm can be rather easily divided according to its refrain:

vv. 1-3, Call for help;	vv. 8-13(14), God's past
vv. 4-7, Lament over God's	concern;
anger;	vv. 14(15)-19, Lament and
	Prayer.

(III) Vv. 1-3. Call for help. The tribe of Benjamin is usually associated with the southern kingdom of Judah (but not always, *cf.,* 1 Kgs 11:13, 32, 36); it is probably mentioned here to fill out the names of the sons through Jacob's favorite wife, Rachel — Joseph (Gen 30:23-24), known through his sons, Ephraim and Manasseh (Gen 48), and Benjamin (Gen 35:16-20). There is another possibility that Benjamin's presence here was influenced by the mention of *man of thy right hand* in v. 17; ben-jamin actually means "son of right hand" (*cf.,* Gen 35:18). The refrain in v. 3, along with the reference to the ark and the cherubim in v. 1, accentuates the startling contrast between God's presence liturgically in the temple and his absence realistically from the people's national life.

Vv. 8-13(14), God's past concern. Israel is frequently compared to a vine (Isa 5:1-7; 27:2-6; Ezek 15:1-8; Hos 10:1; etc.). We think particularly of Isaiah's song of the vineyard, where God declares that "I will break down its wall, and it shall be trampled down, I will make it a waste" (Isa 5:5-6). Without walls, a vineyard was open to the public, for walking and picking the fruit (Luke 6:1). In v. 11, the boundaries reflect the full extent of David's kingdom — never again reached by Israel (2 Sam 8:3; 1 Kgs 4:21, 24-25; etc.). V. 13, *the boar from the forest:* in the Hebrew text of the word "forest" one of its letters is elevated above the others in the same line: some rabbis claimed that this was done to indicate the middle "letter" in the entire book of Psalms; we already saw that Ps 78:38 was the middle verse. There are other explanations! V. 14 seems to be a variation of the refrain (vv. 3, 7, 19) and so belongs at the end of a strophe; yet it also begins the next stanza. The text is not clear.

(IV) It is surprising that God is still called *shepherd of Israel.* In no way does the psalmist doubt God's being a "good shepherd," despite the overwhelming loss and devastation. Again, Israel begins every prayer and discussion with firm faith in God; no question can dislodge the devout Israelite from that position, even though reality may seem to deny it. Even if Ps 80 was composed in the north after the devastation of 732 B.C., its existence was not suppressed after the final collapse of the north in 722/1 B.C. Nothing, "neither death, nor life...nor things present, nor things to come,...will be able to separate us from the love of God in Christ Jesus our Lord" (Rom 8:38-39).

Psalm 81
To The Choirmaster: According To The Gittith. A Psalm Of Asaph.

> [1]Sing aloud to God our strength;
>   shout for joy to the God of Jacob!
> [2]Raise a song, sound the timbrel,
>   the sweet lyre with the harp.
> [3]Blow the trumpet at the new moon,
>   at the full moon, on our feast day.
> [4]For it is a statute for Israel,
>   an ordinance of the God of Jacob.
> [5]He made it a decree in Joseph,
>   when he went out over the land of Egypt.
>   I hear a voice I had not known:

⁶"I relieved your shoulder of the burden;
   your hands were freed from the basket.
⁷In distress you called, and I delivered you;
   I answered you in the secret place of thunder;
   I tested you at the waters of Meribah.   *Selah*
⁸Hear, O my people, while I admonish you!
   O Israel, if you would but listen to me!
⁹There shall be no strange god among you;
   you shall not bow down to a foreign god.
¹⁰I am the Lord your God,
   who brought you up out of the land of Egypt.
   Open your mouth wide, and I will fill it.
¹¹"But my people did not listen to my voice;
   Israel would have none of me.
¹²So I gave them over to their stubborn hearts,
   to follow their own counsels.
¹³O that my people would listen to me,
   that Israel would walk in my ways!
¹⁴I would soon subdue their enemies,
   and turn my hand against their foes.
¹⁵Those who hate the Lord would cringe toward him,
   and their fate would last for ever.
¹⁶I would feed you with the finest of the wheat,
   and with honey from the rock I would satisfy you."

(I) For appreciating Ps 81 in its ancient setting and in our contemporary life, it is helpful to think of it within the liturgy of the feast of Tabernacles in comparison with Pss 50 and 95. The setting of the feast of Tabernacles is detected from several cues within the psalm, especially v. 3, *blow the trumpet, new moon, full moon,* and *our feast day.* On several occasions, Tabernacles is called simply, "the feast," as in 1 Kgs 8:2; Ezek 45:25; and Neh 8:14, "they found it written in the law. . . that the people of Israel should dwell in booths during *the feast* of the seventh month" (*cf.,* Ps 118). The feast was ushered in with trumpets on the first day of the month, the celebration of the new moon (Lev 23:23-25), and again on full moon, the fifteenth day, when the great feast began an octave of celebrations. It concludes now with the feast of *simḥath ha-torah—the Joy of the Torah*, a fact which might have its early echo in vv. 4-5, about *statute, ordinance and decree.* The latter part of Ps 81 refers repeatedly to Israel's wandering in the desert; according to Lev 23:43, Tabernacles was instituted "that your generation may know that I made the people of Israel dwell in booths when I brought them out of the land of Egypt."

By comparing Ps 81 with Ps 95 we discern many similarities, yet some notable differences. In Ps 81:16 "rock" refers to God's care in feeding the people in the wilderness and in the promised land, while in Ps 95:1 Rock is a title for Yahweh, drawn from the rock upon which the temple was built at Jerusalem. This difference may indicate, along with references to the northern Joseph tribes in Ps 81:5, that originally Ps 81 was composed and sung in the northern kingdom of Israel, therefore before 722 B.C. Another difference: in Ps 81:7, God tested Israel; in Ps 95:9, "your ancestors tested" God.

In comparison with Ps 50, we find that God intervenes in Ps 81 more as a grieved parent, who appeals with the people to be faithful; Ps 50 portrays a more severe Judge.

(II) As sung within the liturgy, we suggest this style of execution:

Vv. 1-5b, Hymnic Introduction to the service:
  vv. 1-3, call to praise
  vv. 4-5b, motivation for praise
After v. 5c, solemn preface to the reading of a scripture selection and homily;

Vv. 6-16, Prophetical Oracle, in response to the scriptural reading and homily, is implied; then
  vv. 6+11-16, warns and entreats Israel in the *third* person and concludes with a promise;
  vv. 7-10, addresses Israel in *second* person. Yahweh alone is Israel's God; concludes with a promise.

(III) Vv. 1-5b, this opening, hymnic section has already been discussed in section I.

V. 5c, Rubrical note that an inspired speech is to follow: it may or may not have been spoken aloud (*cf.,* Pss 2:7a; 12:5b, "says the Lord"). We are reminded of the solemn introduction to David's last words, 2 Sam 23:1-2.

Vv. 6 + 11-16, in the Hebrew text, these verses are addressed to Israel in the *third* person (except the last word of v. 16). Spoken by a temple prophet, we sense a mingling of God's kindly pity and the people's stubbornness; the promise at the end in v. 16, shows that God's goodness finally wins the day: *finest of the wheat . . . honey from the rock* repeat in another way the familiar promise of a land, flowing with milk and honey (Exod 3:8, 17; 13:5; etc.), a scene of abundant generosity and idyllic happiness; all this goodness is waiting for Israel simply to pick it up and enjoy it.

Vv. 7-10, another prophetic speech in the intimate form of I-Thou, leads us deeply into the mystery of God, *in the secret place of thunder*, possibly Mount Sinai (Exod 19:18-20; 20:18-26), as reexperienced in the sanctuary (Pss 29; 68:7-8). The beginning of the Decalogue is repeated in vv. 9-10 (*cf.,* Exod 20:2-3; Deut 5:6-7). In fact, the larger setting of vv. 7-10 seems to repeat the majestic introduction to the Deuteronomic decalogue (Deut 5:1-5; *cf.,* Deut 6:4). As Israel proceeds from sin to grace, from stubbornness to obedience to. God's word, the people also follow God's loving call in the wilderness and advance symbolically towards the promised land. The strange conclusion at v. 10b, *open your mouth wide and I will fill it,* makes sense if we compare it to the conclusion to the other section about *finest of the wheat* and *honey from the rock.* Both formulas may be introducing a sacred meal at the sanctuary.

(IV) Ps 81, composed for the final harvest festival, teaches us to celebrate liturgically with "song, timbrel, sweet lyre, harp and trumpet," with full joy, so that the liturgy mirrors the abundance of good things provided by God, *the finest of the wheat* and *honey from the rock.* Just as the Book of

Ecclesiastes was chanted at the feast of Tabernacles as a
healthy warning that all these things can be "vanity," so also
Ps 81 contains a sober note of restraint. Yet the prophetic
oracle is gentle and compassionate. It corrects or refocuses
any excessive joy by drawing us into the mystery of God's
secret place. In an effective dialogue of I-Thou style in vv.
7-10, we sense the enthronement, of "I, the Lord your God
who brought you up from the land of Egypt," in the midst of
ourselves and our community of faith.

Psalm 82
A Psalm Of Asaph.

I
¹God has taken his place in the divine council;
   in the midst of the gods he holds judgment:

II
²"How long will you judge unjustly
   and show partiality to the wicked?   *Selah*
³Give justice to the weak and the fatherless;
   maintain the right of the afflicted and the destitute.
⁴Rescue the weak and the needy;
   deliver them from the hand of the wicked."

⁵They have neither knowledge nor understanding,
   they walk about in darkness;
   all the foundations of the earth are shaken.

III
⁶I say, "You are gods,
   sons of the Most High, all of you;
⁷nevertheless, you shall die like men,
   and fall like any prince."

IV
⁸Arise, O God, judge the earth;
   for to thee belong all the nations!

(I) At first Ps 82 seems so infiltrated with pagan mythology about the assembly of the gods, that it could have only one foot inside the door of divine inspiration — and even then it feels the painful slam of the door! Yet Jesus took the psalm seriously enough as to quote it in a theological discussion of his own divinity (John 10:34). In its few lines Ps 82 reflects a long evolving tradition about pagan gods and arrives at an ultimate decision about who is really divine through norms of human compassion and social justice. The psalm, therefore, is not a speculative discussion about authentic divine attributes; rather, from a very practical viewpoint it condemns Canaanite deities to the same ungodlike fate as would befall venal, self-serving judges, *you shall die like any human being* and collapse into the *darkness* of Sheol (*cf.,* vv. 5-6).

There is no doubt about the mythological allusions: twice, a reference to *gods* — *'elohim* (vv. 1 and 6); once, to *sons of the Most High* (v. 6). A long biblical tradition lies behind a psalm such as this one. The Bible frequently speaks about the assembly of superhuman beings about the throne of God (1 Kgs 22:19-22; Job 1:6, 12; 2:1-6; Pss 29:1; 58:1; Isa 40:1-8), an idea transferred to the temple where Yahweh was surrounded with cherubim or seraphim (Exod 25:22) who seem to come alive (Isa 6:1-4; Ezek 1; 10:9-22; 43:1-5). At times it was more than a matter of majestic literary flair, for in Deut 4:19; 29:25; 32:8-9 and 33:2-3 these lesser gods are acknowledged to be in charge of other nations while Israel belongs to Yahweh alone. Later Jewish interpretation called these lesser gods by a new name — angels, and thus translated *'elohim* in many of these passages, as in Ps 8:5 and here in Ps 82:1. Human beings of high position were sometimes called *'elohim* — *gods* (Exod 4:16; 7:1; Ps 45:7; Deut 19:17) and the prophets will describe the collapse of mighty foreign kings as the descent of the gods to Sheol (*cf.,* Isa 14:4-21; Ezek 28:1-19). Ps 82 by resonating this multi-faceted tradition, is insisting that true divinity whether in the person of God or among God's representatives, is ultimately decided by concern for the weak and destitute; such is the credential for the true God in the Mosaic covenant according to Exod

34:6-7, where Yahweh announced himself as "The Lord, the Lord, a God merciful and gracious...abounding in steadfast love and faithfulness."

(II) In view of this rich, complicated background, it is difficult to date Ps 82 and to determine its principal literary form. E. Beaucamp even calls it "chaotic"! For the following reasons we favor the composition or at least a final editing during the Babylonian exile: a) the gods are no longer taken as a serious threat and are treated as hopelessly reduced to mortal status; b) a weak but still favorable outreach towards gentile nations in v. 8; c) the impact of prophetic preaching, not only in the concern for the poor and needy but also in the use of the literary form of a lawsuit (*cf.,* Isa 1:2-20). These same reasons prompt us to consider Ps 82 as a Prophetic Speech or Oracle, divided according to the following outline:

v. 1, Divine Council Chamber,   vv. 6-7, Verdict and Sentencing,
vv. 2-5, Interrogation and   v. 8, Conclusion; eschatological
   Evidence,   vista.

(III) V. 1. Texts of the ancient Near East and archaeological evidence of temples attest to the common scene of the principal god, presiding over an assembly of lesser or tutelary gods. Originally the Israelite Ps 82 would have opened with "Yahweh," till its change in the elohistic psalter (Pss 42-83) to *'elohim* or *God* [who] *has taken his place in the divine council.*

Vv. 2-5. The defense of the weak and destitute was a primary obligation of kings and judges, as we learn from many ancient Near Eastern texts. The failure to perform this important duty is condemned particularly by the classical prophets (Isa 1:17, 23; 5:23; Mic 2; Jer 5:28-31; Amos 2:6-8). V. 5, *foundations of the earth are shaken:* if human judges do not reflect Yahweh's decisions to care for the poor, then the earth will no longer correspond to heaven's plans for it and so will fall apart. We witness here the close interaction of heaven and earth, the moral and the physical order of the universe.

V. 8, the psalm concludes with a *glimpse* of universal salvation. Israel's universalism evolves out of "secular" obligations which force Israel to perceive the full meaning of its covenantal revelation of Yahweh, the compassionate God. (IV) Ps 82 cautions religion to maintain a firm grounding in the earthly needs of people. The secular world will always set the agenda and very often will provide the impetus, by which we realize the depth and scope of our theological positions. Theology does not contain an exclusive control over its development; such control, in fact, will quickly degenerate into a subtle form of rationalism, ideological systems masking as divine doctrine! Ps 82 particularly in its long, complicated development, shows that Israelite religion did not immediately and definitively reject all other gods. The many stages towards monotheism provide a roadmap for Christianity's dealing with polytheistic religions today.

Psalm 83
A Psalm Of Asaph.

This national lament was prayed at times of extreme military danger, especially when Israel was faced with military invasion. The ten hostile nations (vv. 6-8) may be symbolic of any major onslaught; we cannot document any single alliance of all these countries against Israel. The references to Israel's great victories in vv. 9-12 are drawn from the period of the judges (Judg chaps. 4-5; 7-8), the early time when nomads would invade the land for quick plunder. It is difficult to locate the psalm chronologically, except that it seems quite early, or to identify its place of origin as nothing is said of capital, temple or dynasties. Ps 83 is the last of the Asaph psalms (Pss 50 + 73-83) and also the final one in the Elohist collection (Pss 42-83). It opens with a call for help (v. 1), follows with a lament over a sorrowful situation (vv. 2-8), and ends with a long prayer for help, consisting mostly in the destruction of the enemy (vv. 9-18). For the location of the countries in vv. 6-8, see the map.

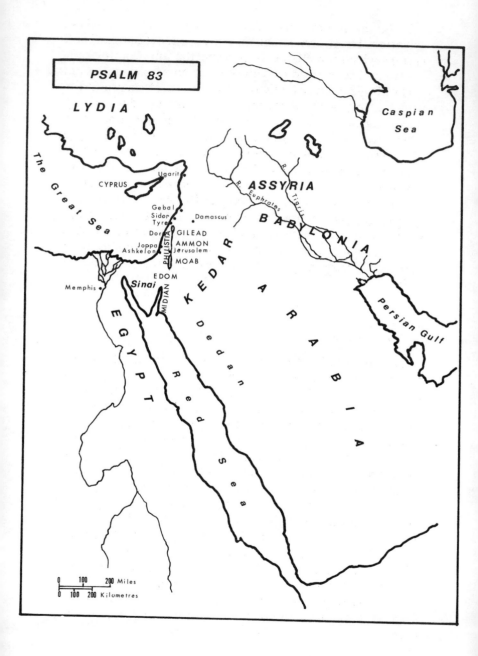

Psalm 84
To The Choirmaster: According To The Gittith. A
Psalm Of The Sons Of Korah.

I-a

¹How lovely is thy dwelling place,
  O Lord of hosts!

-b-

²My soul longs, yea, faints
  for the courts of the Lord;
my heart and flesh sing for joy
  to the living God.

³Even the sparrow finds a home,
  and the swallow a nest for herself,
  where she may lay her young,
at thy altars, O Lord of hosts,
  my King and my God.

-c-

⁴Blessed are those who dwell in thy house,
  ever singing thy praise!   *Selah*

⁵Blessed are the men whose strength is in thee,
  in whose heart are the highways to Zion.

-d-

⁶As they go through the valley of Baca
  they make it a place of springs;
  the early rain also covers it with pools.
⁷They go from strength to strength;
  the God of gods will be seen in Zion.

II-a

⁸O Lord God of hosts, hear my prayer;
  give ear, O God of Jacob!   *Selah*
⁹Behold our shield, O God;
  look upon the face of thine anointed!

-b-

¹⁰For a day in thy courts is better
  than a thousand elsewhere.

I would rather be a doorkeeper in the house of my God
than dwell in the tents of wickedness.
[11]For the Lord God is a sun and shield;
he bestows favor and honor.
No good thing does the Lord withhold
from those who walk uprightly.

III

[12]O Lord of hosts,
blessed is the man who trusts in thee!

(I) We begin a second series of psalms (Pss 84-85, 87-88)
from the levitical clan of the Korahites (see introduction to
Pss 42-43, which opened the other series, Pss 42-49). Again
we sense not only a quiet, ecstatic joy from the presence of
the Lord at the sanctuary, but also an exquisite pain or
nostalgic sorrow suffusing the lines, now that the Korahites
have been demoted and were often bypassed. Even the
dominant meter of Ps 84, despite hymnic elements in vv. 1,
4-5, 7, 10-12, is the 3+2 beat of lamentation. By comparison,
Pss 42-43 were composed at an imposed distance and separation, as the Korahites were blocked from setting out on
pilgrimage; Pss 120-134 (see introduction to Ps 120) were
chanted while on pilgrimage to Jerusalem; Ps 84 seems most
appropriate when the pilgrims came within sight of the Holy
City. At this point even the tired bones and aching muscles
felt a resurgence *from strength to* [new] *strength* (v. 7). The
prayer for the king in vv. 8-9, indicates a pre-exilic
composition.

(II) As a canticle of Zion, Ps 84 can be subdivided:

vv. 1-7, Pilgrimage, in sight of Jerusalem: Joyful exclamation,
   v. 1; motivation for joy in the stanzas: 2-3, 4-5, 6-7;
vv. 8-11, Joy of sojourning in the temple during the time of the
   festival: with a prayer for the king in vv. 8-9; and a quiet meditation in vv. 10-11;
v. 12, Conclusion: blessedness of such a pilgrimage.

The Hebrew text, when compared with the ancient versions, presents a number of difficulties. The text of a popular song, such as Ps 84, could easily be adapted and disturbed by pilgrims.

(III) V. 1, joyful exclamation, inspired by the oracles or blessings of Balaam who "lifted up his eyes, and saw Israel encamping tribe by tribe [as the psalmist glimpsed Jerusalem from afar]. And the Spirit of God came upon him, and he took up his discourse...the oracle of him...who sees the vision of the Almighty: 'How fair are your tents, O Jacob!'" (Num 24:2-5).

Vv. 2-3, motivation for praise, from the joy of the total person, *my soul, my heart, my flesh* with which God is in closest contact as *the living God.* The life of God is felt in intimate desires and sacred aspirations, as when a person is delicately aware of a total environment — like a *sparrow* or *swallow,* swift and certain in settling into its nest, warm and attentive in caring for the young within the nest. Birds may seem to fly in circles and get nowhere, yet their homing instincts are flawless; the Korahites may seem lost in the circles of religious intrigue yet they are confident of finding their home with God.

Vv. 4-5, the *blessed* lines! We find an insinuation not just of dwelling but of praising God for ever, which the Greek Septuagint accentuates to read "for ever *and ever.*" V. 5, *whose strength is in thee:* can also be translated, "whose refuge is in thee." *The highways* [*to Zion*] fill the heart of the psalmist with strong longings, silent prayers, ancient scriptures and memories of Israel's many pilgrimages through its history (*cf.,* Ps 95).

Vv. 6-7, in the environments of Jerusalem, perhaps at the spring of Gihon or the pool of Shiloah, south east of the temple in the Kidron valley (*cf.,* Ps 110:7; Isa 8:6). *The valley of Baca* is translated by the ancient versions as "the valley of weeping," and became the inspiration of the phrase, "in hac lacrymarum valle — in this vale of tears," in the ancient Marian hymn of the church, "Salve, Regina — Hail, Holy Queen." In v. 6c, by changing one vowel in the Hebrew word for pools (*berekoth*) to *berakoth* and by reading another Hebrew word not as *early rain* but (as is more usually the case) as teacher or leader, this line can read: "the cantor entones the blessings," like those described in vv. 4-5 and v. 12. V. 7b, *the God of gods will be seen in Zion:* even though this phrase was derived from a pagan practice of going to the temple to *see* the statues or images of the gods, for Israel it meant, technically, "to approach the temple, or enter it," and realistically to "see" by reliving the great moments of Israel's history within the temple liturgy.

Vv. 10-11. *Doorkeeper* (v. 10b) might be better translated as a reference to the pilgrims "standing at the entrance" (A. A. Anderson).

(IV) Ps 84 has been sung by the church from ancient times to appreciate the presence of the Word Incarnate among us — wondrously as on the feast of the Transfiguration (August 6), corresponding to the Jewish feast of the glorification of Moses (*cf.,* Exod 24:15-18; 34:29-35); symbolically and intimately under the form of bread and wine in the Eucharist; continuously within the sacred edifice, for whose dedication Ps 84 was sung. Like Pss 42-43 this one too prepares us to experience exquisite joy in the sorrow of waiting, longing and approaching. Blessed with the faith of perceiving the Word of God, incarnate in our midst and dwelling within ourselves as a temple of living stones (1 Pet 2:5), we receive a new blessing from Jesus: "Blessed are the eyes which see what you see! For I tell you that many prophets and kings desired to see what you see, and did not see it, and to hear what you hear, and did not hear it" (Luke 10:23-24).

Psalm 85
To The Choirmaster. A Psalm Of The Sons Of Korah.

I-a
¹Lord, thou wast favorable to thy land;
   thou didst restore the fortunes of Jacob.
²Thou didst forgive the iniquity of thy people;

thou didst pardon all their sin. *Selah*
3Thou didst withdraw all thy wrath;
    thou didst turn from thy hot anger.

-b-

4Restore us again, O God of our salvation,
    and put away thy indignation toward us!
5Wilt thou be angry with us for ever?
    Wilt thou prolong thy anger to all generations?
6Wilt thou not revive us again,
    that thy people may rejoice in thee?
7Show us thy steadfast love, O Lord,
    and grant us thy salvation.

II-a

8Let me hear what God the Lord will speak,
    for he will speak peace to his people,
      to his saints, to those who turn to him in their hearts.

-b-

9Surely his salvation is at hand for those who fear him,
    that glory may dwell in our land.

-c-

10Steadfast love and faithfulness will meet;
    righteousness and peace will kiss each other.
11Faithfulness will spring up from the ground,
    and righteousness will look down from the sky.
12Yea, the Lord will give what is good,
    and our land will yield its increase.
13Righteousness will go before him,
    and make his footsteps a way.

(I) As a national lament and prayer, Ps 85 is unusually mild in its tone; it lacks the fierce anger over Jerusalem's horrendous destruction in Ps 74, nor is it as despondent and self-righteous as Ps 44. The psalmist seems to have experienced God's pardon and therefore has a pledge of new forgiveness and restoration. This faith in Yahweh's compassion is accentuated with the prophetic oracle in the second

half of the psalm (vv. 8-13). For many reasons it is associated with the early days after the return from exile: a) no
mention of king or temple; b) a sense of well deserved
chastisement for past sins and of hope for a new Israel; c) the
wearisome life upon seeing the non-fulfillment of the glorious promises of Isa 40-55 and upon facing the drought and
poor crops of those first years back in the land (*cf.*, Hag;
Zech 1-8; Isa 56-59). The theology of Ps 85 can be perceived
through the repetition of key words:

return/restore (in Hebrew, *shub*): vv. 1b, 3b, 4a, 6a, 8b;
land: vv. 1a, 9b, 11a, 12b;
peace (*shalom*): vv. 8b, 10b, 13b;
covenant virtues of *steadfast love* (*ḥesed*), *faithfulness* ('*emeth*),
    righteousness (*ṣedeq*): vv. 7a, 9b, 10ab, 12ab, 14a;
salvation (*yesha'*): vv. 4a, 7b, 9a.

Israel asks God to restore the covenant bond that will
manifest the sturdiness of God's goodness and fidelity,
reaching outward to heaven and earth. Even though the
temple is not yet reconstructed, the psalm has all the ear-
marks of community liturgy.

(II) The psalm proceeds from lament or prayer to prophetic oracle:

vv. 1-7, The prayer opens with	vv. 8-13, The prophetic oracle:
a confession of faith or	v. 8, formal introduction
confidence (vv. 1-3), and is	v. 9, oracle
followed by a lament	vv. 10-13, covenant renewal.
(vv. 4-7);	

(III) Vv. 1-3, these lines are usually interpreted as referring to a past act of deliverance, possibly the return from the
Babylonian exile. However, it is also very possible that the
Hebrew "perfect" form of the verb is not meant to refer to
past time but to impart confidence in Yahweh's favorable
attitude. It is interesting to note that blessings begin with the
land, such an important part of Israel's life. The forgiveness

of sins in v. 2 is always a necessary condition for other gifts.

Vv. 8-9, the prophetic oracle is the center of the psalm, yet adapted from the 1st person to become a statement *about* Yahweh's gift of salvation. It is solemnly introduced — as in Ps 81:6; Hab 2:1, "I will take my stand to watch and station myself on the tower and look forth to see what he will say to me." *Peace* is the kind announced by Isa 57:19-21, that will bring healing "to the far and to the near" but not to the wicked. The oracle prays for God's *glory*, so that the wonder of God's covenantal promises are visible and enjoyable (see Ps 3).

Vv. 10-13 do not state whether the covenantal virtues belong to Yahweh or to Israel; probably it intends a blending of God's full life within the life of the chosen people, reaching into their land and forming the footsteps of God's presence in their midst. We think of the way of God's glory in Isa 40:3-5 or the lovely footprints of the one "who brings good tidings, who publishes peace [and] salvation" (Isa 52:7).

(IV) Even if good memories, as in the first part of Ps 85, can make us dissatisfied with present sorrows, this situation is healthy; it is like the world "groaning in travail" (Rom 8:22). Since we hope for what we do not see but for what we intuit by faith, we have to wait with patience (Rom 8:23-24). These longings are intensified in the Eucharist where we drink the blood of the new covenant for the forgiveness of sin (Matt 26:28), are united with the full body of the Lord and share in the suffering of other members: "if one member suffers, all suffer together" (1 Cor 12:26). All the while, we live in expectation.

Psalm 86
A Prayer Of David.

This individual lament from the postexilic age has an unusual structure. Normally even a lament will close with thanksgiving, not with another expression of sorrow. The different sequence here may be due to a liturgical ceremony about which we are ignorant:

vv. 1-7, Call for help; vv. 8-11, Hymn of confidence;	vv. 12-13, Prayer of thanksgiving; vv. 14-17, Lament and prayer.

Ps 86 draws heavily upon a common font of liturgical phrases; it was written under the shadow of the psalter:

v. 1b—Ps 40:17a, poor and needy

v. 2a—Ps 25:20a, preserve my life

v. 2b—Ps 25:2a, in thee I trust

v. 3—Ps 57:1-2, be gracious to to me; I cry to God

v. 4b—Ps 143:8d; 25:1, I lift up my soul

v. 5a—Ps 25:11, forgiving

v. 5b—Ps 103:8b, abounding in steadfast love

v. 6b—Ps 5:3a; 28:2; 130:2, hearken to the sound of my cry

v. 7a—Ps 77:3a, in the day of my trouble I seek the Lord

v. 7b—Ps 17:6, thou wilt answer me

v. 8—Exod 15:11, who is like thee among the gods?

v. 11a—Ps 27:11a, teach me thy way, Lord

v. 11a—Ps 26:3, I walk in faithfulness to thee

v. 12a—Ps 9:2a, I give thanks with all my heart

v. 13b—Deut 32:22, to the depths of Sheol

v. 14—Ps 54:3, insolent men have risen against me

v. 15—Ps 103:8, merciful and gracious

v. 16a—Ps 25:16a, turn to me and be gracious

v. 16b—Ps 116:16, thy servant, the son of thy handmaid

This psalm manifests the power of memorized Bible texts for personal prayer. These passages, stored away in our subconscious, will spontaneously leap forward with God's direction and consolation for us, especially in times of distress. One text joined to another, especially in the context of daily life, will offer new insights, not anticipated ahead of time. Jewish people chant Ps 86 on the penitential day of Yom Kippur.

Psalm 87
A Psalm Of The Sons Of Korah. A Song.

I

¹On the holy mount stands the city he founded;
² the Lord loves the gates of Zion
more than all the dwelling places of Jacob.
³Glorious things are spoken of you,
O city of God.   *Selah*

II

⁴Among those who know me I mention
Rahab and Babylon;
behold, Philistia and Tyre, with Ethiopia—
"This one was born there," they say.
⁵And of Zion it shall be said,
"This one and that one were born in her";
for the Most High himself will establish her.
⁶The Lord records as he registers the peoples,
"This one was born there."   *Selah*

III

⁷Singers and dancers alike say,
"All my springs are in you."

(I-II) Although the emphasis upon Jerusalem-Zion as universal mother is clear enough, Ps 87 is otherwise so vague that we do not know to whom it is addressed, nor by whom, nor again for what occasion! There is no regular meter or rhythm to the poetry; the ancient translations have quite a few variants. Attributed to the "Sons of Korah," Ps 87 presents a different slant from other Korahite Canticles about Jerusalem, Pss 46-48. All, indeed, manifest an universal scope and center world history about the Holy City. Ps 87 seems to open the gates of the city most widely with family love and unguarded enthusiasm. Such a universal mission for Jerusalem and Zion had its origins in the political empire of David, was reinterpreted when the empire fell apart and spiritualized when the dynasty collapsed. Yet, this kindly openness to gentiles was relegated to the outer edge (Isa 2:2-4; 49:6): it had to wait for the moment when it would move to the center and then transform biblical religion. This dramatic change was strongly hinted at by Jesus and was theologically argued by Paul (Rom 9-11). Because this universal mission was never central to Judaism, we can understand why this psalm was neglected textually and appeared to be something of an embarrassment.

The identity of the pilgrims to Zion is disputed: Jews of the diaspora? or converts/proselytes from the foreigners? Even so, it speaks more of individuals than large groups. The date of the psalm is left equally vague: certainly after the emergence of Babylon as a world power in 612 B.C. If we date the psalm before the Babylonian empire was absorbed by Persia in 539 B.C., then it would have been composed during a time of hardship by one of the most "ecumenical" Israelites in exile! The structure seems rather clear: vv. 1-3, Choice of Zion; vv. 4-6, Zion, universal mother; v. 7, conclusion.

(III) Vv. 1-3, the choice of Jerusalem over all the other sanctuaries of the holy land, over Gilgal, Bethel, Shechem, Shiloh, Beersheba. *The Lord loves the gates,* that place in any walled city where political and social life was most intense (Gen 23:10, 18; Job 29:7; Prov 31:23).

Vv. 4-6, Zion, universal mother. The Greek Septuagint adds the word "mother" to Zion in v. 5. To symbolize the world, the psalm names: two great powers, Egypt (called Rahab — Isa 30:7) and Babylon; two neighboring people, Tyre and Philistia (Ps 83:7; Jer 47:4); and one distant people, Ethiopia (Ps 68:32). Jerusalem appears as the center or "fountain" of life (Ps 68:26), for here is where the river of life, perhaps the rivers of paradise, emerge (Ps 46:4); Jerusalem is the navel of the universe (Ezek 5:5; 38:12) and contains the register or book of life for all the elect (Exod 32:32; Pss 56:8; 69:28; Isa 4:3). Jerusalem is therefore known for its stability and continuity (Ps 125:1-2).

(IV) Through the strong, creative thrust of St. Paul, Christianity took up the universal mission of Judaism, "the mystery...made known to me by revelation...how the Gentiles are fellow heirs, members of the same body and partakers of the promise in Christ Jesus through the gospel ...the mystery hidden for ages in God" (Eph 3:3, 6, 9). In the spirit of Ps 87, this mystery is linked with Jerusalem: "you have come to Mount Zion and to the city of the living God, the heavenly Jerusalem, and to innumerable angels in festal gathering, and to the assembly of the first-born who are enrolled in heaven...and to Jesus, the mediator of a new covenant" (Heb 12:22-24). Ps 87 challenges the church and each of us to open the gates to God's legitimate children, orphans from afar, and to receive them in a dignified way with their cultural richness, religious insights and sacred literature.

Psalm 88
A Song. A Psalm Of The Sons of Korah.

I

¹O Lord, my God, I call for help by day;
   I cry out in the night before thee.
²Let my prayer come before thee,
   incline thy ear to my cry!

II

³For my soul is full of troubles,
   and my life draws near to Sheol.
⁴I am reckoned among those who go down to the Pit;
   I am a man who has no strength,
⁵like one forsaken among the dead,
   like the slain that lie in the grave,
 like those whom thou dost remember no more,
   for they are cut off from thy hand.

III

¹¹Is thy steadfast love declared in the grave,
   or thy faithfulness in Abaddon?
¹²Are thy wonders known in the darkness,
   or thy saving help in the land of forgetfulness?

IV

13But I, O Lord, cry to thee;
in the morning my prayer comes before thee.
14O Lord, why dost thou cast me off?
Why does thou hide thy face from me?
15Afflicted and close to death from my youth up,
I suffer thy terrors; I am helpless.

(I) The bleak, seemingly hopeless and tragic tone of this "gloomiest of all the plaintive Psalms" (Franz Delitzsch), is sustained by a series of key words or synonyms: troubles, Sheol, Pit, dead, slain, grave, cut off, regions dark and deep, horror, shades, Abaddon, land of forgetfulness, cast off, hide thy face, thy wrath, dread assaults, flood, shunned by lover and friend. Some lines delineate the isolated fate of those most unfortunate people, the lepers, who seem "as one dead, of whom the flesh is half consumed [even from] the mother's womb" (Num 12:12); other lines about being *afflicted and close to death from my youth up. . . helpless* (v. 15) may direct us to a person physically disabled in a severe, distorted way, people who are generally kept hidden from view, non-persons who are forced into total inactivity. Often enough religion has no dignified place for them! From the Old Testament into Christian theology little or nothing has been written by disabled people for disabled people, and, for that matter, for everyone of us, who each have our own disabilities. Perhaps, the degraded situation becomes shockingly apparent in the stipulation of the Torah, "Say to Aaron [the priest], None of your generation. . . who has a blemish shall draw near, a man blind or lame, or one who has a mutilated face or a limb too long, or a man who has an injured foot or an injured hand, or a hunchback, or a dwarf, or a man with a defect in his sight or an itching disease or scabs or crushed testicles. . . he shall not come near to offer the bread of his God" (Lev 21:16-21). The gist of this prescription has been repeated in the canon law of the church for many centuries. In reply, the psalmist shares with us one person's attempt to communicate with this silent God and to profess heroic allegiance to a covenant which acclaims God's *steadfast love, faithfulness, wonders and saving help* (literally, justice)—vv. 11-12.

(II) This psalm is a unique dialogue with an absent God, in whose presence, strangely or awkwardly enough, the psalmist still stands — several times the psalmist speaks of being "before God," at times literally "before the face of God," vv. 1-2, 13. The structure has its own unique, creative way! Unlike any other lament, there are no prayers of confidence, no anticipated thanksgiving (see Ps 22). Moreover, the literary form speaks as though God is not present, at one point it either ignores God or presumes divine absence. Yet, it generally addresses God in the second person, "you!"

vv. 1-2, Introductory call for help

vv. 3-5, Lament and description; God is not mentioned

vv. 6-9a, The hostile God

vv. 9b-12, Prayer in the name of the covenant

vv. 13-18, God is addressed as responsible for dread assaults

(III) Vv. 3-5. The psalm presumes the normal theological position of the Old Testament, maintained even by the temple priesthood in New Testament times (*cf.,* Acts 23:6-7), that Sheol, the abode of the dead, is outside of God's concern; the corpse was considered ceremonially unclean. It could not be introduced into a sacred place like the temple, therefore hardly within God's heavenly temple (see Pss 6:5; 16:10). Though still on earth, the psalmist feels like a shadow of a living person.

Vv. 6-9a. The absence of God is enforced by God's continuously heavy hand upon the psalmist. Most pitiably of all, *thou does remember no more;* the psalmist addresses a God who fails to actualize the great redemptive acts of Israel's faith in the person of the psalmist — a clash between theoretical faith and its personal non-realization. V. 8, *my companions shun me*, the Hebrew word for companions presumes someone who has shared and *experienced* (the root meaning of the word) deepest thoughts, intimate feelings, personal hopes. V. 9a has an effective play on words, beginning with my eyes (*'eni*) and ending with sorrow (*'oni*).

Vv. 9b-12, a skillful poignant contrast between covenant faith and the absence of the covenant God, who leaves the psalmist *in the land of forgetfulness: cf.,* Eccles 9:5, "the dead know nothing...the memory of them is lost."

Vv. 13-18, this final lament lays the blame squarely on God's wrath. While morning ought to be a time when "thou dost hear my voice" (Ps 5:3) and dost make me "satisfied with beholding thy form" (Ps 17:15), the psalmist is overwhelmed by the fierce, angry, massive flood waters, always a symbol of God's enemies (Pss 18:4; 42:7; 89:9-10). The full impact of being shunned by *lover and friend* is given by Job 19:13-22, which ends pathetically: "Have pity on me, O you my friends, for the hand of God has touched me," how desperate when a person must appeal to creatures against God!

(IV) Ps 88 does not pretend to be a theological presentation but a realistic sharing of experience. If the psalmist's faith in the covenant loyalty of God had not been so absolute, the problem with God's absence would not have been so cruel and perplexing. With the mystics of all ages the psalmist is being led beyond the power of theological words and positions, into the "dark night of the soul," where God is more present by a person's desire than by liturgical symbol or religious feeling, where love leaps beyond intellectual concepts and therefore leaves the person in darkness, yet this "darkness is not dark to thee, the night is bright as the day" (Ps 139:12). This psalm is ready and waiting for the mystic which we all must become towards the end of our journey towards God. As we pass the last hurdle by blind faith and deep instincts, we rush alone towards God, who, like the prodigal parent, is already awaiting us and drawing us home (Luke 15:20).

Psalm 89
A Maskil Of Ethan The Ezrahite.

I

¹I will sing of thy steadfast love, O Lord, for ever;
  with my mouth I will proclaim thy
    faithfulness to all generations.
²For thy steadfast love was established for ever,
  thy faithfulness is firm as the heavens.
³Thou hast said, "I have made a covenant
  with my chosen one,
  I have sworn to David my servant;
⁴'I will establish your descendants for ever,
  and build your throne for all generations.'"   *Selah*

II-a

⁵Let the heavens praise thy wonders, O Lord,
  thy faithfulness in the assembly of the holy ones!
⁶For who in the skies can be compared to the Lord?
  Who among the heavenly beings is like the Lord,
⁷a God feared in the council of the holy ones,
  great and terrible above all that are round about him?
⁸O Lord God of hosts,
  who is mighty as thou art, O Lord,
  with thy faithfulness round about thee?

-b-

⁹Thou dost rule the raging of the sea;
  when its waves rise, thou stillest them.
¹⁰Thou didst crush Rahab like a carcass,
  thou didst scatter thy enemies with thy mighty arm.
¹¹The heavens are thine, the earth also is thine;
  the world and all that is in it, thou hast founded them.
¹²The north and the south, thou hast created them;
  Tabor and Hermon joyously praise thy name.
¹³Thou hast a mighty arm;
  strong is thy hand, high thy right hand.
¹⁴Righteousness and justice are the
  foundation of thy throne;
  steadfast love and faithfulness go before thee.

-c-

¹⁵Blessed are the people who know the festal shout,
   who walk, O Lord, in the light of thy countenance,
¹⁶who exult in thy name all the day,
   and extol thy righteousness.
¹⁷For thou art the glory of their strength;
   by thy favor our horn is exalted.
¹⁸For our shield belongs to the Lord,
   our king to the Holy One of Israel.

III-a

¹⁹Of old thou didst speak in a vision
   to thy faithful one, and say:

-b-

"I have set the crown upon one who is mighty,
   I have exalted one chosen from the people.
²⁰I have found David, my servant;
   with my holy oil I have anointed him;
²¹so that my hand shall ever abide with him,
   my arm also shall strengthen him.
²²The enemy shall not outwit him,
   the wicked shall not humble him.
²³I will crush his foes before him
   and strike down those who hate him.
²⁴My faithfulness and my steadfast love shall be with him,
   and in my name shall his horn be exalted.
²⁵I will set his hand on the sea
   and his right hand on the rivers.
²⁶He shall cry to me, 'Thou art my Father,
   my God, and the Rock of my salvation.'
²⁷And I will make him the first-born,
   the highest of the kings of the earth.

-c-

²⁸My steadfast love I will keep for him for ever,
   and my covenant will stand firm for him.
²⁹I will establish his line for ever
   and his throne as the days of the heavens.

³⁰If his children forsake my law
  and do not walk according to my ordinances,
³¹if they violate my statutes
  and do not keep my commandments,
³²then I will punish their transgression with the rod
  and their iniquity with scourges;
³³but I will not remove from him my steadfast love,
  or be false to my faithfulness.
³⁴I will not violate my covenant,
  or alter the word that went forth from my lips.
³⁵Once for all I have sworn by my holiness;
  I will not lie to David.
³⁶His line shall endure for ever,
  his throne as long as the sun before me.
³⁷Like the moon it shall be established for ever;
  it shall stand firm while the skies endure."   *Selah*

IV-a

³⁸But now thou hast cast off and rejected,
  thou art full of wrath against thy anointed.
³⁹Thou hast renounced the covenant with thy servant;
  thou hast defiled his crown in the dust.
⁴⁰Thou hast breached all his walls;
  thou hast laid his strongholds in ruins.
⁴¹All that pass by despoil him;
  he has become the scorn of his neighbors.
⁴²Thou hast exalted the right hand of his foes;
  thou hast made all his enemies rejoice.
⁴³Yea, thou hast turned back the edge of his sword,
  and thou hast not made him stand in battle.
⁴⁴Thou hast removed the scepter from his hand,
  and cast his throne to the ground.
⁴⁵Thou hast cut short the days of his youth;
  thou hast covered him with shame.   *Selah*

-b-

⁴⁶How long, O Lord? Wilt thou hide thyself for ever?
  How long will thy wrath burn like fire?
⁴⁷Remember, O Lord, what the measure of life is,
  for what vanity thou hast created all the sons of men!

⁴⁸What man can live and never see death?
  Who can deliver his soul from the power of Sheol?

Selah

⁴⁹Lord, where is thy steadfast love of old,
  which by thy faithfulness thou didst swear to David?
⁵⁰Remember, O Lord, how thy servant is scorned;
  how I bear in my bosom the insults of the peoples,
⁵¹with which thy enemies taunt, O Lord,
  with which they mock the footsteps of thy anointed.

V

⁵¹Blessed be the Lord for ever!
  Amen and Amen.

(I) Just as the Second Book of the Psalter (Pss 42-72) concluded with an important Davidic psalm, the Third Book (Pss 73-89) also closes with a still more elaborate psalm centering on the Davidic dynasty. From its initial composition, Ps 89 displayed its rich, delicately interlaced unity as shown in the research of J.-B. Dumortier and R. J. Clifford. The poet drew upon ancient traditions about the creation of the universe and the formation of the people Israel and then linked these stories with the promises given to David for an everlasting dynasty. David would be the Lord's instrument to sustain the good order of the world and to insure the fulfillment of the Mosaic covenant. A serious defeat, however, has not only jeopardized God's promises to David, but the entire universe was liable to fall apart and creation be undone. The psalm's principal purpose is to serve as a liturgical lament over military defeat and is general enough to express the people's sorrow and dismay over any defeat. As such it can be compared with several other psalms: Ps 74 bemoans the desecration of the temple; Ps 77 and 80, a major military loss; Ps 83, another serious rout of the army, this time associated with battles in the far away days of the Judges. All these psalms recall ancient events of colossal proportions whose significance was enhanced with the passing of time. The wondrous deeds of Yahweh, the basis for future faith but the source of present sorrow in their non-fulfillment, are woven into these psalms, sometimes at the beginning (Ps 44) or at the end (Ps 77), or in the middle (Pss 74, 80, 83). When the dismay comes last as in Ps 89, the classic form of a national lament is still being followed.

(II) The key words of the Mosaic covenant — steadfast love and fidelity, in Hebrew *ḥesed we'emeth* — link the entire psalm compactly together: vv. 1, 2, 5, 8, 14, 24, 33 and 49. Steadfast love denotes a *close bond* of blood and loyalty, fidelity attests to the *strength* of this bond (see Ps 12). God is united with the universe as its creator in order to center the world around the covenant with his chosen people Israel; the peace and fertility of this world are then entrusted to the Davidic dynasty. This interaction will be seen in many details as we proceed through the psalm, but first we view the overall unity of this magnificent poem:

vv. 1-4, Grand hymnic intro-
    duction
  v. 1, invitatory
  vv. 2-4, motivation drawn
    from creation and from the
    covenant with David
vv. 5-18, Hymn to Yahweh
  vv. 5-8, Supreme in heav-
    enly assembly
  vv. 9-14, victorious in creation
  vv. 15-18, supreme in
    earthly assembly

vv. 19-37, Hymnic Oracle, hon-
    oring the Davidic king
  v. 19a, new introduction
  vv. 19b-27, King, Yahweh's
    lieutenant
  vv. 28-37, Divine promises
vv. 38-51, Reversal of the
    Dynasty
  vv. 38-45, lament
  vv. 46-51, prayer
  v. 52, Conclusion to Book
    Three of the Psalter

(III) Vv. 1-4, Grand, hymnic introduction introduces the covenantal virtues of steadfast love and fidelity (Exod 34:6-7; Hos 2:19-20), to be repeated eight more times in this psalm. Here they are attached to two visible symbols of stability and concern: the heavens and the dynasty. These opening lines show an intricate arrangement of key words: the literary form of "inclusion," by which a section opens

and closes on the same words: *for ever* and *all generations* in
vv. 1 and 4; and the other literary form of "chiasm," from the
Greek word Chi or "X," by which significant words in the
downward stroke are reversed in their order upward: in v. 2,
establish and make firm (*banah — kun* in Hebrew); in v. 4,
make firm and establish (*kun — banah* in Hebrew; unfortunately not that evident in RSV translation).

Vv. 5-8, Cosmic hymn to Yahweh Creator. The opening
lines (vv. 5-8) are sung by a choir representing the heavenly
court of Yahweh, here called *the assembly of the holy ones,*
in Hebrew, "the sons of the gods — *bene'elim,*" as in Ps 29:1;
see also Ps 82. The covenant virtues are first seen in the
celestial throne room.

The next lines (vv. 9-14) draw upon Canaanite mythology
to review God's conquest of hostile, chaotic forces to secure
peace and fertility across the universe. For the Canaanites
this was an annual celebration, when the god Baal conquered the angry sea gods which had roared from the Medi-
terranean during the winter season but were now quieted in
death as spring brought new life from the soil and among the
livestock. From this Canaanite background we understand
that creation could be undone each winter; for Israel it was
fragile insofar as it depended upon a human response to
God's offer of the covenant. This creation myth was associated with the exodus out of Egypt in Isa 50:9-10 and with
the establishment of the Jerusalem temple in Ps 46. This
section closes with the covenantal promises of *steadfast love
and faithfulness.*

Vv. 15-18 are probably to be sung by a special choir
during a liturgical possession; the temple setting here corresponds to God's celestial sanctuary in vv. 5-8. The procession is indicated: *who walk in the light of thy countenance.*
"Countenance" would inspire remembrance not only of the
glorious temple where Yahweh was enthroned, but also of
the glorious deeds of creation and those in the history of
Israel like the exodus, Mount Sinai, the settlement in the
land, and the Davidic conquests, all of which symbolically
reenacted and spiritually relived God's great deeds for
Israel.

Vv. 19-37, Hymnic oracle in honor of the Davidic king.
This section, of course, is linked with the coronation ceremony of new kings (see Ps 2) which centered particularly in
the adoption-formula that God is Father and the king is son
(v. 26). What is unique to this poem, however, is the attribution to the king of what had been acclaimed of Yahweh:

vv. 21-23, the arm of the Lord strengthens the king against enemies
   as the arm of the Lord scatters the sea monsters in v. 10;
v. 24a, steadfast love and fidelity are with the king, as they are the
   herald of Yahweh in v. 14;
v. 24b, the horn (glorious strength) of the king is exalted as Yahweh exalts the horn of all the people in v. 17;
v. 25, the king rules over sea and river, as Yahweh rules and crushes
   the rebellious sea in v. 9.

Another, more elaborate chiasm is folded into vv. 28-37
which detail the promises to the king. The downward stroke
is reversed in the upward stroke of the Greek letter chi or
"X":

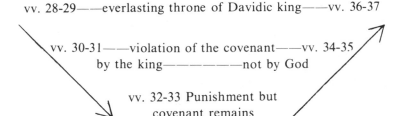

vv. 28-29——everlasting throne of Davidic king——vv. 36-37

vv. 30-31——violation of the covenant——vv. 34-35
by the king—————not by God

vv. 32-33 Punishment but
covenant remains

Vv. 38-51, Lament and prayer over military reversal. The
lament in vv. 38-45 finds the people covered with shame;
their prayer in vv. 46-51 is desperate. The lament begins with
an abrupt reversal: *But you* [O Lord]! The people shout to
God: *How long?* and question God's fidelity to the covenant. If the king is mocked (v. 51), isn't God also put to
shame?

(IV) Ps 89 is frequently and prominently quoted in the
New Testament:

vv. 3-4,   in Acts 2:30, Peter's pentecostal discourse;

v. 20,   in Acts 13:22, Paul's discourse at Pisidian Antioch;

vv. 26-27, in 1 Pet 1:17 and Rev 1:5, speaking of Christ's sufferings;

v. 11,   in Luke 1:51, during Mary's *Magnificat;*

vv. 50-51, in Heb 11:26, abuse suffered for Christ;

v. 52,   in Luke 1:68, during Zachary's canticle, the *Benedictus;*

v. 7,   in 2 Thess 1:10 (Septuagint, Greek reading), Christ glorified by the saints.

In accord with this psalm of lament, these references speak of suffering, mostly Christ's but also our own, which lead to a renewal of the covenant by which God's steadfast love and fidelity are fully confirmed in Christ's resurrection.

Ps 89 weaves together Canaanite mythology and the Mosaic covenant, chaos and creation, political and military reversals. For us these details might be compared to popular piety and perhaps popular mythology, to God's covenantal promises to the church and the church's indefectibility, to the collapse of world order and the necessity of re-creating a new world out of chaos, to the mammoth struggles for justice and peace against oppressive regimes. The inter-weaving of such key dramatic themes from modern life not only puts religion in an effective relation with our world, but these motifs and attitudes, some of them from the secular world or from foreign "pagan" religions, also become instrumental, now as in biblical times, for new insights into the full scope and fierce struggles of establishing God's kingdom in our midst.

BOOK IV
(PSALMS 90-106)

Psalm 90
A Prayer Of Moses, The Man Of God.

I
¹Lord, thou hast been our dwelling place
   in all generations.
²Before the mountains were brought forth,
   or ever thou hadst formed the earth and the world,
   from everlasting to everlasting thou art God.

II
³Thou turnest man back to the dust,
   and sayest, "Turn back, O children of men!"
⁴For a thousand years in thy sight
   are but as yesterday when it is past,
   or as a watch in the night.

⁵Thou dost sweep men away; they are like a dream,
   like grass which is renewed in the morning:
⁶in the morning it flourishes and is renewed;
   in the evening it fades and withers.

⁷For we are consumed by thy anger;
   by thy wrath we are overwhelmed.

⁸Thou hast set our iniquities before thee,
  our secret sins in the light of thy countenance.

⁹For all our days pass away under thy wrath,
  our years come to an end like a sigh.
¹⁰The years of our life are threescore and ten,
  or even by reason of strength fourscore;
  yet their span is but toil and trouble;
  they are soon gone, and we fly away.

¹¹Who considers the power of thy anger,
  and thy wrath according to the fear of thee?
¹²So teach us to number our days
  that we may get a heart of wisdom.

III

¹³Return, O Lord! How long?
  Have pity on thy servants!
¹⁴Satisfy us in the morning with thy steadfast love,
  that we may rejoice and be glad all our days.
¹⁵Make us glad as many days as thou hast afflicted us,
  and as many years as we have seen evil.
¹⁶Let thy work be manifest to thy servants,
  and thy glorious power to their children.
¹⁷Let the favor of the Lord our God be upon us,
  and establish thou the work of our hands upon us,
  yea, the work of our hands establish thou it.

(I) Book Four of the psalter (Pss 90-106) begins here. This collection lacks any clear lines of choice; in fact, eleven of the psalms are untitled or "orphaned." Because the title of Ps 90 attributes it to Moses, the rabbis have attempted to explain this and the next ten psalms according to the blessing of Moses upon the eleven tribes (not twelve, because the tribe of Simeon was punished — Num 25:14). Another scholarly attempt proposes that the sequence of psalms in Book Four is in accord with the order of prayers/ceremonies for the feast of Tabernacles. We cannot be certain.

Similar to the sapiential literature, Ps 90 remains aloof from the history of Israel and its great, redemptive events. In this way it preserves a more moderate, calm positioning. This fact also means that the psalm will be marked with ambiguities, even with the quick jumps which we associate with the disconnected verses in sapiential literature like Proverbs. The psalm is plagued with other problems: the Hebrew text comes to us in poor condition; the ancient versions are not too helpful in correcting it. For all these reasons it is not easy to identify the occasion of the psalm's composition nor of its use. Because of vv. 5-6, some associate it with a drought. Better, however, to call these lines along with vv. 7-8 a liturgical formula for communal confession of sin. We also find the rich, penitential word, *return* (in Hebrew, *shub*) in vv. 3 and 13. It has a different meaning in each case yet by this diversity one enriches the other; each, moreover, introduces a principal part of the psalm.

(II) The psalm opens with a statement of confidence in the eternal God, always *there* despite the passing of human life (vv. 1-2). The next major section (vv. 3-12) is sapiential in character and delays over the fragile, short span of human existence. The final major section (vv. 13-17) is a communal lament and prayer for help. As L. Jacquet remarked, the first major section by itself would remain stiff and distant; the second major part by itself would lack depth and the tragic proportions we now find here.

(III) This title is the only instance of attributing a psalm to Moses and as already mentioned has aroused curious attention among the rabbis. We find parallels with the "First Book of Moses," where Gen 1-3 speaks of the creation of the universe (Ps 90:2) and the return of humankind to dust (Ps 90:3), and with the "Fifth Book of Moses," where Deut 32:7, 36 speak of "the days of old" (Ps 90:4) and the spent "power" of God's people (Ps 90:9-10); Deut 33:27, moreover, refers to "the eternal God" (Ps 90:2c). Finally, both the title and the last chapter of Deuteronomy refer to Moses as *the man of God*, someone with charismatic authority to break through all difficulties and enunciate a message of new hope and strong certainty, like the other ancient "men of God," Elijah (1 Kgs 17:18, 24) and Elisha (2 Kgs 4:7, 9, 21) who brought the dead back to new life, a hint how God over-comes transitory human existence.

Vv. 1-2, Prayer of Confidence in the eternal God, always present to create life across the universe, including the "ever-lasting" mountains (Ps 76:4). The idea will be echoed in Ps 102:25, "Of old thou didst lay the foundation of the earth."

Vv. 3-12, Meditation on fragile human life. In vv. 3-4, the return to dust may allude to Gen 3:19, "you are dust, and to dust you shall return"; however, the Hebrew word for "dust" is different. Here it properly means "crushed" or "humiliated" as in Isa 57:5 or Ps 34:18, "crushed in spirit," preparing the way for the penitential section to follow in vv. 13-37. 2 Pet 3:8-10 reflects upon the *thousand years in thy sight* [and the] *watch in the night* to encourage Christians to persevere till the second coming of the Messiah. Vv. 7-8 indicate that the psalm could have been used for communal confession of sin. *Secret sins* are open before God "who knows the secrets of the heart" (Ps 44:21; *cf.,* Jer 12:3). In vv. 9-10 the reference to 70 or 80 years is not according to the normal life span at that time. The average age of Israel's kings, from Rehoboam to Jehoiakim, was forty-four, and we presume that these princes received better care than their subjects. David reached only 70 years (2 Sam 5:4). The psalm therefore asserts that even at best, life is *but toil and trouble.*

Vv. 11-12 admonish us to make the best use of our short life (*cf.,* Gal 6:10; Col 4:5, "conduct yourselves wisely... making the most of the time").

Vv. 13-17, the penitential prayer for help appeals to the covenant God *with thy steadfast love* (Exod 34:6-7; Pss 12 and 89) and to the renewal of *thy glorious power,* a vague reference perhaps to the wonders in Israel's history.

(IV) In Jesus we see the eternal God plunged into our fragile human nature, "beset with weakness" and so able to "deal gently with the ignorant and wayward." He is able to "sympathize with our weakness [and] in every respect has been tempted as we are." "He learned obedience through what he suffered [and so is] designated by God a high priest

after the order of Melchizedek" (Heb 4:15; 5:2, 8-10). Therefore, Jesus is exalted as "the first and the last, the living one;
I died, and behold I am alive for evermore, and I have the
keys of Death and Hades" (Rev 1:17-18). In Jesus, therefore, "the perishable puts on the imperishable, and the mortal puts on immortality" and for this reason "death is
swallowed up in victory. . . . Thanks be to God who gives us
the victory through the Lord Jesus Christ" (1 Cor 15:54-57).

Psalm 91

I

¹He who dwells in the shelter of the Most High,
  who abides in the shadow of the Almighty,
²will say to the Lord, "My refuge and my fortress;
  my God in whom I trust."

II

³For he will deliver you from the snare of the fowler
  and from the deadly pestilence;
⁴he will cover you with his pinions,
  and under his wings you will find refuge;
  his faithfulness is a shield and buckler.
⁵You will not fear the terror of the night,
  nor the arrow that flies by day,
⁶nor the pestilence that stalks in darkness,
  nor the destruction that wastes at noonday.

⁷A thousand may fall at your side,
  ten thousand at your right hand;
  but it will not come near you.
⁸You will only look with your eyes
  and see the recompense of the wicked.

⁹Because you have made the Lord your refuge,
  the Most High your habitation,
¹⁰no evil shall befall you,
  no scourge come near your tent.

11For he will give his angels charge of you
    to guard you in all your ways.
12On their hands they will bear you up,
    lest you dash your foot against a stone.
13You will tread on the lion and the adder,
    the young lion and the serpent you
        will trample under foot.

III

14Because he cleaves to me in love, I will deliver him;
    I will protect him, because he knows my name.
15When he calls to me, I will answer him;
    I will be with him in trouble,
    I will rescue him and honor him.
16With long life I will satisfy him,
    and show him my salvation.

(I) Just as Ps 90 extended the lament at the end of Ps 89, Ps 91 ends by answering the fear of Ps 90 about the fragile quickness of human existence: *with a long life I will satisfy him* (v. 16). Ps 91, moreover, introduces the pilgrim to the temple; Pss 92-100 provide the liturgical celebration. Several biblical traditions merge in Ps 91: the sapiential position that God protects the just person (Job 5:17-26; Prov 3:13-26); liturgical influences of pilgrimages (Pss 17:8, "hide me in the shadow of thy wings"; similarly 27:5; 31:20), of entrance liturgies (Pss 15; 24; 26), and of priestly or prophetic oracles (Pss 12:5 or 89:19-37); an important Deuteronomic contact shows up by comparison with Deut 32:8, 11, 22-24, 30, 33. A succession of frightful images appear: snares and traps (v. 3), pestilence or epidemics (vv. 5-6), war (vv. 4b, 7) and dangerous animals (v. 13), yet a protective calm from God's presence pervades the psalm. That all these influences and images blend so smoothly, testifies to the psalmist's long contemplation and quiet spirit of confidence. For reasons just mentioned the psalm acquired an important role in the piety of Israel and the church, not just for night prayers but also for the exorcism of demons and as a healing service for the sick. At times individual verses were copied on sacred parchment and worn as prayers, begging God's protection on a journey.

(II) This prayer of confidence is easily subdivided: vv. 1-2, an introduction, welcoming the pilgrim to the sanctuary; ritually v. 2b was spoken by the pilgrim; vv. 3-13, a priestly sermon of encouragement, about the blessings of God's presence at the sanctuary which will follow the pilgrims on their way home and through life; vv. 14-16, a concluding oracle, spoken in God's name.

(III) Vv 1-2, the pilgrim is welcomed into the secret intimacy of Yahweh. If "truly thou art a God who hidest thyself" (Isa 45:15), God receives his faithful people into that divine embrace, symbolized by the darkness of the Holy of Holies and by the invisible but real presence of Yahweh above the ark between the wings of the cherubim (Exod 25:22; 1 Kgs 8:10-12). With Israel's stress upon a personal God, this awesome presence connoted a covenant inscribed upon the heart (Jer 31:31-34) and exercised by loving "with all your heart, and with all your soul, and with all your might" (Deut 6:5). *Shadow of the Almighty*, not only refers to God's gentle care, supporting the people with eagle's wings (Deut 2:11) and abiding with them between the wings of the cherubim (Pss 17:8; 36:7), but also to an eternal concern reaching back as far as Abraham who worshipped God the Almighty — *'el shaddai* (see Ps 68:14).

Vv. 3-13, priestly instruction/encouragement. V. 5, *terror of the night:* just as morning symbolized new life (Pss 5:3; 17:15; 88:13), night is a time of fear and evil, for at night the firstborn of Egypt (Exod 12:29) and the army of Sennacherib (Isa 37:36) were destroyed by avenging angels. *The arrow that flies by day* reads differently in the old Latin psalter: "*a daemonio meridiano* — from the noonday devil," a phrase which gave rise to many religious applications condemning luxury, lazyness, false security, voluptuousness, etc. Vv. 7-8 are influenced by military images; we think of the reference to the "Lord, a man of war" in Exod 15:3. V. 11 has influenced a long tradition about the guardian angel which persists throughout the Old and New Testament, into apocryphal literature of more popular origin, into the piety of many faithful people. A fine Old Testament example is the Book of Tobit. As these texts are studied, the angels are not superstitious beings, distracting from God, but rather instruments to reveal God's intimate love and continuous concern for each person. V. 13, referring to the lion, adder and serpent, now harmless creatures, may reflect in a vague way the prophetic image of the new paradise of universal peace (Isa 11:6-9).

Vv. 14-16, Oracle, promising long life and salvation. Many liturgical expressions resonate here (Pss 23:6; 50:15, 23). We are intrigued by a hint of messianic salvation at the end of the long life. At least the faithful old man Zachary reflects such an interpretation: "Lord, now lettest thou thy servant depart in peace,...for mine eyes have seen thy salvation" (Luke 2:29-30).

(IV) As A. Maillot-A. Lelièvre remark, Ps 91 promises no immunization from trouble; God grants protection in such a way that each trial strengthens and purifies God's servant. This idea is at the root of the sapiential books. Such a person is protected like Jesus as angels descend and ascend upon the son of man (John 1:51) or like Jacob as he began his perilous journey north to Haran (Gen 28:12). God's servant will find himself or herself at peace, strongly in control, sensing God's presence, arriving at eternal glory. The devil misquoted this psalm in terms of an easy, quick victory in tempting Jesus (Matt 4:6). Jesus cites v. 13 after sending forth the 70 disciples on a difficult but victorious apostolate (Luke 10:19).

Psalm 92
A Psalm. A Song For The Sabbath

I

¹It is good to give thanks to the Lord,
  to sing praises to thy name, O Most High;
²to declare thy steadfast love in the morning,
  and thy faithfulness by night,

³to the music of the lute and the harp,
  to the melody of the lyre.

II

⁴For thou, O Lord, hast made me glad by thy work;
  at the works of thy hands I sing for joy.
⁵How great are thy works, O Lord!
  Thy thoughts are very deep!
⁶The dull man cannot know,
  the stupid cannot understand this:
¹⁰But thou hast exalted my horn like that of the wild ox;
  thou hast poured over me the fresh oil.
¹²The righteous flourish like the palm tree,
  and grow like a cedar in Lebanon.

(I-II) From the way that this psalm acquired a prominent place in the Sabbath liturgy of the temple (Exod 29:39-40), accompanying the libation of wine (Sir 50:15), according to the Mishna, we can appreciate its spirit and purpose. The psalmist and the entire congregation who rest with God on the seventh day after "the work which he had done in creation" (Gen 2:3) join in thanksgiving for the goodness of earth and life. The chaotic enemies have been overcome; the work of God's hand is manifest all around. All glory and thanksgiving to Yahweh, whose sacred name is repeated seven times in Ps 92, again consonant with the Sabbath. After a hymnic introduction (vv. 1-3), Yahweh is thanked for his righteous and providential care.

(III) Vv. 1-3, the psalmist invites others to join in the happy moment of song with musical instruments and a meditative type of melody. The morning praise (*cf.,* Pss 5:3; 30:5) will extend into the night, as the psalmist is surrounded with Yahweh's covenant love and faithfulness (Exod 34:6-7).

Vv. 4-15, Thanksgiving. The *works* of the Lord include the marvels of the created world and the redemptive acts in the history of the covenant; all of these are celebrated, reenacted and relived in the temple services. *The dull* and *the stupid* (v. 6) may be intelligent people but incapable or unwilling to recognize God's hand at work, not only creating and redeeming but also demanding that these good things be properly shared with all his family (Pss 49:10; 73:22). The anointing in v. 10 is difficult to explain; if the psalmist was a priest, as Maillot-Lelièvre suggest, then it refers to his own consecration as a priest. Palm trees and cedar (v. 12) suggest strength and regal magnificence (for the symbolism of palms and cedars, see 1 Kgs 6:29; 7:2, 7; 9:11 in the building program of Solomon; Isa 9:14, representative of Israel's rulers; and Ezek 40:16, 22, a vision of the temple.)

(IV) With Jesus who "rejoiced in the Holy Spirit," we pray: "I thank thee, Father, Lord of heaven and earth, that thou hast hidden these things from the wise and understanding and revealed them to babes" (Luke 10:21). God has blessed us with every spiritual blessing in the heavenly places, as we are united in church where the riches of his graces are lavished upon us (Eph 1:1-8). Here we await the eternal Sabbath.

Psalm 93

I

¹The Lord reigns; he is robed in majesty;
   the Lord is robed, he is girded with strength.
 Yea, the world is established; it shall never be moved;
² thy throne is established from of old;
   thou art from everlasting.

II

³The floods have lifted up, O Lord,
   the floods have lifted up their voice,
   the floods lift up their roaring.
⁴Mightier than the thunders of many waters,
   mightier than the waves of the sea,
   the Lord on high is mighty!

III

⁵Thy decrees are very sure;

holiness befits thy house,
O Lord, for evermore.

(I) To appreciate a series of psalms, honoring Yahweh as King and Creator (Pss 47, 93, 96-99), it is helpful to review two major lines of religious practice in Israel: 1) the official, "orthodox" line which stressed God's intervention within Israel's history and was formulated in the classic "creeds" like Deut 26:5-10 or in the ancient poetry outside the psalms (Exod 15; Num 23-24; Deut 32-33; Judg 5); and 2) the line of popular piety, less controlled and still more open to Canaanite religious practices, motifs and language, more tolerant of polytheism, interested if not obsessed with fertility and therefore with creation-centered ritual. Some of the earliest hymns in the Psalter come from this latter background (*i.e.,* Pss 19A or 29). The two lines never remained cleanly distinct of one another; they were continually overlapping.

We can draw upon the example of a Catholic church with its statues of popular saints and its main eucharistic altar. While orthodoxy strongly defended the prerogatives of the "main altar" and its ceremonies honoring Israel's experience of Yahweh in Egypt, Sinai, wilderness and settlement of the land, the people drifted continually towards the "statues" and their significance for healing the sick, for contacting the dead, for enhancing fertility in the land and in the homes. Orthodox religion was aided not only by its Mosaic authority but also by the political scene. To acquire the promised land for the poor and needy, for those coming from the desert and for the serfs and former slaves of petty Canaanite kings, Israel rallied against a religion which supported the city temples and their ruling dynasties. Yet Israel was still attracted to the features of fertility and grandeur in the indigenous Canaanite religion. The two lines crisscrossed in a love-hate relationship.

When David conquered Jerusalem and secured eternal promises for his dynasty, and later when Solomon constructed the magnificent temple, Israel entered into a way of life and worship 90% Canaanite. Notice the opposition of the prophet Nathan in 2 Sam 7:4-7 to erecting a temple. With the conquest of other countries, dynasty and temple acquired new glory in Israel and it seemed that God's promises were totally fulfilled (*cf.*, Ps 87). The temple ritual began to stress Yahweh's title as king and so (like the Canaanites) offered strong religious support for the Davidic king (Pss 2, 89 and 110). Orthodoxy combined the two lines, yet still maintained the primary importance of Yahweh's role as personal God of the covenant, which did not begin with cosmic creation but at Sinai. The convergence appears quite clearly in Ps 68, but also in other psalms which centered creation motifs at Jerusalem (Ps 46). This situation of closely uniting temple with Yahweh's heavenly palace, Davidic dynasty with Yahweh's royalty was challenged by prophets (Jer 7 and 26) and ended with the Babylonian exile (587-539 B.C.).

After the return from exile and the revival of temple worship, royalty was celebrated exclusively with Yahweh in mind. The Davidic psalms were chanted only in view of the distant, messianic age, to be ushered in by a new "David" (see Ps 2). The psalms, honoring Yahweh as King, anticipated the messianic age liturgically; they acclaimed Yahweh as world king and re-creator according to all the hopes of the covenanted people. Psalms like 47, 93, 96-99, propose a messianic age without a Davidic messiah. God alone appears as king. This celebration of Yahweh-King entered into most sabbath ceremonies, when Israel lived in the peace and joy of the first creation (see Ps 92), but it was particularly solemnized on the feast and during the octave of Tabernacles, the final harvest festival, 15-22 of Tishri in Sept-Oct.

Jewish tradition in the Mishna, similar to the title of Ps 93 in the Greek Septuagint, places the singing of this psalm on the eve of the Sabbath, opening the great day of rest and happiness when the earth was first inhabited and anticipating the final, eternal sabbath.

From this historical background, we can recognize the

difficulty of dating Ps 93; it belongs to the long tradition, reaching back most probably to the reign of Solomon when it absorbed many Canaanite/Ugaritic expressions and motifs and yet was much at home in the exile and postexilic age when an archaizing tendency revived many of these same expressions. The style of the psalm is rapid, enthusiastic and yet carefully cadenced. Attractive transitions are seen, from speaking *about* Yahweh in vv. 1 and 4, to a sudden address *to* Yahweh in vv. 2-3 and 5.

(II) The psalm opens in vv. 1-2, where a cosmic setting is provided. The liturgical action is orchestrated in vv. 3-4. The final v. 5 associates the wide-ranging mythological language of the preceding verses with the moral precepts of the covenant and with their home at the Jerusalem temple.

(III) Vv. 1-2, Enthronement of Yahweh and stability of the world. The opening acclamation, *the Lord reigns*, unlike that for the enthronement of earthly kings (2 Sam 15:10; 1 Kgs 1:11), places the name of the divine king first, to emphasize that it is none other than Yahweh who is king. This does not mean that Yahweh was never before king or that the Lord reacquires what had been lost — no more than the proclamation after the Eucharistic consecration, "Christ has died, Christ is risen, Christ will come again," means that Christ is dying or rising for the first time or that his death and resurrection are being repeated due to a deficiency in the events at Jerusalem. Rather the mystery is being continuously actualized in the lives of the worshipers. Nor does the enthronement of Yahweh depend upon the creation or re-creation of the universe; these acts are mentioned later and are due to Yahweh's royal presence, not vice versa.

The language, *robed* and *girded*, come from the military field and denote what we have seen already (Pss 2 or 46) that Israel like other semitic people viewed creation as a mortal battle against chaos. Canaanites linked this struggle with the yearly event of overcoming the hostile forces of winter; the Israelites associated it with the moral order of sin and conversion where Yahweh triumphs in the lives of his people. *Cf.*, Isa 51:9-10, "Awake, awake, gird yourself with strength, O arm of the Lord; awake, as in days of old. . . Was it not thou that didst cut Rahab in pieces, that didst pierce the dragon? Was it not thou that didst dry up the sea, the waters of the great deep; that didst make the depths of the sea a way for the redeemed to pass over?" In this Isaian passage the creation story is associated with the exodus out of Egypt, in our psalm with the renewal of life through temple worship, particularly at the harvest festival of Tabernacles.

V. 2 refers to Yahweh's enthronement above the ark of the covenant (*cf.,* Exod 25:17-22) but attention is focused upon the person of Yahweh; in the Hebrew the verse ends unusually and very emphatically with the second person pronoun, "You!"

V. 3 incorporates Ugaritic/Canaanite words for sea monsters (as did Isa 51:9-10). Another example is present in Ps 29, where Yahweh reigns supreme above all opposition and grants extraordinary peace to his people, assembled in the temple. This peace is as certain as the Lord is mighty, but from Israel's side it always carries a silent warning that the people must be faithful and obedient to the Lord's covenant. The results of disobedience can hit as disastrously as the flood in Noah's days (Gen 6-9).

V. 5 is an excellent example of Israel's way of integrating the Canaanite myths of creation within its own religious renewal. Here the words emphasize obedience to the covenant decrees and therefore to the norms of justice and compassion within the community. Through strong moral compliance with the Lord's will, Israel adorns the house of the Lord with holiness. The way by which the Lord lives effectively in the daily lives of his people determines the holiness of liturgy and temple.

(IV) The magnificent hymn of Ps 93 extends sanctuary or church across the universe and unites the royalty of Yahweh or Jesus, which we acclaim in worship, with our everyday lives in family, neighborhood and country, with the stability of the seasons of the year and with the cycles of life in our farmland, in our rivers and oceans and in the sweep of open air. Whether it is a strong moral fiber in our lives, or whether it is the ecological well-being of fresh air and clean water —everything centers upon God and our obedient, loving response to God. Peace such as this is not easily achieved, nor should it be gratuitously taken for granted. Storms threaten us, as they did the disciples with Jesus on the sea of Galilee. Through Jesus' words, "Peace! Be still!" the wind will cease and a great calm spread through our lives and family/community (Mark 4:39). We cannot survive the crossing without the presence of Jesus, who will rise from the dead again in our lives and there be enthroned (*cf.,* Eph 1:15-23). Thus we inch closer to the moment when "the kingdom of the world has become the kingdom of our Lord and of his Christ, and he shall reign for ever and ever" (Rev 11:15).

Psalm 94

A confident statement that God does not tolerate for ever the injustices of scheming and avarious judges who manipulate the law for themselves and their friends. The first half of the psalm (vv. 1-15), a national lament, lays before us the principles and larger setting; the second half (vv. 16-23) applies these practically within the life of the individual. It is difficult to decide whether Ps 94 was composed originally for community prayer or for private recitation and individual consolation. According to the Septuagint and the Mishna, it was to be communally sung on the fifth day of the week (Wednesday).

The psalm is rich in its variety of literary forms: invocations, questions, laments, narratives, imprecations or curses, instruction, confidence, outrage. To write this way, the poet had to be exceptionally sincere, strong and honest. His was not a groveling obedience before authority; he responded with the independence of the classical prophets (*cf.,* Amos 5:7; Hos 7:1; Isa 1:23; Jer 2:8; etc.).

The psalm manifests an intricate internal development —according to E. Beaucamp. After the introduction (vv.

1-2), we find the following parallels and chiastic structure
(see Pss 19:1; 89:1-4, 28-37): vv. 3-6 and vv. 20-23, first and
last strophes, the arrogance of the lawless; vv. 7-11 and vv.
16-19, second and second-to-last strophes, the questioning;
vv. 12-15, the central, key strophe that Yahweh cares for his
heritage.

Psalm 95

I-a

¹O come, let us sing to the Lord;
   let us make a joyful noise to the rock of our salvation!
²Let us come into his presence with thanksgiving;
   let us make a joyful noise to him with songs of praise!
³For the Lord is a great God,
   and a great King above all gods.
⁴In his hand are the depths of the earth;
   the heights of the mountains are his also.
⁵The sea is his, for he made it;
   for his hands formed the dry land.

-b-

⁶O come, let us worship and bow down,
   let us kneel before the Lord, our Maker!
⁷For he is our God,
   and we are the people of his pasture,
   and the sheep of his hand.

II

O that today you would hearken to his voice!
⁸ Harden not your hearts, as at Meribah,
   as on the day at Massah in the wilderness,
⁹when your fathers tested me,
   and put me to the proof, though they had seen my work.
¹⁰For forty years I loathed that generation
   and said, "They are a people who err in heart,
   and they do not regard my ways."
¹¹Therefore I swore in my anger
   that they should not enter my rest.

(I) Like Ps 81, this psalm also originated as a processional or entrance hymn, and included a further liturgical service of scripture reading, homily and response. Ps 95, however, was composed at Jerusalem and shows the imprint or influence of Deuteronomy and Second Isaiah (Isa 40-55). Because the latter two biblical sources are closely associated with the thought patterns of the former kingdom of Israel, Ps 95 represents a remnant of this northern background, long after the kingdom was destroyed in 721 B.C. We are inclined to place the composition of Ps 95 in the early postexilic age when the pain of the exile was still felt and the people did not yet find themselves at rest and thoroughly at home (Hag 1:4-6). The insistence upon "today" (v. 7d) is common in Deuteronomy (Deut 4:30; 5:3; 6:1; 7:11; etc.); the celebration of Yahweh as supreme over all other gods, as creator of the heavens and the earth and as shepherd of the flock Israel, happens frequently in Second Isaiah (Isa 40:11; 41:21-24; 48:13). In some way Ps 95 folds the journey from exile into a procession and service at the Jerusalem temple. There at Jerusalem the people behold the rock upon which the altar of sacrifice or the Holy of Holies was placed and they easily transform this rock into a symbol for Yahweh. Jerusalem psalms frequently acclaim Yahweh as "Rock," in Pss 18:2; 78:35; 89:26 (see introduction to Ps 18).

(II) The psalm combines a hymn of praise with a prophetic oracle. If the Hebrew text is uneven in meter and division of lines, this literary disturbance is probably due to the liturgical action that accompanied the psalm:

1) The Hymn of Praise: vv. 1-7c

Procession to Sanctuary	Adoration within Sanctuary
call to process and praise, vv. 1-2	call to adore and praise, v. 6
motivation, vv. 3-5	motivation, v. 7abd

2) [The Reading of Scripture + Homily]
3) The Response: Prophetic Oracle, vv. 7d-11

(III) As indicated above, the hymnic section consists of two parts, one to accompany the procession towards the sanctuary or temple, the other for the ceremony of adoration before the Holy of Holies. For vv. 1-5, we are suggesting a processional march, beginning at a sacred place like the spring of Gihon (*cf.,* 1 Kgs 1:38-40, here Solomon was crowned king) and then proceeding up the Kidron valley with the towering rock of the temple in view. The entire congregation sang at the end of each line, perhaps continuously, vv. 1-2, encouraging each other to "come...shout... come forward...shout, shout"; the schola or choir sang lines of motivation: Yahweh is king, greater than all gods, creator of the sea, mountains and dry land, therefore of everything. "Sea" may remind them not only of the fierce struggles at creation but also of the spring of Gihon, whose source of life-giving water was transferred symbolically to the temple (Ps 46); mountains perhaps embody the "threat" to Jerusalem from the "Mountain of Offense," to the southeast where Solomon had once built temples to the deities of his wives (1 Kgs 11:17). Yahweh is supreme!

Vv. 6-7 were chanted after the assembly had climbed the mountain of the Lord, entered the temple through the "Gate Beautiful," and were now before the Holy of Holies. As they are prostrate on the ground in adoration, the schola sings: *we are the people of his pasture, the sheep of his hand.*

After a scripture reading and homily — perhaps along the style of what we find in Neh 8:4, 6, 8, 9-12 — the service concluded with a warning (vv. 7d-11) to take to heart what had been heard. Here the temple prophet linked the journey of the people's lives with the march of the Israelites through the Sinai wilderness. They grumbled, complained and tested God's patience (Exod 17:2-7; Num 20:13). Even though the people are "resting" before the Lord in adoration, nonetheless unless their hearts are obedient to the Lord, they will be driven out of their land, as once happened during the exile or like their ancestors who died in the wilderness (Num 14:20-23). "Rest" is a rich theological term, not only in the Book of Deuteronomy but also in books composed under its influence like Joshua, Samuel and Kings (Deut 3:8-11; Josh 1:13; 2 Sam 7:11). "Rest" means protection from enemies and peace within the promised land; like the land it is God's gift.

(IV) Ps 95, as mentioned already, combines various journeys, a tradition that continues from the Old into the New Testament:

1) journey of the people through the desert in the days of Moses;
2) journey from exile back to the land;
3) liturgical journey into the sanctuary;
4) spiritual journey from a hardened to an obedient heart;
5) journey into paradise and rest with God (Heb 4:4, 9-10).

The Epistle to the Hebrews speaks of God's rest on the seventh day and of Jesus' journey through life, death and resurrection, till Jesus too, like the people in the psalm, arrives at rest before the Holy of Holies (Heb 4:14-16; 8:1-2; 9:24).

Ps 95, moreover, has been the traditional invitatory hymn, introducing the daily prayer of the church. The line, "*today* if you hear his voice," was heard to announce a new grace for each new day, feast or season of the year. A new refrain was composed to honor each occasion of the liturgical year: "Today, Christ has risen! Today Christ is the King of martyrs... or of confessors! Today Christ is born for us!" These refrains adapt the psalm to Easter, the feast of martyrs or confessors of the faith, or Christmas. In many different ways we are being called upon a journey from sin or weakness to resting with the Lord. We rest in the grace of Easter or Christmas; we share in the triumph of the saints —already on earth through the liturgy, in anticipation of the full glory of heaven, where we enter with Christ behind the veil into the Holy of Holies (Heb 4:14; 10:19-22).

Ps 95 can be sung at the dedication of a new church, according to an ancient ritual book, *Pontificale*.

Psalm 96

I-a

¹O sing to the Lord a new song;
  sing to the Lord, all the earth!
²Sing to the Lord, bless his name;
  tell of his salvation from day to day.
³Declare his glory among the nations,
  his marvelous works among all the peoples!

-b-

⁴For great is the Lord, and greatly to be praised;
  he is to be feared above all gods.
⁵For all the gods of the peoples are idols;
  but the Lord made the heavens.
⁶Honor and majesty are before him;
  strength and beauty are in his sanctuary.

II-a

⁷Ascribe to the Lord, O families of the peoples,
  ascribe to the Lord glory and strength!
⁸Ascribe to the Lord the glory due his name;
  bring an offering, and come into his courts!
⁹Worship the Lord in holy array;
  tremble before him, all the earth!

-b-

¹⁰Say among the nations, "The Lord reigns!
  Yea, the world is established, it shall never be moved;
  he will judge the peoples with equity."
¹¹Let the heavens be glad, and let the earth rejoice;
  let the sea roar, and all that fills it;
¹² let the field exult, and everything in it!
  Then shall all the trees of the wood sing for joy
¹³ before the Lord, for he comes,
  for he comes to judge the earth.
  He will judge the world with righteousness,
  and the peoples with his truth.

(I) Another of the enthronement psalms honors Yahweh as Israel's king (see Ps 47). Here we meet an anthology or medley, drawn from other psalms and from Second Isaiah (Isa 40-55). Therefore as L. Jacquet remarked, Ps 96 may be considered the parent of hymnology. While creating little that is new, it was creative of a new hymnic form!

v. 1a = Pss 33:3a; 98:1a; Isa 42:10a — Sing to the Lord a new song.
v. 4b = Pss 48:1; 95:3 — Great is the Lord, greatly to be praised.
vv. 1-9 = Ps 29:1-2 — Ascribe to the Lord, O families of the peoples,   glory and strength.
v. 10b = Ps 93:1c — The world is made firm, never to be   moved.
v. 10c = Ps 9:8b — He judges the peoples with equity.
v. 11a = Ps 91:1 — Let the heavens be glad and earth rejoice.
v. 11b = Ps 98:7a — Let the sea roar and all that fills it.
v. 13 = Pss 98:9; 9:8a — Before the Lord for he comes, for he comes to judge the earth... with righteousness and the peoples with his truth.

The Book of Chronicles quoted the entire Ps 96, placing it in between sections of Pss 105 and 106. Chronicles is associating the singing of the psalm with the occasion when David brought the ark to the tent in Jerusalem:

1 Chron 16:8-22 = Ps 105:1-15;
1 Chron 16:23-33 = Ps 96;
1 Chron 16:34-36 = Ps 106:1, 47-48.

The Septuagint added a title: "when the house [or temple] was built after the captivity." Ps 96, therefore, is a temple psalm. It has found abundant use within the ancient Christian liturgy. The willingness to use and adapt it becomes evident when we find a strong Christian accommodation in the old Latin version of v. 10, "Say among the nations, 'The Lord reigns *from the cross*'" a phrase that occurs in the famous Christian hymn, *Vexilla regis prodeunt*, by the bishop of Poitiers, Venantius Fortunatus (+ A.D. 609).

(II) The psalm has two major parts:

introduction or call to praise: vv. 1-3   7-9
motivation for praise: vv. 4-6   10-13

(III) We comment on a couple verses. V. 1, *sing a new song*, is drawn from Isa 42:10. What Second Isaiah anticipated in the new exodus out of exile back to the homeland, the psalm finds *new* in the liturgy where God's great redemptive acts in the history of Israel are actualized as a new experience of grace. V. 2, *tell of his salvation* translates a Hebrew word, *basar*, which is often rendered, "announce the good news" (Isa 40:9 and 52:7) and lies behind our English word "gospel." The psalm extends the meaning of Isaiah into a more universal scope. V. 5a, *gods...idols*, an effective play on words in the Hebrew, *'elohim... 'elilim*. The psalmist is not so much challenging the existence of other gods as their effectiveness; what more demeaning situation could there be for a god! V. 7 avoids the polytheism of Ps 29:1, "Ascribe to the Lord, *O heavenly beings- ...glory and strength*," a curious theological correction of Ps 29 by a later scribe. V. 9 removes Ps 29's raucous sound of thunder from the sanctuary. The psalm ends with an extraordinary, universal sweep. In the forlorn days of the postexilic age psalms such as 96-99 enabled the people not just to survive and keep faith till the Messiah came, but also to anticipate interiorly the wonder of that great moment.

(IV) From the background of Ps 96 we may want to reread the great gospel of hope in chap. 8 of Romans.

Psalm 97

This postexilic psalm, honoring Yahweh as King (see Ps 93), expands upon the theme of justice in Ps 96 and even more freely draws upon other psalms, especially Pss 18:7-15; 50:1-6 and 77:16-20, as well as upon Second Isaiah. We cite these examples:

v. 1   Isa 49:13; 42:10, 13; 51:5 — let the earth rejoice and the many isles be glad;

v. 3   Isa 42:25 — fire burns up his adversaries;
v. 6   Isa 40:5 — all the peoples behold his glory;
v. 7   Isa 42:17; 45:16 — all worshipers of images are
          put to shame;
v. 11 Isa 58:10; 60:1 — light dawns for the righteous.

As a "hymn-writer," the author of this medley seems closer
to laity, their concern for justice and their obsession at times
with God's marvelous intervention, than to the priests or
levites as in Ps 96 with its many ritual acts of praise.

The first section (vv. 1-6) presents the theophany or wondrous appearance of the Lord within the sanctuary; already
there is special concern for justice. The second section (vv.
7-12) offers the results of this theophany for the good and
for the wicked. V. 2 has an interesting parallel between
clouds and thick darkness and *righteousness and justice*
—not just in the mythological sense found with other
nations, that these virtues are the special gifts of deity — but
also in a truly mystic sense that righteousness and justice
lead to joy and peace beyond all anticipation. Their results
are among the special secrets of Yahweh. The final day of
the Lord, the eschatological triumph, the creation of the
new heaven and the new earth: all of these terms for the end
of the world will not unlock their secret by our investigating
the numbers in the Book of Daniel (chaps. 7-9) or the weird
symbols in the Book of Revelation, but by the practice of
righteousness and justice in the name of the covenant Lord.

Psalm 98
A Psalm.

I

¹O sing to the Lord a new song,
    for he has done marvelous things!
His right hand and his holy arm
    have gotten him victory.
²The Lord has made known his victory,
    he has revealed his vindication in the
    sight of the nations.

³He has remembered his steadfast love and faithfulness
to the house of Israel.
All the ends of the earth have seen
the victory of our God.

II-a

⁴Make a joyful noise to the Lord, all the earth;
break forth into joyous song and sing praises!
⁵Sing praises to the Lord with the lyre,
with the lyre and the sound of melody!
⁶With trumpets and the sound of the horn
make a joyful noise before the King, the Lord!

-b-

⁷Let the sea roar, and all that fills it;
the world and those who dwell in it!
⁸Let the floods clap their hands;
let the hills sing for joy together

-c-

⁹before the Lord, for he comes
to judge the earth.
He will judge the world with righteousness,
and the peoples with equity.

Like the two preceding psalms, Ps 98 acclaims Yahweh as
king over the universe (see Ps 93). Here, however, the
address to Yahweh as King is not accorded the same prominent place (v. 6) as in Pss 96:13 or 97:1, but a worldwide
participation is accentuated. The salvation of Israel, the
involvement of the peoples of the world and the transformation of the physical universe, all these motifs move forward
triumphantly at once. In fact, Yahweh's own personal victory seems wrapped up with these other movements, especially in v. 1b, *His right hand and his holy arm have gotten
him victory.* Yet attention focuses upon the person of the
Lord, the victorious one. Ps 98 has been influenced, not only
by other psalms honoring Yahweh King (or else, all draw
upon a common liturgical repertoire at the temple), but also
by Second Isaiah. For instance, the combination of *victory*

(in Hebrew, salvation) and *vindication* (in Hebrew, justice or righteousness) in v. 2 occurs frequently in chaps. 40-55 of Isaiah (46:13; 47:12; 51:5); the phrase, *all the ends of the earth*, is another favorite of Second Isaiah (45:22; 52:10). It is better not to overemphasize universal salvation. If read carefully, Ps 98 might be saying no more than that other nations are beholding what Yahweh is doing for Israel (see v. 3). V. 9, however, seems to end more generously and include the peoples of the world in the triumph of God's righteousness. The psalm anticipates this moment liturgically.

The ritual actions of the temple liturgy in vv. 4-6, particularly involving music and singing, echo the sounds of the universe: the sea, floodwaters and hills (vv. 7-8). The final line ends with the word, *equity*, that which is morally right and leads to one's destination of peace and joy with God. The final, glorious kingdom of God is not achieved simply by liturgy, nor by studying apocalyptic predictions, but by justice and righteousness. Liturgical anticipation keeps hopes alive and even gives a foretaste of the future, enabling us to persevere in justice.

Vv. 1-3 call upon Israel to praise Yahweh; vv. 4-9 summon a full orchestration of temple musicians and singers (vv. 4-6) and of universal "sights and sounds" (vv. 7-8), till we reach the climactic line: *before the Lord, for he comes* (v. 9). The occasion for the original composition seems to have been the return from exile, but the psalm extends to all God's redemptive acts or *marvelous things* (v. 1) for his covenanted people.

Psalm 99

I

¹The Lord reigns; let the peoples tremble!
   He sits enthroned upon the cherubim;
      let the earth quake!
²The Lord is great in Zion;
      he is exalted over all the peoples.

³Let them praise thy great and terrible name!
Holy is he!

II

⁴Mighty King, lover of justice,
thou hast established equity;
thou hast executed justice
and righteousness in Jacob.
⁵Extol the Lord our God;
worship at his footstool!
Holy is he!

III

⁶Moses and Aaron were among his priests,
Samuel also was among those who called on his name.
They cried to the Lord, and he answered them.
⁷He spoke to them in the pillar of cloud;
they kept his testimonies,
and the statutes that he gave them.

⁸O Lord our God, thou didst answer them;
thou wast a forgiving God to them,
but an avenger of their wrongdoings.
⁹Extol the Lord our God,
and worship at his holy mountain;
for the Lord our God is holy!

(I) The psalms honoring Yahweh as King (Pss 93; 96-99) come to an end almost with anticlimax, certainly more down to earth! The excitement of singing a new song (96:1), the mythological references to the roaring sea (98:7), the trembling earth (97:4) and the mountains melting like wax (97:5), all this agitation subsides. The influence of Second Isaiah is not felt; if anything, we are closer in tone to First Isaiah in the three *Holy, Holy, Holy* (vv. 3, 5 and 9 — Isa 6:3), in the mention of Jacob (v. 4 — Isa 2:3, 5), and in the insistence upon justice (Isa 1:21-26). All these reasons point to the pre-exilic age for the time of composition.

(II) If we divide the psalm into three stanzas (Maillot-Lelièvre), then the following sequence emerges: vv. 1-3,

Yahweh is honored by all the nations for his grandeur; vv. 4-5, the *Davidic king* is celebrated for the exercise of justice; vv. 6-9, the *great intercessors,* Moses, Aaron and Samuel, are reverenced. The three stanzas conclude with a congregational response to Yahweh's holiness, only each time the verse is longer and more elaborate.

(III) Vv. 1-3, the stanza opens with the acclamation: *The Lord reigns* (see Ps 93). *The peoples tremble:* normally the verb, to tremble, is used of mountains (Ps 18:7), or the depths of the sea (Ps 77:16), or the entire earth (Ps 17:18). Such exalted liturgical language, echoing ancient Canaanite myths, has been quieted; the word "peoples" makes us think more realistically of neighboring countries. The exaggeration remains, however, for there is no evidence that any of these nations *en bloc* converted or ever worshiped Yahweh, unless as vassals or tributaries in the days of David (*cf.,* Ps 87). The Lord's enthronement *upon the cherubim* has already been met in the psalms (Pss 17; 18:10); these passages also draw upon another image, the Lord's presence *in the pillar of cloud* (here, v. 7; also Ps 18:10-11). We find ourselves within the temple liturgy which reenacted ancient traditions about the pillar of cloud in the days of Moses and about the cherubim in the early sanctuary at Shiloh. The stanza ends quickly but emphatically: *Holy is he!* Holiness always bespeaks wonder, transcendence, indefectibility, separateness from human weakness, summarized brilliantly by Hos 11:9, "I am God, no human being, the Holy One in your midst." Yet the prophet was honoring this transcendent God for his compassion, as the preceding verse enunciates: "my compassion grows warm and tender. I will not execute my fierce anger." Nothing, it seems, is more transcendent or mysterious about God than God's closeness and loving concern for us.

Vv. 4-5 are sung for the reigning king at Jerusalem; he is praised for the exercise of justice, as in Ps 72:1-2. Other commentators will continue the praise of Yahweh into these lines. The Lord's *footstool,* according to the parallel refrain in v. 9, would be the *holy mountain* where the temple is constructed (*cf.,* Isa 60:13, "The glory of Lebanon shall come to you [Jerusalem],...to beautify the place of my sanctuary; and I will make the place of my feet glorious").

Vv. 6-9, in a style somewhat didactic, rather sober for a hymn, the great intercessors of Israel are mentioned: *Moses* (*cf.,* Exod 14:15, where Moses divides the Reed Sea; 17:11, when Moses extends his arms in prayer for the army; 32:11, where Moses' prayers preserve Israel from the Lord's anger and extinction); *Aaron* (*cf.,* Num 16:41-50, where Aaron's prayers and ritual action with incense stop a plague and make atonement); and *Samuel* (*cf.,* 1 Sam 7:8, where "the people of Israel said to Samuel, 'Do not cease to cry to the Lord our God for us.'"). Because of the santuary setting of this psalm, with the Lord's enthronement within the Holy of Holies, it is not unusual to give attention to temple priests and to mediators between Israel and God, not only for prayer and ritual actions, but also, as in this psalm, for preaching the Lord's will for justice and his desire to forgive. For this preachers drew upon Israel's long tradition, reaching back to Moses when the Lord *spoke to them* and led them *in a pillar of cloud* (Exod 13:21-22; 33:9-10).

(IV) Ps 99 beautifully blends: awesome holiness with Yahweh as a forgiving God; liturgical action with the daily practice of justice; Israel as a chosen people with their relation to other peoples; sanctuary with world. In such a setting Yahweh is king.

Psalm 100
A Psalm For The Thank Offering.

I-a
¹Make a joyful noise to the Lord, all the lands!
2   Serve the Lord with gladness!
    Come into his presence with singing!

-b-
³Know that the Lord is God!
    It is he that made us, and we are his;
    we are his people, and the sheep of his pasture.

II-a

⁴Enter his gates with thanksgiving,
and his courts with praise!
Give thanks to him, bless his name!

-b-

⁵For the Lord is good;
his steadfast love endures for ever,
and his faithfulness to all generations.

(I) The short doxology of Ps 100 concludes either Pss 96-99 honoring Yahweh as King, or the larger collection of liturgical psalms, for the most part hymns of praise (Pss 91-99). As the title points out, *for the thank offering*, this psalm accompanied a thanksgiving service (Lev 7:12-15). Ps 100, however, would seem more closely atuned to the preparatory ceremonies of a solemn entry into the temple courtyards. Later, after the initial hymns and prayers, the priest burned a small part of the offering upon the altar, the larger part was used for a sacred meal, as we read in Deut 26:10-11. "you shall rejoice in all the good which the Lord your God has given to you and your house, you, and the Levite, and the sojourner who is among you." The final line of Ps 100, stressing the covenant virtues of steadfast love and faithfulness (*cf.,* Exod 34:6-7; Ps 89:1-2), strengthens the faith that all of life is to be reunited with its "home" in God who made a special covenant with Israel. The dominant note in the psalm is one of joy. Other important key words also appear: *serve, come, enter, give, bless.* We meet a prolific use of action words.

(II) The divisions within the psalm are easily recognizable: vv. 1-3, a call to praise while processing to the temple; vv. 4-5, praise while entering through the courtyard gates. Each section is like a mini hymn:

call to praise:	vv. 1-2	v. 4
motivation:	v. 3	v. 5

(III) V. 1, *all the lands:* the Hebrew has the singular and probably refers only to the land of Israel; we must be cautious in attributing universal recognition and worship of Yahweh to Old Testament passages. V. 2, *serve*, refers to ritual actions, as in Pss 134:1; 135:1-2; but we are particularly reminded of the ceremony of renewing the covenant in Josh 24, where Israel is summoned to decide, in dramatic fashion, whether to serve Yahweh or the other gods. Joshua's words then ring out, defiantly, magnificently: "as for me and my house, we will serve the Lord" (Josh 24:15). V. 3, *know:* implies an experiential outreach which makes every part of the human person and of community, to vibrate the wonders of the liturgical acclamation: *The Lord is God* — there is no other god! *He made us* by choosing us as his special people (Exod 19:5-6; Deut 7:6-8).

(IV) Joy was certainly the dominant note of Israel's liturgy; they worshiped the living God (*cf.,* Pss 42:2; 84:2; Luke 20:38). This joy was not flighty and unsubstantial, for it was grounded in the bond of the Mosaic covenant, stronger than any blood relationship; but neither was the joy produced exclusively by reasoning and discussion, even if drawn from sacred tradition. Joy came spontaneously, and therefore could overcome every obstacle; it resulted from the experience, individually and communally, that Yahweh is God in every moment and circumstance of life. Therefore, we should always be ready for a thanksgiving service.

Psalm 101
A Psalm Of David.

I
¹I will sing of loyalty and of justice;
  to thee, O Lord, I will sing.

II
²I will give heed to the way that is blameless.
  Oh when wilt thou come to me?

  I will walk with integrity of heart
  within my house;

³I will not set before my eyes
  anything that is base.

III

I hate the work of those who fall away;
  it shall not cleave to me.
⁴Perverseness of heart shall be far from me;
  I will know nothing of evil.

⁵Him who slanders his neighbor secretly
  I will destroy.
The man of haughty looks and arrogant heart
  I will not endure.

⁶I will look with favor on the faithful in the land,
  that they may dwell with me;
he who walks in the way that is blameless
  shall minister to me.
⁷No man who practices deceit
  shall dwell in my house;
no man who utters lies
  shall continue in my presence.

IV

⁸Morning by morning I will destroy
  all the wicked in the land,
cutting off all the evildoers
  from the city of the Lord.

(I) This royal psalm initiates a new series of "Psalms of David," namely Pss 101-3, 108-110, 138-144. These are one of three main groups within the final fifty psalms of the psalter. We will also meet a series of "Hallelujah" Psalms (Pss 105-107, 111-118, 135-136, 145-150 — introduced by Ps 104), and the "Gradual" psalms (Pss 120-134, introduced by Ps 119).

Ps 101, according to H.-J. Kraus and E. Beaucamp, could have functioned as a discourse from the throne, enunciating the king's "platform" or pledge to righteous action. Some will locate the psalm within the coronation ceremonies, but it could have been repeated on any royal anniversary or special festival. The psalm seems to draw upon sapiential tradition; after all, the early book of Proverbs like the late book of Sirach originated in schools for noble youth (*cf.,* Prov 8:15, "By me [wisdom] kings reign, and rulers decree what is just"; and Sirach's reference to "my school," Sir 51:23).

(II) The structure is rather closely knit (H. A. Kenik), particularly within the Hebrew text: v. 1, hymnic introduction; vv. 2-3a, general statement about the moral conduct appropriate for the king; vv. 3b-7, specific recommendations, first in the negative (vv. 3b-5) and then in the positive form (vv. 6-7). In the conclusion, v. 8, justice shall prevail across the land of Israel.

(III) V. 1, *I will sing of loyalty and justice* (in the Hebrew, steadfast love and justice — ḥesed - mishpaṭ); to seek these virtues is a joy for the king, worthy of a song. These are the basic qualities of the Mosaic covenant (Exod 34:6-7), confided to the king (Ps 89:1-2; Isa 55:3). Vv. 2-3a, the opening protestation of the king includes a prayer, sincere and ingenuous, *When wilt thou come to me?* V. 2, *integrity of heart:* throughout the psalm, the king seeks more than external conformity to the law; there are repeated references to honesty, concern and even humility (the opposite of arrogance in v. 5), an emphasis in Prov 11:20; 17:20, "a person of crooked mind does not prosper." The king who is guardian of the temple must manifest the "clean hands and pure heart" expected of all pilgrims in Ps 24:4. V. 8, *morning by morning,* the preferred time for administering justice at the city gate or in other official posts (*cf.,* 2 Sam 15:2; Jer 21:12, "Execute justice in the morning, and deliver from the hand of the oppressor him who has been robbed, lest my wrath goes forth like fire").

(IV) Sooner or later most persons acquire some position of authority over others, whether as parent or teacher, as "elder statesperson" in the neighborhood, as learned or experienced in one or other profession or art, as an elected or ordained overseer. On anniversaries Ps 101 provides a healthy format for an examination of conscience. We seek both interior wholesomeness and external justice; we respect the bond of covenant — steadfast love and righteousness; we pray in the midst of it all, *Oh when,* [*Lord,*] *wilt thou come to me?* (v. 2).

Psalm 102

I

¹Hear my prayer, O Lord;
  let my cry come to thee!
²Do not hide thy face from me
  in the day of my distress!
 Incline thy ear to me;
  answer me speedily in the day when I call!

³For my days pass away like smoke,
  and my bones burn like a furnace.
⁴My heart is smitten like grass, and withered;
  I forget to eat my bread.
⁵Because of my loud groaning
  my bones cleave to my flesh.
⁶I am like a vulture of the wilderness,
  like an owl of the waste places;
⁷I lie awake,
  I am like a lonely bird on the housetop.
⁸All the day my enemies taunt me,
  those who deride me use my name for a curse.
⁹For I eat ashes like bread,
  and mingle tears with my drink,
¹⁰because of thy indignation and anger;
  for thou hast taken me up and thrown me away.
¹¹My days are like an evening shadow;
  I wither away like grass.

II

¹²But thou, O Lord, art enthroned for ever;
  thy name endures to all generations.
¹³Thou wilt arise and have pity on Zion;
  it is the time to favor her;

the appointed time has come.
¹⁴For thy servants hold her stones dear,
and have pity on her dust.
¹⁵The nations will fear the name of the Lord,
and all the kings of the earth thy glory.
¹⁶For the Lord will build up Zion,
he will appear in his glory;
¹⁷he will regard the prayer of the destitute,
and will not despise their supplication.

¹⁸Let this be recorded for a generation to come,
so that a people yet unborn may praise the Lord:
¹⁹that he looked down from his holy height,
from heaven the Lord looked at the earth,
²⁰to hear the groans of the prisoners,
to set free those who were doomed to die;
²¹that men may declare in Zion the name of the Lord,
and in Jerusalem his praise,
²²when peoples gather together,
and kingdoms, to worship the Lord.

III
²³He has broken my strength in mid-course;
he has shortened my days.
²⁴"O my God," I say, "take me not hence
in the midst of my days,
thou whose years endure
throughout all generations!"

IV
²⁵Of old thou didst lay the foundation of the earth,
and the heavens are the work of thy hands.
²⁶They will perish, but thou dost endure;
they will all wear out like a garment.
Thou changest them like raiment, and they pass away;
²⁷ but thou art the same, and thy years have no end.
²⁸The children of thy servants shall dwell secure;
their posterity shall be established before thee.

(1) The fifth of the seven penitential psalms (the others are

Pss 6, 32, 38, 51, 130 and 143) reflects the pain and loneliness of a critically sick person (vv. 5 and 23); words for sin and pardon are conspicuously absent. Sickness unites the psalmist closely with the people of Israel, whose holy city Jerusalem and its temple have been destroyed (vv. 14 and 16). This bond with a discouraged and even (it would seem) a rejected people, reminds us of Paul's statement: "I could wish that I myself were accursed and cut off from Christ for the sake of my family, my kinspersons by race" (Rom 9:3), because as Paul also wrote, "if one member suffers, all suffer together" (1 Cor 12:26). The poet drew upon a rich tradition: a) of prayers, as we will notice in vv. 1-6; b) of hymns, as in vv. 12, 25-27; c) of prophetic hopes, especially as enunciated by Second and Third Isaiah (chaps. 40-55 & 56-66) in vv. 13, 22, 28; d) possibly of sapiential tradition in v. 28. Sickness provided the leisure, perhaps the emotional necessity to plummet ancient religious sentiment, in order to survive a critical period, and to come out of it more hopeful than before. Because of Second and Third Isaiahs' influence, we place the psalm in the postexilic period.

(II) The psalm is best considered a single composition, even if the meaning slips from an individual lament to a communal expression of pain, and from lament to prophetic hope. Because of the latter, personal distress could not destroy an individual's faith.

vv. 1-11, individual lament;   vv. 23-24, individual lament;
vv. 12-22, communal lament   vv. 25-28, hymnic conclusion.
   with aspects of prophetic
   hope and hymnic praise;

(III) Vv. 1-11, the opening verses resonate a long tradition of prayer and lament:

Hear my prayer, Pss 39:12;   *incline ear,* Pss 31:1; 71:2
  65:2   *answer speedily,* Pss 69:17;
my cry, Pss 18:6; 39:12; 40:1   143:7
hide face, Pss 13:1; 27:9; 69:17   *day I call,* Ps 56:9

day of darkness, Pss 59:16;   *days pass like shadow,* Pss
77:2   37:20; 90:9; Isa 51:6
bones burn, Job 30:30; Jer 20:9 *eat ashes,* Job 2:8; Isa 58:5
dry up like grass, Isa 40:6-8   *drink tears,* Pss 42:3; 80:5
vulture and owl, Isa 34:11;
   Zeph 2:14

With such a repetitious cry for help, the psalmist is not
seeking to overcome God's deafness nor to trust in multi-
plicity of words; rather the personal need to sustain an
attitude of prayer despite fearful temptations to give up,
necessitate such repetition. V. 6, *vulture* and *owl*, the former
word is difficult to identify in the Hebrew, but in any case
the psalmist identifies himself or herself with two unclean
objects, to express isolation from community worship.
While drawing upon liturgical language for prayer, the
psalmist is ostracized by its rules!

Vv. 12-22 blend praise and sorrow, prophetic tradition
and lament. V. 12 cites Lam 5:19, except that the psalm
states that God's *memory* (RSV, *name*) *endures to all generations.* Prophetic promises for Zion/Jerusalem not only
sharpen hope but also are expressed with delicate sensitivity: *thy servants hold her stones dear, and have pity on her
dust* (*cf.,* Isa 49:13; 52:2; Jer 29:10; 30:18). We are reminded
of Jesus' tears over Jerusalem (Luke 19:41-44). If even the
dust and stones are held so dear, how more precious are the
children (Luke 23:27-31). From abysmal sorrow the psalmist reaches out to the nations of the world (vv. 15 and 22), to
unborn generations (v. 18), to prisoners doomed to die (v.
19). We hear the echo of Isaiah (Isa 40:5; 41:5; 52:10; 59:19;
60:2) and are reminded of the allusion to unborn children in
Ps 22:31. The psalmist determinately records a statement of
confidence for everyone to see, like a Jeremiah (30:2) or a
Job (19:24). A magnificent certitude emerges that God has
heard the psalmist's cry.

Vv. 25-28, a hymnic conclusion, again drawing upon
Second Isaiah who confessed Yahweh as the First and the
Last, always fulfilling promises and therefore leaving us

with a pledge for the final accomplishment of the divine will (Isa 48:12). These final lines about the heavens' wearing out like a garment repeat an opening reflection, *my days pass away like smoke;* yet now there is firm security in God's creative presence. The psalm ends with hope for new generations.

(IV) The Epistle to the Hebrews quotes vv. 25-27, that Jesus who brings all promises to completion always existed and spans the creation of planet earth and its dissolution (Heb 1:10-12). This same Jesus, according to Hebrews, has also gone the full route of our human existence, even to be tempted as we are (Heb 4:15). Lament and hymns, frustration and hope blend together in Jesus' life as in Ps 102. Biblical faith leads not just to victory but also to a delicacy of love and a tender compassion. There is an *appointed time* (v. 13) for the triumph of faith.

Psalm 103
A Psalm Of David.

I

¹Bless the Lord, O my soul;
   and all that is within me, bless his holy name!
²Bless the Lord, O my soul,
   and forget not all his benefits,

II

³who forgives all your iniquity,
   who heals all your diseases,
⁴who redeems your life from the Pit,
   who crowns you with steadfast love and mercy,
⁵who satisfies you with good as long as you live
   so that your youth is renewed like the eagle's.

III

⁸The Lord is merciful and gracious,
   slow to anger and abounding in steadfast love.
⁹He will not always chide,
   nor will he keep his anger for ever.

> [10]He does not deal with us according to our sins,
>   nor requite us according to our iniquities.
> [11]For as the heavens are high above the earth,
>   so great is his steadfast love toward those who fear him;
> [13]As a father pities his children,
>   so the Lord pities those who fear him.
> [14]For he knows our frame;
>   he remembers that we are dust.
>
> [15]As for man, his days are like grass;
>   he flourishes like a flower of the field;
>
>   IV
> [19]The Lord has established his throne in the heavens,
>   and his kingdom rules over all.

(I) In this lovely, optimistic psalm, thanksgiving easily blends into hymnic praise, sinfulness enables one to settle into God's gracious compassion, individual concerns about health reach outward to God's covenant with Israel and the heavenly throne that spans the universe. Ps 103 glistens with memorable lines: *As the father pities his children, so the Lord* ... (v. 13) or *he remembers that we are dust* (v. 14). It *almost* seems as if it were good to be sick and to recall one's sinfulness, in order to appreciate more the Lord's steadfast love, were it not for the thrice repeated key phrase that we be counted among *those who fear him* (vv. 11, 13, 17). Ps 103 belongs to the spirituality of Second and Third Isaiah (Isa 40-55, 56-66), prophets who preached and wrote during the exile and the early postexilic age: v. 9 echoes Isa 57:16, "I will not contend for ever nor will I always be angry"; vv. 15-16's comparison of human life with the grass of the field parallels Isa 40:6-8; and v. 11, the Lord's steadfast love, as high above us as the heavens are above the earth, seems modeled upon Isa 55:9. Gentle spirituality such as this which blossoms out of the dead soil of exile and the dismal terrain of the early postexilic age may not be able to explain adequately the mystery of sin and pain, yet it speaks convincingly to our faith about *the steadfast love of the Lord*

...from everlasting to everlasting (v. 17). Ps 103 may date in the silent stretch of the postexilic age, perhaps around 450 B.C. and was composed after the psalmist's health had revived.

(II) Despite the transitions from exalted hymn to God's pardon for sin, from personal expressions to communal words, we sense a fragile yet real unity in the psalm.

vv. 1-2, Introduction, and vv. 19-22, conclusion, in hymnic style;
vv 3-5 and 6-18, two expressions of thanksgiving, first for forgiveness and healing, second for the Lord's gracious acts through the Mosaic covenant.

(III) V. 1, *bless*, that is, we joyfully recognize and proclaim God's wondrous, redemptive presence in our lives (*cf.,* Ps 104:1). *O my soul:* the Hebrew word *nephesh* can realistically mean throat (Isa 5:14; Hab 2:5) and metaphorically indicate longing, desire, craving, energetically seeking, in this case the Lord (Hos 4:8; Prov 16:26; Ps 42:1-2).

Vv. 3-5 show that the psalmist was close to death; his or her return to health belongs to a consistent pattern of the Lord's steadfast love. In v. 5, the phrase, *as long as you live,* is difficult in the Hebrew, literally, "your adornment" or "your strength"; because of the translation in ancient versions (Septuagint, "your desire"; and the Syriac, "your body"), Maillot-Lelièvre may be correct in suggesting a realistic yet metaphorical designation for sexual vitality and hope for a family. Life *renewed like the eagle's* (*cf.,* Isa 40:31) may refer to the legend of the phoenix bird which as it flew towards the sun, burned away its old feathers and acquired new ones.

Vv. 6-18, from a long meditation upon the Mosaic covenant (Exod 34:6-7) and prophetic preaching (Hos 11:1; Isa 1:2-4; Jer 3:4, 19; 4:22; Isa 63:16), life's experiences are seen to deepen the realization of the Lord's personal, tender love. The prophets, who announced Israel's punishment for violating the covenant, also interpreted the punishment in terms of God's love, even his tenderness. The psalmist continues this religious development: where Second Isaiah used the metaphor of grass and the flower of the field to compare the transitoriness of human life with God's everlasting word, the psalmist becomes more personal and thinks, instead, of God's steadfast love.

Vv. 19-22, a glorious finale. The Lord's heavenly throne is surrounded with angels, mighty ones and all his hosts: *cf.*, Pss 29:1-2, 10; 82; 148:1-4. This extraordinary psalm which first concerned itself with an individual's sickness and sinfulness concludes with a vision of the Lord's works across heaven and earth.

(IV) Like the psalmist, we too at first tend to attribute our sickness to personal sin and God's anger. Without soft sentimentalism, Ps 103 seems almost to leap, in quiet excitement and quick, strong strides of faith, from personal healing to covenant renewal, from Israel to the world. Yet the Lord appears less as a mighty God and Creator, almost totally as loving parent. This family bond is shared with the world. It is the covenant perception within a human, physical experience that created this hymn of extended, grateful arms.

Psalm 104

I

¹Bless the Lord, O my soul!
O Lord my God, thou art very great!
Thou art clothed with honor and majesty,
² who coverest thyself with light as with a garment,
who hast stretched out the heavens like a tent,
³ who hast laid the beams of thy chambers on the waters,
who makest the clouds thy chariot,
who ridest on the wings of the wind,
⁴who makest the winds thy messengers,
fire and flame thy ministers.

II

⁵Thou didst set the earth on its foundations,
so that it should never be shaken.

⁶Thou didst cover it with the deep as with a garment;
    the waters stood above the mountains.
⁷At thy rebuke they fled;
    at the sound of thy thunder they took to flight.
⁸The mountains rose, the valleys sank down
    to the place which thou didst appoint for them.
⁹Thou didst set a bound which they should not pass,
    so that they might not again cover the earth.

III

¹⁰Thou makest springs gush forth in the valleys;
    they flow between the hills,
¹¹they give drink to every beast of the field;
    the wild asses quench their thirst.
¹²By them the birds of the air have their habitation;
    they sing among the branches.
¹³From thy lofty abode thou waterest the mountains;
    the earth is satisfied with the fruits of thy work.
¹⁴Thou dost cause the grass to grow for the cattle,
    and plants for man to cultivate,
    that he may bring forth food from the earth,
¹⁵ and wine to gladden the heart of man,
    oil to make his face shine,
    and bread to strengthen man's heart.
¹⁶The trees of the Lord are watered abundantly,
    the cedars of Lebanon which he planted.
¹⁷In them the birds build their nests;
    the stork has her home in the fir trees.
¹⁸The high mountains are for the wild goats;
    the rocks are a refuge for the badgers.

IV

¹⁹Thou hast made the moon to mark the seasons;
    the sun knows it time for setting.
²⁰Thou makest darkness, and it is night,
    when all the beasts of the forest creep forth.
²¹The young lions roar for their prey,
    seeking their food from God.
²²When the sun rises, they get them away
    and lie down in their dens.

23 Man goes forth to his work
  and to his labor until the evening.

V

24 O Lord, how manifold are thy works!
  In wisdom hast thou made them all;
    the earth is full of thy creatures.
25 Yonder is the sea, great and wide,
  which teems with things innumerable,
    living things both small and great.
26 There go the ships,
  and Leviathan which thou didst form to sport in it.

VI

27 These all look to thee,
  to give them their food in due season.
28 When thou givest to them, they gather it up;
  when thou openest thy hand,
    they are filled with good things.
29 When thou hidest thy face, they are dismayed;
  when thou takest away their breath, they die
    and return to their dust.
30 When thou sendest forth thy Spirit, they are created;
  and thou renewest the face of the ground.

VII

31 May the glory of the Lord endure for ever,
  may the Lord rejoice in his works,
32 who looks on the earth and it trembles,
  who touches the mountains and they smoke!
33 I will sing praise to my God as long as I live;
  I will sing praise to my God while I have being.
34 May my meditation be pleasing to him,
  for I rejoice in the Lord.
35 Let sinners be consumed from the earth,
  and let the wicked be no more!
  Bless the Lord, O my soul!
  Praise the Lord!

(I) Called "the pearl of the psalter," Ps 104 draws upon the rich culture of the "fertile crescent," ranging from Egypt, across the Holy Land, Lebanon and Syria, into Mesopotamia (modern Iraq). It reaches deeply into Israelite traditions, benefits from the Jerusalem liturgy, and all the while manifests an independent creative touch. Out of a total of 269 Hebrew words, there are 93 different substantives or adjectives (the names of God, not included), 63 verbs and 21 other words equally distinct. The poet could play with language with the same exquisite ease as the Lord made sport with sea monsters (v. 26; Job 40:29). Within Israel's tradition the poet interacted with the days of creation in Gen 1:1—2:4a, as can be detected:

1st day—creation of light—
  Ps 104:1-2a
2nd day—creation of firmament—vv. 2b-4
3rd day—separation of heaven and earth—vv. 5-9

4th day—sun, moon, stars—
  vv. 19-20
5th day—fish created—vv. 25-26
6th day—animals, humankind—
  vv. 21-23, 27-28

The psalmist was no passive copyist, and from reading the two compositions of Gen 1 and Ps 104, the psalm at once appears more elegant and lively. The psalmist is delicately perceiving and inferring *why* and *how* God the Creator acts, while Gen 1 is more concerned with *what* God was making. Even though there is a didactic aspect of Ps 104 (v. 24), still it avoids the lapidary style and the repetition of phrases in Gen 1. Ps 104 stresses God the Creator rather than creation; God compassionate rather God omnipotent; the universe, not passively accepting its proper place, but trembling at God's touch (v. 32), stretching out its shimmering, taut tent cloth in the heavens (such is the appearance of the sky as hot and cold air interact in the atmosphere). In Ps 104 even the lion's roar is presented as a prayer to God for food (v. 21)!

Other comparisons have been noted, especially with the hymn to the sun god Aten by the Egyptian pharaoh and famous monotheist, Akhenaten (ca. 1364-1347 B.C.) but also with Mesopotamian hymns to the god Enlil. We should not overlook the possible relation in Ps 104 with the temple liturgy at Jerusalem. Here the temple was built upon the holy mountain. Once the oceans surged around it angrily but the Lord quieted them as he subdued nations and kingdoms before the city walls; and from here a sacred stream of water flowed to bring life throughout the land (Ps 46; 48). These scenes may be reenacted again in Ps 104:5-10. These facts seem to point to a peaceful and prosperous time in the pre-exilic period, perhaps Uzziah (783-742 B.C.), Hezekiah (715-687 B.C.) or Josiah (640-609 B.C.). The strong interaction with Gen 1, therefore, would have been with the early, oral form of this creation account.

. (II) The psalm can be subdivided according to Yahweh's presence in the world:

vv. 1-4, Introductory call to praise, Yahweh in the heavenly throne room;

vv. 5-9, Yahweh, creating the universe in a battle against chaos;

vv. 10-18, Yahweh, Dispenser of food;

vv. 19-23, Yahweh, Master of the Seasons;

vv. 24-26, Yahweh, Lord of earth and sea;

vv. 27-30, Yahweh, Master of life and death;

vv. 31-35, Glorious finale.

(III) Vv. 1-4, From the heavenly throne room of Yahweh, a call to praise reverberates across the sky and echoes within the soul of the psalmist (*cf.,* Ps 103:1). The verbs in vv. 2-4 are in the participle form as though right at this moment "Thou, Lord, art the one covering thyself with light, stretching out the heavens,. . . walking on the wings of the wind." The word, *bless,* weaves a long liturgical tradition, into the psalm, whereby the Lord was being recognized and acclaimed for wondrous deeds among the people Israel; this joy overflowed into a sacred meal and thereby was experienced anew (*cf.,* Gen 24:27; Exod 18:10-12; 1 Kgs 8:56-61). The image of the Lord's *chambers* or palace over the heavenly waters corresponds with Semitic cosmogony that the sky was like a sturdy firmament that kept the waters above from roaring down upon the earth; above these ocean waters rose the Lord's dwelling (Amos 9:6; Ps 18:6b-15) which in turn was reflected in the Jerusalem temple (Ps 29:9-10). The clouds become Yahweh's chariots; the wings of the wind, his messengers. Both clouds and winds remind us of the heavenly court, prompt in doing the Lord's will (Pss 8:10; 29:1-2, 82; 103:20; Job 1:6). The relation of this scene with the Lord's enthronement between the wings of the cherubim in the Jerusalem temple comes to mind (Ps 17). Later Jewish tradition tended to identify these heavenly beings with the angels.

Vv. 5-9 reflect the battle against chaos, usually found in creation texts (Gen 1:1-2; Pss 2:1-3; 8:2; 89:9-12). This same struggle is read into God's redemptive acts for Israel (Isa 50:2; 51:9-10, 20), to show that the Lord was himself involved in Israel's battle for freedom and grace, and this battle in turn affected the peace of the universe. The taming of primeval chaos in v. 9 is repeated almost verbatim in Jer 5:22, again as a comparison, negatively in Jeremiah's speech, with the people Israel.

Vv. 10-18, Yahweh, Dispenser of food and water, grain, oil and wine. These were considered the staple of life: grain (Ps 105:16); oil for many purposes like anointing the body for health, royal coronation (Deut 28:40 and Ps 89:20), worship (Lev 2:4) and lighting a home (Matt 25:3-8); wine to gladden the heart (Judg 9:13; Eccles 10:19; Sir 40:20).

Vv. 19-23, Yahweh is master of the seasons of the year, for the Lord created the moon and the sun for this purpose (Gen 1:14; Sir 43:6-8). Because Israel's religious festivals evolved around the agricultural seasons (*cf.,* Lev 23:3, 10-13, 22, 40; Deut 26:1-4), Israel's celebration of them completed the cycle and returned the fruits of the earth to the Lord, their creator.

Vv. 27-30, Yahweh, master of life and death. The cycle of life-death-new life depends upon the Lord. This rhythm was apparent in the fields, among the livestock, in their families. Israel, as God's chosen people, possessed a divine pledge of continuity. The psalm does not apply this cycle to the individual nor to universal salvation, but by its explicit pledge of sending the spirit to re-create *the face of the ground,* and by the strong individual note in the conclusion: *I will sing as long as I live...bless the Lord, O my soul,* some kind of implicit faith in personal immortality, even of universal salvation, is lurking behind the words.

Vv. 31-35, the psalm ends like Pss 105 and 106 with *Praise the Lord,* in Hebrew, *Hallelujah,* constituting with these two psalms a small "Hallelujah collection" (*cf.,* Ps 101, introduction).

(IV) Doctrinally, Ps 104 proclaims the goodness of God's world, sin has no place within it and sinners are consumed (v. 35). God's spirit within creation provides a cleansing force; evil returns to the dust out of which God forms a new creation. In this way the entire universe is comparable to the Jerusalem temple where sin, sickness and death have no place (*cf.,* Ps 16).

Liturgically, Ps 104 was chanted by the Jewish people: on the morning of *Yom Kippur* (providing a pledge that new life will emerge out of penance and sorrow), on the evening of the new moon (to consecrate another month of life), and on the sabbath office between *Simhat ha-torah* ("Joy of the Law," final day of the octave of Tabernacles) up till the feast of Pasch, therefore giving a promise throughout the winter season that spring rains and the gentle gift of the spirit will bring new life. The Greek church sings Ps 104 daily in its vesper service, in gratitude for the life of the waning day and in anticipation of new life after the passing of night. Greek and Latin churches have given Ps 104 a prominent place in the celebration of Pentecost. The psalm praises God who *ridest on the wings of the wind* (v. 3) — the Hebrew and Greek word for "wind" is identical with that for "spirit." Pentecost, therefore, reconsecrates the totality of life in the universe. Even where it has succumbed to sin or death, in some ways like Jesus on the cross and in the tomb, on Pentecost we pray that "thou, O God, *sendest forth thy Spirit* [and] *they are created and thou renewest the face of the ground."* This renewal extends through the entire period after Pentecost in the church calendar, as Jesus' healing the sick and sowing the good news of the word in the hearts of the poor transform life and the entire universe. In accord with the psalm, Pentecost sends forth people, missioned by the Spirit, to the four corners of the universe.

Psalm 105

I

¹O give thanks to the Lord, call on his name,
   make known his deeds among the peoples!

⁴Seek the Lord and his strength,
   seek his presence continually!
⁵Remember the wonderful works that he has done,
⁶O offspring of Abraham his servant,
   sons of Jacob, his chosen ones!

II

⁸He is mindful of his covenant for ever,
   of the word that he commanded, for
   a thousand generations,

¹⁰which he confirmed to Jacob as a statute,
   to Israel as an everlasting covenant,
¹¹saying, "To you I will give the land of Canaan
   as your portion for an inheritance."

III-a

¹²When they were few in number,
   of little account, and sojourners in it,
¹⁴he allowed no one to oppress them;
   he rebuked kings on their account,
¹⁵saying, "Touch not my anointed ones,
   do my prophets no harm!"

-b-

¹⁷he had sent a man ahead of them,
   Joseph, who was sold as a slave.

²⁰The king sent and released him,
   the ruler of the peoples set him free;

22to instruct his princes at his pleasure,
and to teach his elders wisdom.

-c-
26He sent Moses his servant,
and Aaron whom he had chosen.
27They wrought his signs among them,
and miracles in the land of Ham.
28He sent darkness, and made the land dark;
they rebelled against his words.

34He spoke, and the locusts came,
and young locusts without number;
35which devoured all the vegetation in their land,
and ate up the fruit of their ground.

-d-
39He spread a cloud for a covering,
and fire to give light by night.
40They asked, and he brought quails,
and gave them bread from heaven in abundance.

IV
43So he led forth his people with joy,
his chosen ones with singing.

Praise the Lord!

(I) During the Babylonian exile (587-539 B.C.), two major religious leaders sustained the people's faith, one was the prophet Ezekiel and the other was the "Great Unknown," a prophet who composed the second part of the Book of Isaiah (chaps. 40-55). Ps 105 belongs to the latter circle. With Second Isaiah the psalmist stressed: a) the new exodus back to the promised land (Isa 40:3-5; 43:1-7; etc.) with little or no attention to organization of life once the people are back; b) attention to the ancient patriarchs (Isa 41:8; 51:2); and c) strong interaction with the traditions in the Book of Deuteronomy. The first two aspects are obvious even from a quick reading of Ps 105, but the last point of contact with Deuteronomy may need some exposition:

v. 1—Deut 32:3, call upon the name;

v. 4—Deut 12:5, seek the sanctuary;

v. 5—Deut 7:18, the wonderful works;

v. 5—Deut 1:16, judgments he uttered;

v. 6—Deut 7:7, the Lord chose you;

v. 8—Deut 7:9, thousand generations;

v. 11—Deut 32:9, portion for inheritance;

v. 24—Deut 6:3, multiplication of people.

Ps 105 will insist that the land is a promise and a gift; it seems to infer as well that this basic religious truth of Israel can be easily forgotten (a key word in the psalm is "to remember," vv. 5, 8, 42). Therefore, Israel must be reminded: of the patriarchs, sojourners for their lifetime; of Joseph, a prisoner for two years (Gen 41:1) before becoming a teacher of foreigners; of Israel, many generations enslaved in Egypt and an entire generation wandering in the wilderness. Only through God's intervention could such a people acquire the promised land.

(II) Ps 105 then is a hymn of new hope in God's ancient promises. According to R. J. Clifford, it can be divided:

vv. 1-6, Invitation to praise and remembrance;
vv. 7-11, Land is promised to the patriarchs;
vv. 12-41, Wandering of God's people:
  vv. 12-15, Patriarchs amidst hostile kings, yet protected;
  vv. 23-28, Israel in Egypt, oppressed yet freed;
  vv. 16-22, Joseph in Egypt, prisoner yet released
  vv. 39-41, Israel in the wilderness, yet protected and fed;
vv. 42-45, Conclusion, restating key themes.

(III) Vv. 1-6. The meditation upon the patriarchs in Ps 105 is unique among the psalms. By reflecting upon God's promises to them, the psalmist is performing an act of worship, as the phrase, "seek the Lord," means. Several key words are introduced here: servant or chosen one (vv. 6, 9-10, 15, 17, 25, 26, 42-43) and remembrance (vv. 5, 8, 42).

"Remembrance" implies actualizing anew and experiencing now the Lord's ancient promises and prodigies. Israel is called to *give thanks* for what is received only in hope, from a distance (Rom 8:24-25; Heb 12:8-31).

Vv. 7-11. The promise of land to the patriarchs becomes the basic law or covenant in the Bible; all else flows from this gracious gift of God, whether it be the ten commandments that keep Israel united as a people before the one God or the sanctuary liturgy. All is done as seeking and receiving from God. Another key word is introduced, "land or earth," or else "portion": vv. 7, 11, 12, 16, 23, 27, 30, 31, 32, 33, 35, 36, 41. We note that the Hebrew word for land is ambiguous; *'eretz* can refer either to a specific land or to all the earth. Like this word, the psalm seems to look in two directions, sometimes towards the promised land of Israel and separation from the nations, other times towards all the earth where Yahweh is also supreme and where Israel now worships in exile. As often in the Old Testament, the salvation of the nations remains ambiguous. Another key word comes into the text at v. 11, "saying," and will be repeated in synonyms for "word" or "promise" (vv. 14-15, 19, 27, 42). In exile Israel had to rely upon the Lord's word and in it to find life, hope and worship.

Vv. 12-15, while living as a wanderer, the patriarchs not only *rebuked kings* but were also designated *prophets* (spokespersons for God whose word endures) and *anointed ones,* greater than the anointed kings and presaging Israel's victory over the world (*cf.,* Gen 20:7).

Vv. 16-22, while a prisoner, Joseph is summoned to instruct foreign princes and elders.

Vv. 23-28, in Egypt God protects his people so marvelously, that the Egyptians are *glad when they depart.* A strong chiasm (a literary feature whereby the upward stroke repeats the order of the downward stroke, like the letter "chi" or "X" in the Greek language) is present in the central verses:

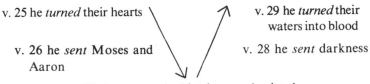

v. 25 he *turned* their hearts

v. 26 he *sent* Moses and
    Aaron

v. 29 he *turned* their
    waters into blood

v. 28 he *sent* darkness

v. 27 they wrought his signs and miracles

The story of the plague differs from Exod 7-11 and Ps 78, in one way among others by placing the plague of darkness first (v. 28). By contrast the Lord immediately provided Israel with light for their departure from Egypt (v. 39).

Vv. 39-41. Just as Egypt, the land of plenty, was ravaged with many plagues which were destructive of life, the wilderness abounded with bread, meat and water which the Lord rained down from heaven.

Vv. 42-45 rehearse all the key words: remember, servant, chosen one, promises, and land. Israel goes forth triumphantly and is now to live as the Lord's obedient people. The cultic refrain, *Hallelujah*, concludes Ps 105 (see introduction to Ps 101).

(IV) Pss 103 and 105 surround the brilliant psalm about nature (Ps 104) with a strong sense of Israel's sacred history and ancient traditions. God as Creator is always understood within the context of God the Redeemer of Israel. Our own bond or covenant with God provides a family setting of love and concern in which every other material aspect of life is viewed. The psalm further emphasizes that without God we wander hopelessly, but under God's basic "law" or promise (v. 10) our wandering leads to a promised land. Yet most attention is given to the *way* towards that land, not to the land itself — despite the fact that a key word in the psalm is land! Thus we never forget that land is a promise. That the promise exceeds our merit and ability is continually brought to our attention as we are fed with *bread from heaven in abundance* (v. 40). We go forth, or rather we are *led forth with joy* (v. 43); we cannot begin without God's invitation. As the liturgy celebrates this continuous exodus in its sacred processions, we joyfully approach our heavenly homeland.

Psalm 106

Like the sermons in the Book of Deuteronomy, the auto-biographical writing in Nehemiah, or the prayers in Third Isaiah, especially 59; 61:1-3; 63:7—64:11, the pervading attitude of Ps 105 is hopeful sorrow over sin. It leads, not just to a forgiving God, but to a peaceful reunion with God during the quiet and sombre days of the postexilic period. If we must type the psalm, we prefer to call it a communal lament within a liturgy of song, confession of sin and promise of grace. Coming upon the heels of Ps 105, this psalm cannot avoid comparison with the latter. While Ps 105 views Israel's history from *God's* viewpoint of promise and ever-lasting covenant, Ps 106 surveys the same history from the *human* viewpoint of sin plus an abiding sense of Yahweh's enduring covenant. Both psalms belong to the psalter, address the same God. Both are united by the word *Halle-lujah! Praise the Lord!* (see the introduction to Ps 101). Today as in ancient times we need both psalms within our canonical scriptures, Ps 105 to lift us up and Ps 106 to reprove, Ps 105 to absorb God's sweep of history and Ps 106 to admit our faults for our betterment. It is a strong and solid spirituality to recognize that we are not swept along by mammoth powers of evil but are answerable in a responsible way for our own deeds and misdeeds; it is a consoling spirituality that God listens to us even in our sins.

Ps 106 is quoted within 1 Chron 16 in a medley of psalms:

1 Chron 16:7-22 = Ps 105:1-15   1 Chron 16:34 = Ps 106:1
            16:23-33 = Ps 96:1-13a   16:35-36 = Ps 106:47-48

The psalm, therefore, was composed some years before 1-2 Chron, *i.e.,* before 450 B.C., but after the return from exile in 537 B.C. because of vv. 27 and 47.

We adopt the division of A. Deissler, recognizing the interweaving of various liturgical forms:

Title — Praise the Lord-Hallelujah!

vv. 1-3, Entry Chant

vv. 4-5, Prayer

vv. 6-22, Israel's ingratitude in desert

vv. 23-27, Yahweh's mercy and justice

vv. 28-44, Further disobedience in the land

vv. 45-46, New Grace of Yahweh

v. 47, Prayer

v. 48, Doxology, concluding Book Four of the Psalter

BOOK V
(PSALMS 107-150)

Psalm 107

I

¹O give thanks to the Lord, for he is good;
   for his steadfast love endures for ever!
²Let the redeemed of the Lord say so,
   whom he has redeemed from trouble
³and gathered in from the lands,
   from the east and from the west,
   from the north and from the south.

II

⁴Some wandered in desert wastes,
   finding no way to a city to dwell in;
⁵hungry and thirsty,
   their soul fainted within them.
⁶Then they cried to the Lord in their trouble,
   and he delivered them from their distress;
⁷he led them by a straight way,
   till they reached a city to dwell in.
⁸Let them thank the Lord for his steadfast love,
   for his wonderful works to the sons of men!
⁹For he satisfies him who is thirsty,
   and the hungry he fills with good things.

III

¹⁰Some sat in darkness and in gloom,
   prisoners in affliction and in irons,
¹¹for they had rebelled against the words of God.
   and spurned the counsel of the Most High.
¹²Their hearts were bowed down with hard labor;
   they fell down, with none to help.

¹³Then they cried to the Lord in their trouble,
   and he delivered them from their distress;
¹⁴he brought them out of darkness and gloom,
   and broke their bonds asunder.
¹⁵Let them thank the Lord for his steadfast love,
   for his wonderful works to the sons of men!
¹⁶For he shatters the doors of bronze,
   and cuts in two the bars of iron.

IV

¹⁷Some were sick through their sinful ways,
   and because of their iniquities suffered affliction;
¹⁸they loathed any kind of food,
   and they drew near to the gates of death.
¹⁹Then they cried to the Lord in their trouble,
   and he delivered them from their distress;
²⁰he sent forth his word, and healed them,
   and delivered them from destruction.
²¹Let them thank the Lord for his steadfast love,
   for his wonderful works to the sons of men!
²²And let them offer sacrifices of thanksgiving,
   and tell of his deeds in songs of joy!

V

²³Some went down to the sea in ships,
   doing business on the great waters;
²⁴they saw the deeds of the Lord,
   his wondrous works in the deep.

²⁵For he commanded, and raised the stormy wind,
   which lifted up the waves of the sea.

²⁸Then they cried to the Lord in their trouble,

and he delivered them from their distress;
²⁹he made the storm be still,
and the waves of the sea were hushed.

³¹Let them thank the Lord for his steadfast love,
for his wonderful works to the sons of men!
³²Let them extol him in the congregation of the people,
and praise him in the assembly of the elders.

VI
⁴³Whoever is wise, let him give heed to these things;
let men consider the steadfast love of the Lord.

(I) The original psalm of thanksgiving consisted of vv. 1-22. It was composed under the influence particularly of Second Isaiah (chaps. 40-55) and Job, in order to express communal gratitude for the return from exile. Two sets of refrains provide key words and basic religious insights: *trouble* and *distress*, too serious for anyone to be able to extricate themselves by their own resources; God's *wonderful works*, beyond Israel's ability and merit; *sons of men*, a phrase always accentuating human weakness (*cf.*, Ps 8:4); God's *steadfast love*, pointing out a bond of affectionate loyalty between God and the people. Human weakness and distress require God's strong, protective and tender care all the more immediately. The people are close to death, and in the second and third stanzas they are guilty of sin. Even in the first and fourth stanzas where sin is not mentioned, the imagery points to demons who inhabit desert places (Isa 34:12-15; Tob 8:3; Lev 16:21-22) and to the sea monsters (Pss 74:13-14; 89:9-10). Later the psalm was expanded, under sapiential influence (*i.e.,* Proverbs), first with the addition of a fourth stanza (vv. 23-32) that was modeled upon the other three and then with the strongly sapiential conclusion (vv. 33-43).

(II) The structure of Ps 107 is easily recognized:

vv. 1-3, Introductory call to *give thanks*
vv. 4-32, where each of the four stanzas follow the same pattern:

	travel by land	imprison-ment	sickness	travel by sea
description of distress	vv. 4-5	10-12	17-18	23-27
prayer refrain	6	13	19	28
deliverance	7	14	20	29-30
thanksgiving refrain	8-9	15-16	21-22	31-32

vv. 33-42, God's power over the world (vv. 33-38), and care for the afflicted (vv. 39-42); finally, advice from the sages (v. 43).

(III) Vv. 1-3, Call to *give thanks*. Especially in its final verse, it is adapted to the ingathering of God's people. The refrain, *his steadfast love endures forever*, repeated continuously in the Great Hallel (Ps 136), originated in the postexilic age. Religiously it views every moment of Israel's history as related to God's inner self and personal concern. A similar insight is contained in the word *redeem*, twice repeated in v. 2; that Hebrew word began in the secular arena for blood relative (Lev 25:23-55) and was transferred to the religious (*cf.*, Ps 19, also Isa 35:19; 43:1; 51:10; 62:12).

Vv. 4-9, travel by land in *desert wastes*, always dangerous, and if one loses the way, certain death. The refrain in vv. 8, 15, 21 and 31, links this deliverance with all of the Lord's *wonderful works* in the long history of Israel. The Lord's care of Israel in the wilderness in the days of Moses continues with the present generation; the Lord is always "the same" (Ps 102:37), "from everlasting to everlasting" (Ps 106:48).

Vv. 10-16, imprisonment and execution are attributed to a deliberate rebellion against God's word; callously they *spurned the counsel of the Most High*. When Israel had done this in Moses' day and would not accept the invitation to go directly into the promised land, "the Lord said to Moses, 'How long will this people *despise* me? And how long will they not believe in me, in spite of all the signs which

I have wrought among them? I will strike them...and
disinherit them, and I will make of you a nation greater and
mightier than they'" (Num 14:11-12). Again the Lord's
steadfast love prevails and *he shatters the doors of bronze* to
set them free (*cf.,* Isa 45:2; Herodotus refers to the hundred
bronze gates at Babylon — A. A. Anderson).
    Vv. 17-22, illness close to death, due again to willful sin.
God saves the person from *the gates of death,* a phrase that
will be repeated by Jesus in Matt 16:18 in promising everlasting protection to Peter and the church. It is God's healing word which brings the dying person back to life. Here as
in Isa 57:18-19 and elsewhere in the Bible, physical health
and spiritual obedience to God's word go hand in hand (*cf.,*
Gen 3:19, 22, where sin brings the curse of sickness and
death). God does not simply remove the symptoms; his
healing word reaches to the radical cause of sickness. In the
Hebrew text, vv. 21-26 begin with an inverted letter "nun," a
curiosity without adequate explanation; the rabbis claimed
that it was due to a change or transposition of verses, an
explanation which did not please Rabbi Jedudah ha-Nasi,
famous redactor of the Mishnah or code of Jewish laws at
the beginning of the third century. He would not tolerate
any such dislocation in God's word; he explained that here
and in Num 10:35-36 where it happens again, we have a
book within a book, so precious are the verses — B. J.
Roberts. This stanza closes the original psalm with sacrifice
in the temple and a sacred meal.
    Vv. 23-32, dangers of sea travel. Here the influence of
Second Isaiah is no longer in evidence and we find parallels
with images of dangerous sea travel in the sapiential books
of Proverbs and Sirach (Prov 23:34; 30:18-19; 31:14; Sir
43:24-25). Only for a brief period during the reigns of
Solomon and Jehoshaphat (1 Kgs 9:26-28; 22:49) did Israel
have a fleet of ships, at Ezion-geber, sailing in the direction
of the Red Sea. That of Jehoshaphat was wrecked before it
got underway, confirming Israel's fear of the sea. Even
sailing in the Sea of Galilee is marked with sudden storms
(Mark 4:35-41).

V. 43. This conclusion reminds us of the sapiential addition to the prophecy of Hosea (14:9).

(IV) Ps 107 embraces the totality of life; it reaches into the most desperate moments of our existence, and enables us to realize that God's steadfast love — the bond of love and blood which unites us as kinspersons — embraces and cares for the tender roots of our lives. Even when we have rebelled or wandered, when we have ventured recklessly into dangers, moral and physical, always the bond of love claims its own and God comes to our aid. But we must cry to the Lord in our trouble and distress and appeal to our common blood relation with God, according to one of the refrains. At these moments we find that Jesus calms the storm at sea (Mark 4:39), compassionately provides bread in the wilderness (Matt 14:13-21), releases the chains of prisoners (Luke 4:18), and asks all who are weary to come to him (Matt 11:28).

Psalm 108
A Song. A Psalm Of David.

The author combines material from two preexisting psalms: Ps 57, an individual lament; and Ps 60, a national lament; yet in doing so, he or she produced something new with much less emphasis upon sorrow and a new expression of thanksgiving in vv. 1-5 and consolation in vv. 6-13.

Ps 108:1-5 = Ps 57:7-11
Ps 108:6-13 = Ps 60:5-12

This uprooting of verses from their original setting shows that in ancient times biblical interpretation was not confined to historical studies but was primarily a pastoral undertaking to meet new expectations and demands. The psalm shows a creative hand at work. The author lived in the postexilic age. By its present position in the psalter we are being introduced to a small collection of Psalms of David (Pss 108-110).

Psalm 109
To The Choirmaster. A Psalm Of David.

(I) In this psalm we are brought to the side of a person, calumniated (vv. 4, 20, 29) and condemned without a hearing (vv. 7 and 31), dejected and possibly sick (vv. 23-24), deserted by friends (v. 25). We think of the prophet Jeremiah whose words seem to resonate within the psalm, especially his curses in Jer 18:21-22. According to some scholars, in the long section cursing the enemy (vv. 6-20), the psalmist is quoting the adversary's charge against himself. Yet it seems more likely that one person composed the entire psalm. There are many identical words found in the curses (vv. 6-20) and again in the laments (vv. 1-5, 21-31), and the wicked person would hardly be quoting the prophet Jeremiah.

(II) The structure of the psalm is quickly perceived:

vv. 1-5, Introductory lament;
vv. 6-20, Curse of enemy;
vv. 21-29, Continuation of lament;
vv. 30-31, Vindication, to be celebrated within an assembly.

(III) The psalm opens abruptly, almost defiantly, *Be not silent, God;* do not act like those false gods who "have mouths, but do not speak; eyes, but do not see; ears, but do not hear; noses, but do not smell; hands, but do not feel..." (Ps 115:5-7). *God of my praise* reflects a plaintive plea with God by Jeremiah (17:14). Within the imprecation (v. 16), we find that the enemy has violated the prophetic injunction: "do justice, love kindness, walk humbly with your God" (Mic 6:8). The new lament (vv. 21-29) recalls the prayers in other psalms. For expressing words of gratitude to God, the psalmist avoids the normal expression for a liturgical assembly but speaks of being *in the midst of the throng* (v. 30). Are some of his accusers among the temple personnel and so their "sacred" assembly is repudiated? Or is he thinking simply of a wide circle of acquaintances?

(IV) For appreciating the vindicative psalms within the

spirituality of the Bible and today, see the commentary on
Ps 69.

Psalm 110
A Psalm Of David.

I

¹The Lord says to my lord:
"Sit at my right hand,
till I make your enemies
your footstool."

II

²The Lord sends forth from Zion
your mighty scepter.
Rule in the midst of your foes!

III

³Your people will offer themselves freely
on the day you lead your host
upon the holy mountains.
From the womb of the morning
like dew your youth will come to you.

IV

⁴The Lord has sworn
and will not change his mind,
"You are a priest for ever
after the order of Melchizedek."

V

⁵The Lord is at your right hand;
he will shatter kings on the day of his wrath.
⁶He will execute judgment among the nations,
filling them with corpses;
he will shatter chiefs
over the wide earth.

VI

⁷He will drink from the brook by the way;
therefore he will lift up his head.

(I) In Ps 110 we meet what may well be one of the oldest psalms in the psalter, whose Hebrew text and interpretation modulated through the centuries. This long history not only permitted a variety of applications but also surrounded God's messianic plans with mystery. Not even the highest authorities in Jesus' day were sure of the precise meaning. By quoting the psalm Jesus silenced his adversaries: "nor from that day did anyone dare to ask him any more questions" (Matt 22:46). If Ps 110 is the most quoted of all psalms in the New Testament, the citations are discreetly confined to vv. 1 and 4 and move away from secular royalty (where the psalm originated with the Davidic dynasty) and its right to control the temple and religious matters. The New Testament also avoids the rights of priests to determine secular government as we see this power granted to priests in Sir 45:24-25 and 1 Macc 14:41-43. The New Testament emphasizes first the mysterious origin of the Messiah (Matt 22:41-46) and then the priestly prerogatives of the Messiah (Heb 5:5-10). Because of these difficulties and uncertainties Ps 110 could not be called upon to settle disputes, and its ability to gather and sustain a rich, versatile body of traditions made it an extraordinarily effective tool for plummeting into theological depths.

Ps 110 blends three major forms of leadership: a) the *prophetic*, since it begins with a rubric designating a prophetical oracle, *The Lord says,* literally, *the oracle of the Lord—ne'um yahweh*, found only this single time in the psalter but frequently with the prophets (of its 361 occurrences, 167x in Jeremiah; 83x in Ezekiel; 23x in Isaiah; 21x in Amos; etc.); b) the *royal*, since like Ps 2 it functioned as a coronation hymn for a new king; see v. 3; and c) the *priestly*, as is evident in v. 4. One or other of these aspects will emerge supreme at different times of Israelite history, a simple statement which reflects traumatic tension and at times political upheaval. Little wonder that Ps 110 found itself at the eye of the hurricane in the controversy between Jesus the Jew and some other Jewish leaders as well as between the early Jewish disciples of Jesus and their Jewish neighbors.

(II) We understand Ps 110 as originally representing the coronation ceremony of a new Davidic king. For general background, see Ps 2. For more specific details of the ceremony, we can tentatively propose the following schema:

v. 1, the crown prince is led to the royal "throne" in the temple, at the "pillar";

v. 2, presentation of the scepter, symbol of authority;

v. 3, anointing with oil and utterance of the consecratory formula, the heart of the ceremony; from this moment onward the crown prince is king;

v. 4, the new king is acclaimed according to the titles of the ancient Jebusite royalty of pre-Davidic Jerusalem;

vv. 5-6, the king is Yahweh's lieu-tenant, "holding the place" of Yahweh towards all Israel;

v. 7, drinking of the life-giving waters, either at the sacred place of the Gihon spring in the Kidron valley to the east of Jerusalem where Solomon was crowned king (1 Kgs 1:39-40), or in the Jerusalem temple where this water, spiritually or typologically, was thought to originate, to give life to the entire city and country (*cf.,* Ps 46:4).

(III) V. 1, *The Lord said to my lord:* literally in the Hebrew, "The Oracle of Yahweh [addressed] to my lord [the new king on this day of enthronement]." Jesus' words as cited in the Gospels (Matt 22:44; Mark 12:36; Luke 20:42) are drawn from the Greek Septuagint translation which twice used the same word, *kurios,* "The Lord said to my Lord," enhancing the divine origin and relationship of the Davidic king, but not claiming divinity. In the postexilic age, when the dynasty disappeared, its revival remained God's mysterious, messianic promise. *Sit at my right hand:* certainly a place of honor (1 Kgs 2:19; Ps 45:9) and of power (Ps 80:17), here referring either to the pillar at the right of the Holy of Holies within the temple and reserved for royalty (2 Kgs 11:14; 23:3), or to the palace and other royal buildings directly south of the temple. Because directions were taken, facing east, one of the Hebrew words for "south" was "righthand" (Josh 17:7). *enemies your footstool: cf.,* Josh 10:24; for a more favorable interpretation of loyalty to Yahweh, Ps 99:5. V. 2, *Lord sends forth from Zion:* Jerusalem is considered the center of the universe (Ezek 5:5; 38:12). Other nations are considered only in relation to Israel, Yahweh's chosen people; that all nations find their peace in terms of Israel is at least a step towards universal salvation.

V. 3, for this crucial verse, the divine word by which the crown prince is constituted king, there are two major traditions, the Hebrew and the Greek. Very often the Greek is derived from the same Hebrew consonants but different vowels: *i.e., your people,* in Hebrew *'ammi,* reads in Greek "with you," translated from the Hebrew *'immi;* or *your youth,* in Hebrew *yalduteka,* reads in Greek *"I have begotten you,"* translated from the Hebrew *yelidtika.* The RSV generally follows the Hebrew, except that it reads *upon the holy mountains* (in Hebrew, *harre-kodesh*), a correction of the actual Hebrew text, *hadre-kodesh* = *in holy splendor.* In Hebrew the letters "d" and "r" are almost identical in shape.

Hebrew, in literal translation	*Greek Septuagint*
Your people offer themselves freely in the day of your power (*)	With you is dominion in the day of your power
in holy splendor	in the splendor of the holy ones (**)
from the womb, from the dawn	from the womb before the morning star
yours the dew of your youth	I have begotten you.

(*) with a slight change, the Hebrew can read, "in the day of your birth."

(**) "holy ones" refers to the divine assembly — see Ps 82.

As in Ps 2:7 the king is considered in a most special way Yahweh's "son," and the coronation, the day of his birth. As such the king is representative of all the people who are also called Yahweh's children (Exod 4:22; Hos 11:1). The mysterious relationship of the king to Yahweh is stated clearly in the Greek, more mystically in the Hebrew, as *dew* not only symbolized God's special blessing (Ps 133:3) but also a mysterious origin (Job 38:28, "Has the rain a father, or who has begotten the drops of dew?"; *cf.,* Judg 6:37-40).

V. 4, *priest for ever after the order of Melchizedek:* according to ancient tradition (Gen 14:18), Melchizedek was a priest-king of Salem (=Jerusalem, *cf.,* Ps 76:2) and provided a title for the pre-Davidic, Jebusite kings of the city. When David conquered the city, he acquired the rights of its royalty and therefore its honorary titles. Normally, liturgical functions were fulfilled by levitical priests of the family of Eli or of Zadok (2 Sam 8:17). Yet on important occasions kings offered sacrifices: *i.e.,* David (2 Sam 6:17-18; 24:25) and Solomon (1 Kgs 8:5). If the word, Melchizedek, is not left as a proper name but is translated into what it means (my king, righteousness) the verse could read, "Thou art a priest forever, because I have spoken right-eously, my king." We do not favor this latter interpretive translation for these reasons: relation of Melchizedek in Gen 14 with Jerusalem; Jewish tradition before and after the time of Jesus which developed interesting stories, relating Melchizedek to Abraham, the messiah and heavenly beings; the Epistle to the Hebrews which develops an eternal priest-hood of Jesus the messiah from this reference to the messiah-priest Melchizedek (Heb 5:6; 7:17, 21).

Vv. 5-7. It is possible that the "he" who acts in these verses, shattering kings, executing justice and drinking from the brook, refers to the Davidic king — except in the first and last line: *The Lord is at your right hand* and *he* [the Lord] *will lift up his* [the king's] *head.* In oriental style these lines speak of the king's victorious reign and of the ritual drinking of "holy water" in v. 7 (see above).

(IV) *Theologically,* the long, convoluted history of Ps 110 indicates that there is no simple, easy way of listing Old Testament texts to *prove* the true Messiah; once we accept Jesus as Lord and Savior, then we can profitably use these texts to explore the mysterious origin and role of the Mes-siah. *Historically,* the complicated way of Israelite politics by which the Scriptures referred to kings who assume the office of priest (Ps 110:4) or of priests who claimed royal power (Zech 3:1-10; 6:9-14 admittedly difficult verses) show that we cannot find in the Bible a single definition of priesthood. Rather priestly functions were evolving according to political, religious needs of individual moments of time, always with traditional roots, but also with dramatic changes. *Liturgically,* our church ritual ought to remain sensitively in touch with the full life of people, an important part of which is political leadership, so that the means of economic stability, social justice and international peace are blessed. *Spiritually,* Ps 110 consecrates Jesus as *our* king and Messiah, ruler of each moment and part of our lives, as the resurrected Jesus sends the Spirit into our hearts (Acts 2:34-35). This messianic king was crowned with thorns and mocked with a scepter or reed in his hands (Matt 27:27-30). Here we witness a fulfillment of royal psalms with dramatic reversal!

Psalms 111-112

Pss 111 and 112, though separate poems, share rhythm, vocabulary and larger ideas; they seem to have been composed by the same poet-teacher. Each follows an acrostic or alphabetical arrangement (see Pss 9-10), and so accentuate a didactic purpose, Ps 111 to remember the great works of the covenant God, Ps 112 to inspire covenant fidelity and righteousness. The subject matter dictated the major attitude so that Ps 111 leans towards a hymn and a song of thanksgiving while Ps 112 tilts definitely in the direction of a Wisdom psalm. While Ps 111 directs the praise to God, Ps 112 looks towards the righteous person:

> righteousness that endures for ever for God (Ps 111:3)
> and for the Lord's servant (Ps 112:2);
> God's works are established in Ps 111:8; the righteous
> person is established in Ps 112:6;

God (Ps 111:8) or the heart of the just person (Ps 112:8) is
   steady;
Remembrance is made of Yahweh's works (Ps 111:4) or
   of the righteous person's (Ps 112:6);
Graciousness and mercy are the qualities of the Lord (Ps
   111:4) or of the just person (Ps 112:4 — in this verse the
   Hebrew omits the word "Lord").

Pss 111-112 are also joined by the introductory word *Hallelujah* or *Praise the Lord!* This word, outside of the alpha-
betic arrangement whereby each half verse begins with the
next letter of the Hebrew alphabet, may have been added so
that Pss 111-112 introduce the "Egyptian Hallel," Pss 113-
118. See Ps 113, commentary.

These two psalms are difficult to date; most commentators favor a postexilic period when the sapiential movement
flourished. If an individual sang these poems in *the company of the upright, in the congregation* (Ps 111:1), this
assembly may have been gathering in the home rather than
in the temple, possibly for the celebration of the paschal
meal. Ps 111:3-9 seems to allude to paschal events like the
covenant (Exod 34:6-7), the sacred food of the manna
(Exod 16) and the remembrance of the Lord's great deeds
(Exod 12:25-27).

Psalm 113
Praise The Lord!

I

¹Praise, O servants of the Lord,
   praise the name of the Lord!

²Blessed be the name of the Lord
   from this time forth and for evermore!
³From the rising of the sun to its setting
   the name of the Lord is to be praised!

II

⁴The Lord is high above all nations,

and his glory above the heavens!

5Who is like the Lord our God,
  who is seated on high,
6who looks far down
  upon the heavens and the earth?

III

7He raises the poor from the dust,
  and lifts the needy from the ash heap,
8to make them sit with princes,
  with the princes of his people.
9He gives the barren woman a home,
  making her the joyous mother of children.
  Praise the Lord!

(I) Popular in Judaism and in Christianity, Ps 113 begins the "Egyptian Hallel" (Pss 113-118), songs of praise, as the word *Hallel* means, assigned to the three pilgrimage festivals (Pasch, Pentecost and Tabernacles), sung also on Hannukah, and on the first day of each month (new moons) except New Years. Pss 113-114 were sung earlier in the paschal meal, Pss 115-118 after the dinner (*cf.,* Matt 26:30). The psalm has been influenced by the Canticle of Hannah (1 Sam 2:1-10); in fact, Ps 113:7-8 is a quotation from 1 Sam 2:3a-d; v. 9 is very similar to 1 Sam 2:5cd. While this connection with the canticle of Hannah alludes to the case of the sterile wife, blessed by God with children, to exemplify the Lord's concern for people who are scorned and seemingly cursed (Gen 16:2; 20:18; 1 Sam 1:5), still Ps 113 also reaches outward to all Israel, scattered from their homeland to the east and the west (v. 3), reduced to poverty and helplessness both in their own country and abroad (v. 7; *cf.,* Isa 54; Hag 1:5-6). Ps 113 belongs more properly, we think, to the postexilic age.

(II) As a hymn of praise, Ps 113 is well adapted for sanctuary worship as well as for family celebration, as on the occasion of the paschal meal. It can be easily divided for antiphonal singing: vv. 1-3, the call to praise, sung by the entire congregation; the two other stanzas provide motivation and acclaim Yahweh: vv. 4-6, in exalted grandeur; vv. 7-9, in the care of the lowly. Yahweh directs the greatest use of divine power to the tender care of poor and lonely people.

(III) Vv. 1-3. Although the phrase, *servants of the Lord,* can refer to levites or priests, as in Pss 134:1; 135:1, here it seems to reach outward to all Israel, as in Pss 69:35-36; or 90:13, 16. *The name of the Lord* indicates that most mysterious, intimate aspect of Yahweh, revealed only to Israel and actively concerned for the chosen people. Name, like vocation (*cf.,* Gen 17:5; Matt 16:18), indicates the main thrust of a person's activity (see Ps 8). V. 3, *From the rising of the sun to its setting,* refers to the diaspora of Israel, who since the exile has been scattered across the ancient Near East (Ps 50:1; Isa 43:3-6; Mal 1:11).

Vv. 4-9. The question, *Who is like the Lord,* reminds us of Pss 18:31; 35:10; 71:19; etc. This question formula in hymns is intended to stir congregational interest and interaction. According to v. 9, Israel does not lose hope of once again being the mother of many children, as in Isa 54:1, "Sing, O barren one, who did not bear; break forth into singing... you who have not been in travail! For the children of the desolate one will be more than the children of her that is married" (Isa 54:1). *Praise the Lord:* this final phrase is to be transferred as a title to Ps 114.

(IV) Ps 113 acts as a bridge between the Canticle of Hannah (1 Sam 2:1-10) and Mary's *Magnificat* (Luke 1:47-55). It harmonizes with a continual New Testament motif that whoever would lose their life will save it (Luke 9:24), and like Jesus, who "emptied himself [of godhead] and taking the form of a servant, being born in human likeness ...became obedient unto death....Therefore God has highly exalted him" (Phil 2:7-9).

Psalm 114
Praise The Lord!

I

¹When Israel went forth from Egypt,
   the house of Jacob from a people of strange language,
²Judah became his sanctuary,
   Israel his dominion.

II

³The sea looked and fled,
   Jordan turned back.
⁴The mountains skipped like rams,
   the hills like lambs.

III

⁵What ails you, O sea, that you flee?
   O Jordan, that you turn back?
⁶O mountains, that you skip like rams?
   O hills, like lambs?

IV

⁷Tremble, O earth, at the presence of the Lord,
   at the presence of the God of Jacob,
⁸who turns the rock into a pool of water,
   the flint into a spring of water.

(I) Everyone praises the high artistic quality of this psalm: regular parallelism, brevity of expression, imaginative figures, surprise and wonder, strength and power — all this within eight verses! A series of twin phrases achieves at once cohesiveness and momentum: Israel-Judah; Egypt-people of strange language; sea-Jordan; flee-turn back; mountains-hills; rams-lambs; Lord-God of Jacob; rock-flint. Particularly in the Hebrew text one can feel the pulse of immediate excitement: the psalm opens with an infinitive construction, to be translated, "In Israel's going forth"; later the statement of wonder (vv. 3-4) and then the questions or exclamations, how can this be (vv. 5-6); concluding with *tremble at the presence . . . at the presence* of God and the participles, literally "turning the rock into a pool of water, the flint into a spring of water." The great redemptive deeds of the exodus, God's care in the wilderness, and the settlement in the land are seen and heard to be happening *now*. The place and date of composition are difficult to determine. Some scholars like H.-J. Kraus place the original poem near the banks of the Jordan river at the sanctuary of Gilgal and its later revision at Jerusalem; others reach into the late pre-exilic age at the time of the Deuteronomic reform at Jerusalem under King Josiah (640-609 B.C. — *cf.*, 2 Kgs 22:1-23:25; Deut 12). The psalm reflects a period when north and south were united, therefore before the death of Solomon in 922 or else after the destruction of the northern kingdom in 721 B.C. and its gradual absorption into the south under King Hezekiah or King Josiah. In the Greek Septuagint, the Vulgate and other ancient versions Pss 114-115 are listed as a single psalm (Ps 113), possibly because almost all of Ps 114 is an introduction to praise (vv. 1-7) with only v. 8 for motivation; Ps 115 would be thought to .continue the latter, yet its spirit and style are very different. Ps 114 belongs to the "Hallel," see Ps 113.

(II) The hymn of praise is easily divided into doublets: vv. 1-2, 3-4, 5-6, 7-8.

(III) V. 1. *Strange language* probably refers to the difficult Egyptian language, particularly in its hieroglyphic form of writing. Vv. 3-4 link together the crossing of the Reed Sea and the River Jordan and transfer the wonders of one event to the other (*cf.*, Josh 4:23, "For the Lord your God dried up the waters of the Jordan for you until you passed over, as the Lord your God did to the Red Sea..."). Although other psalms and biblical passages present the crossing of the sea as a mammoth battle against chaotic forces and link God's act of creation with it (*cf.*, Ps 74:12-17; Isa 51:9-10), here the response is joyful, even playful, judging from the questions in vv. 5-6. The mountains' skipping like rams removes the awesome fear of earthquake and lightning as surrounded Mt. Sinai when the Lord came down to speak with Moses (Exod 19:16-25; 20:18-20). V. 8, *a pool* [and] *a spring of water,* these words remind us of Second Isaiah's lyrical portraits of the new exodus out of Babylon, as in Isa 41:18b, "I will make the wilderness a pool of water, and the dry land springs of water"; also Isa 43:20; 44:3-4.

(IV) Dante heard the melody of this psalm from the boat that was transporting the just towards Purgatory (*Purgatorio,* chap. 2, #46); they had been liberated from their "Egypt" and were now approaching the "wilderness" through which they must pass before entering the promised land of heaven. Jews sing it before the paschal meal, celebrating their ancestors' release from slavery; Christians sing it for Sunday vespers and especially during the octave of Easter, the new Passover from death to new life.

Psalm 115

I

¹Not to us, O Lord, not to us,
 but to thy name give glory,
  for the sake of thy steadfast love and thy faithfulness!
²Why should the nations say,
 "Where is their God?"

II

⁴Their idols are silver and gold,
 the work of men's hands.
⁵They have mouths, but do not speak;
 eyes, but do not see.

III

¹²The Lord has been mindful of us; he will bless us;
 he will bless the house of Israel;
 he will bless the house of Aaron;
¹³he will bless those who fear the Lord,
 both small and great.

IV

¹⁶The heavens are the Lord's heavens,
 but the earth he has given to the sons of men.
¹⁷The dead do not praise the Lord,

nor do any that go down into silence.
18But we will bless the Lord
from this time forth and for evermore.
Praise the Lord!

(I) Because Ps 115 modulates into different literary forms
with irregular meter, it is best to understand and interpret
these changes according to a liturgical ceremony. A sinful,
but penitential people are rejecting their fears and false
alliances and are receiving a new blessing as the Lord's
covenant people. The ceremony would fit periods of
national, religious revival which occurred in the preexilic
age, during the great reforms of King Hezekiah (715-687/6
B.C. — *cf.,* 2 Kgs 18-19; 2 Chron 29-32) and of King Josiah
(640-609 B.C., — *cf.,* 2 Kgs 22:1-23:30; 2 Chron 34-35); a
postexilic date, however, may be more appropriate, according to the studies of K. Luke.

(II) The ceremony opens with a "confession" of community misdeeds (vv. 1-2), continues with a rejection and curse
of other gods (vv. 3-8) and with a dialogue between priests
and worshipers that ends with a priestly blessing (vv. 9-15);
hymnic praise concludes the psalm (vv. 16-18). When the
psalm was later joined with Ps 114, certainly in Egypt and
possibly in Palestine, the hymnic features became more
accentuated.

(III) Vv. 1-2. The phrase, *give glory*, is frequently asso-
ciated with a confession of sin and a new consecration to
Yahweh by the total community, as when Achan was con-
fronted with his preservation of pagan amulettes (Josh 7:19,
"Then Joshua said to Achan, 'My son, *give glory* to the Lord
God of Israel, and render praise to him; and tell me now
what you have done; do not hide it from me'"; also 1 Sam 6:5;
Isa 12:1). Confession of sin glorifies God's strength in re-
moving sin from the community, at times God's mercy.
Some aspects of the same ceremony are reflected in Mic
7:7-20, along with the question, "Where is your God?" as
well as in Ezek 36:22-38.

Vv. 3-8, Ridicule and curse of an enemy's gods was a

common enough practice in the ancient Near East. The Assyrians made sport of Yahweh in 2 Kgs 18:33-35 and the prophet Elijah mocked the god Baal in 1 Kgs 18:27. In the covenant renewal ceremony of Josh 24, a stirring demand was put to the people: "Choose this day whom you will serve, whether the gods [of] your ancestors. . . or the gods of the Amorites. . .; but as for me and my house, we will serve the Lord" (Josh 24:15). *Cf.,* Isa 44:9-20; Jer 10:1-10; Wis 13:10-19.

Vv. 9-15, a dialogue between priests and worshipers, similar in some ways to Pss 15 and 24. As liturgically executed in the postexilic age, three groups of people were indicated: *house of Aaron,* the priestly tribe (Ps 135:20 adds "house of Levi"); *house of Israel,* the laity; and *those who fear the Lord,* gradually a technical term for proselytes or for those gentiles who believed in Yahweh but did not accept circumcision and Jewish dietary laws (Acts 10:2, 22; 13:26).

Vv. 16-18, hymnic conclusion. Life is reaffirmed as God's special gift; therefore, the dead are excluded (see Ps 6:5; also Isa 38:18-19). *From this time forth and for evermore:* is this a vague, implicit affirmation of what v. 17 denied — that after death we will continue to bless the Lord? It seems that Israel was never satisfied with the rejection of a person's conscious survival after death, necessary (it seemed) to avoid the polytheistic notion of afterlife among other peoples: eventually, a doctrinal advance was reached in Dan 12 or 2 Macc 7. V. 18, *Praise the Lord:* this final phrase is to be transferred to the beginning of Ps 116 as its title.

(IV) As we pray this psalm to renew our own covenant with the Lord, we will glorify God by identifying and rejecting the false gods in our personal life, our nation and our world. Ours may not be made of silver and gold, but perhaps of oil or automobiles or TV; and we may have allowed ourselves to be pulled away from the Lord towards false values and loyalties. Perhaps our "contraceptive culture" has pulled us to our knees before false gods as we put many luxuries and selfish interests before the sharing of life with children or neighbors, with the sick or shut-in's.

Psalm 116
Praise The Lord!

I

¹I love the Lord, because he has heard
my voice and my supplications.
²Because he inclined his ear to me,
therefore I will call on him as long as I live.

II

³The snares of death encompassed me;
the pangs of Sheol laid hold on me;
I suffered distress and anguish.
⁴Then I called on the name of the Lord:
"O Lord, I beseech thee, save my life!"

III

⁵Gracious is the Lord, and righteous;
our God is merciful.
⁶The Lord preserves the simple;
when I was brought low, he saved me.
⁷Return, O my soul, to your rest;
for the Lord has dealt bountifully with you.

⁸For thou hast delivered my soul from death,
my eyes from tears,
my feet from stumbling;

⁹I walk before the Lord
in the land of the living.
¹⁰I kept my faith, even when I said,
"I am greatly afflicted";
¹¹I said in my consternation,
"Men are all a vain hope."

IV

¹²What shall I render to the Lord
for all his bounty to me?
¹³I will lift up the cup of salvation
and call on the name of the Lord,
¹⁴I will pay my vows to the Lord

in the presence of all his people.
[15]Precious in the sight of the Lord
is the death of his saints.
[16]O Lord, I am thy servant;
I am thy servant, the son of thy handmaid.
Thou hast loosed my bonds.
[17]I will offer to thee the sacrifice of thanksgiving
and call on the name of the Lord.
[18]I will pay my vows to the Lord
in the presence of all his people,
[19]in the courts of the house of the Lord,
in your midst, O Jerusalem.
Praise the Lord!

(I) Although Ps 116 is clearly one of thanksgiving to accompany ritual action in the temple (vv. 9, 14, 18, 19), it also enables us to look behind the moment of gratitude to the dark time of distress. The psalmist was once quite sick (vv. 3 and 8), falsely accused (v. 11), possibly bound in chains for execution (vv. 3 and 16). Upon deliverance, the psalmist is intent not only to fulfill vows but to do so publicly in the temple with the full attention of Jerusalem (vv. 18-19). Yet, the psalmist is not mesmerized with public ceremony; features of private or personal piety continually appear, from the very first words, *I love the Lord,* and continued even with several late Aramaic expressions (vv. 7 and 12).

These Aramaisms lead to a date late in the postexilic age. Ps 116 is divided into two poems in the Greek Septuagint and Latin Vulgate, as Ps 114 (vv. 1-9) and Ps 115 (vv. 10-19). Ps 116 begins the second part of the "Egyptian Hallel" (see Ps 113) and would have been sung by Jesus, immediately before leaving the upper room for Gethsemane. This psalm which thanks God for preservation from death prepares Jesus for death; to resolve this mystery, we are helped by reading Heb 4:7-10.

(II) The psalm can be read according to the following plan of A. Deissler:

vv. 1-2, profession of faith

vv. 3-4, former distress

vv. 5-11, Chant of praise and confidence

vv. 12-19, Sacrifice of Thanksgiving

(III) Vv. 3-4. The serious illness of the psalmist is accentuated in its mystery and pain if the psalmist was also a levite. Some will interpret the words in v. 16ab, *thy servant, the son of thy handmaid*, as a person dedicated to divine service from birth. Because Yahweh was the God of life and because no sick person could enter the temple, serious illness was a severe trial to any Israelite, but particularly to a priest or levite whose purpose in life was seriously threatened (see Ps 16). For *Sheol*, see Pss 6:5; 16:10. V. 4, *I called:* grammatically the word is in the incomplete tense, and therefore states, "I kept calling on the name of the Lord."

Vv. 5-11. These lines are rich in the covenantal theology of a merciful God (Exod 34:6-7), echoing other psalms like Ps 112:4 and prophetic preaching like Isa 54:1-8. V. 6, *simple*, does not refer to lazyness or scoffing at knowledge (Prov 1:22, 32) but to people who seem too honest for their own good, too trustful and therefore vulnerable. The Greek Septuagint reads "infants." V. 7, *your rest:* a rich theological word with profound meaning for a stance of faith and prayer before God (see Ps 95:11). V. 10 is quoted by St. Paul in 2 Cor 4:13 according to the Greek form, "I believed, and so I spoke" the message of salvation. This Greek rendition is not a poor translation from the Hebrew: we are dealing with two traditions in reading and adapting the text. V. 11b, literally, "everyone is a liar," is quoted by Paul in Rom 3:4, to show that the inability of some to believe and accept the gospel does not nullify the gospel. The psalmist, likewise, was strong in personal loyalty and faith, even if all others condemned him.

Vv. 12-19, Sacrifice of Thanksgiving. *What shall I render the Lord?* — certainly no gift will ever be adequate; we do not "pay" God for God's mercy. The psalmist will publicly testify and offer a sacrifice of thanksgiving. V. 13, *cup of salvation,* probably a reference either to a cup of wine, poured out on the altar in worship of God (Num 28:7) or to a communion banquet where the psalmist celebrated the Lord's goodness with family and friends (Ps 23:5; 1 Cor 10:16).

(IV) In offering thanksgiving to God, Ps 116 allows us to remember the former sorrow. That too has become a real part of ourselves; to ignore it and suppress it only cause future guilt or trauma. Our pain has become ourselves in our offering to God. Ps 116 weaves expressions of personal piety into public ceremonial phrases; such a blend prevents worship from being stilted, mechanical or routine. The verse, *Precious in the sight of the Lord is the death of his saints* (v. 15) provides the ultimate act of faith; even if God does not save us from death — and eventually such will be the case — the moment is "precious." Here is faith that overcomes even death (1 Cor 15:54-57).

Psalm 117

> ¹Praise the Lord, all nations!
>   Extol him, all peoples!
> ²For great is his steadfast love toward us;
>   and the faithfulness of the Lord endures for ever.
>   Praise the Lord!

This shortest of all psalms is readily adaptable to any number of liturgical occasions. As a quick but incisive hymn of praise, strong and clear in its reliance upon the covenant virtues of steadfast love and faithfulness (Exod 34:6-7), flashing an insight of universal salvation, Ps 117 can introduce or conclude a liturgical ceremony or an individual part of it. It would seem best suited as an invitatory psalm (like Ps 95). In Rom 15:11 St. Paul cites v. 1 in a context that includes three other Old Testament texts "in order [to show] that the Gentiles might glorify God for his mercy." Without Paul's citation, the question of universal salvation would rise in discussing a psalm that calls upon *all nations* and *all peoples* to praise and extol the Lord. Yet, we ought not to be too generous in what we attribute to the psalmist. When we look at the motivation *why* the gentiles are to praise Yahweh, it is because of Yahweh's steadfast love *for us*, that is, for the Israelites! It is possible that gentiles, at least some of them, could be impressed with what the Israelite God has done for his people and yet not be converted. A similar idea is present, we think, in Isa 40:3-5, where "all flesh shall see" the "glory of the Lord" manifest in the return of Israel to their homeland. "Seeing" or "admiring" is not necessarily "believing" and "accepting"! Furthermore, we should not discount the real possibility of exaggeration in religious fervor and liturgical celebration. Yet, after registering these serious hesitations, nonetheless we recognize that the gentiles in Ps 117 take notice of what is happening in Israel. There is an agreement that they are capable of conversion and attachment to the chosen people. Texts like Ps 117 were keeping alive a universal outreach somewhere within the religious synthesis of Israel and so preparing for an apostle Paul. The explication of this insight was to take its full toll of years and controversy.

Ps 117 is usually placed in the postexilic age, for the reason that it would be more at home after than before the preaching of Second Isaiah (Isa 40-55), who also saw the nations interacting in a positive way with the new exodus of Israel. Yet, if our reasoning is correct, Ps 117 could have originated in an earlier period, alongside such texts as Gen 12:2-3; 18:18; 22:18 in which all nations will find blessings in Abraham. V. 2, *Praise the Lord:* this final phrase really belongs as a title at the beginning of Ps 118.

Psalm 118
Praise The Lord!

I

¹O give thanks to the Lord, for he is good;
his steadfast love endures for ever!

²Let Israel say,
  "His steadfast love endures for ever."
³Let the house of Aaron say,
  "His steadfast love endures for ever."
⁴Let those who fear the Lord say,
  "His steadfast love endures for ever."

II

⁵Out of my distress I called on the Lord;
  the Lord answered me and set me free.
⁶With the Lord on my side I do not fear.
  What can man do to me?
⁷The Lord is on my side to help me;
  I shall look in triumph on those who hate me.
⁸It is better to take refuge in the Lord
  than to put confidence in man.
⁹It is better to take refuge in the Lord
  than to put confidence in princes.

¹⁰All nations surrounded me;
  in the name of the Lord I cut them off!
¹¹They surrounded me, surrounded me on every side;
  in the name of the Lord I cut them off!
¹²They surrounded me like bees,
  they blazed like a fire of thorns;
  in the name of the Lord I cut them off!
¹³I was pushed hard, so that I was falling,
  but the Lord helped me,
¹⁴The Lord is my strength and my song;
  he has become my salvation.

¹⁵Hark, glad songs of victory
  in the tents of the righteous:
  "The right hand of the Lord does valiantly,
¹⁶ the right hand of the Lord is exalted,
  the right hand of the Lord does valiantly!"
¹⁷I shall not die, but I shall live,
  and recount the deeds of the Lord.
¹⁸The Lord has chastened me sorely,
  but he has not given me over to death.

¹⁹Open to me the gates of righteousness,
   that I may enter through them
   and give thanks to the Lord.

²⁰This is the gate of the Lord;
   the righteous shall enter through it.

²¹I thank thee that thou hast answered me
   and hast become my salvation.

III

²²The stone which the builders rejected
   has become the head of the corner.
²³This is the Lord's doing;
   it is marvelous in our eyes.
²⁴This is the day which the Lord has made;
   let us rejoice and be glad in it.
²⁵Save us, we beseech thee, O Lord!
   O Lord, we beseech thee, give us success!

IV

²⁶Blessed be he who enters in the name of the Lord!
   We bless you from the house of the Lord.
²⁷The Lord is God,
   and he has given us light.
   Bind the festal procession with branches,
   up to the horns of the altar!

V

²⁸Thou art my God, and I will give thanks to thee;
   thou art my God, I will extol thee.

²⁹O give thanks to the Lord, for he is good;
   for his steadfast love endures for ever!

(I) This psalm turns out to be very complex, not on purpose, of course, nor because of the psalmist's ineptitude, but on account of adaptation to liturgical ceremonies at the Jerusalem temple and also on account of reinterpretation by the rabbis and New Testament writers. Explained as simply as possible, Ps 118 belonged to the entrance liturgy, possibly at a temple gate called "Gate of Righteousness" (v. 19); we know from ancient and modern practice that gates or decorative arches within a sacred area can be given special names. At Mount Sinai, along the 4000 steps leading to the top, a pilgrim passes through "the Door of Confession," where the monk St. Stephen heard confessions and granted absolution. Ps 118 along with Pss 15 and 24 provides an entrance liturgy on the occasion of solemn thanksgiving to God.

(II) According to E. Beaucamp, Ps 118 has indications of being sung when pilgrims gratefully came to Jerusalem for the feast of Tabernacles, the final harvest festival: v. 15 refers to "tent," the booths in which pilgrims lived during the eight day festival; v. 24, to "the day," corresponding to the custom of calling Tabernacles simply "the feast" (*cf.*, Neh 8:14; Ps 81:4); v. 25, to the refrain, "Hosannah" (see below); v. 27, to lights, prominent at the feast of Tabernacles; and to the "*lulab,*" or bundle of "branches" from myrtle, willow, palm and citron (Lev 23:40). Recited also on the feast of Passover, Ps 118 accompanied the rite of filling the fourth cup of wine (Mark 14:26). This psalm concludes the "Egyptian Hallel" — see Ps 113.

Maillot-Lelièvre offer a more elaborate dramatization:

1) introduction

priest:	v.	1a	2a	3a	4a
people or choir:	v.	1b	2b	3b	4b

2) Thanksgiving from individuals:

prisoner	vv. 5-7	merchant	vv. 10-14	——	sick	vv. 17-19	
priest	v. 8	priest	v. 15ab	v. 16a	priest	v. 20	
people	v. 9	people	v. 15c	v. 16b			

3) Interaction between individual, priest and people:

individual	v. 21	——	——	——	v. 28
priest	vv. 22-23a	v. 24a	v. 25a	v. 26a	v. 27
people	v. 23b	v. 24b	v. 25b	v. 26b	v. 29

A. A. Anderson offers a simpler division of parts, based

upon the situation in the preexilic period when the king
would represent the people:

vv. 1-4, Congregational   vv. 22-28, ritual interaction
   thanksgiving   v. 22 proverbial expression
vv. 5-21, Individual thanks-   v. 23-24 praise
   giving sung by the king   v. 25, prayer
                           vv. 26-27 priestly blessing
                           v. 28 response of king
                           v. 29 congregational conclusion

These suggestions, tentative and to a certain extent imaginative, attempt to make sense out of scattered pieces of evidence; they are models for a creative use of psalms within
our own pastoral setting. In the exegesis below we propose a
general subdivision of verses.

(III) Vv. 1-4, communal thanksgiving, consisting of traditional formulas: *for he is good* (Pss 92:1; 100:5; 107:1); *his
steadfast love endures for ever* (Pss 107:1; Ezr 3:11). In Ps
136 *steadfast love* explains the entire history of the cosmos
and of Israel; Ps 118 unites this national and even cosmic
history of the Lord's goodness to the help given to individuals. The refrain echoes the basic quality of the covenant and
its God (Exod 34:6-7).

Vv. 5-21, individual thanksgiving, sung either by the king
or as an interaction between various categories of people
with priest and congregation. V. 5, *distress:* similar to Ps
116:3; Lam 1:3. The phrase, *set me free* reflects the desire of
nomads to roam the open spaces of the wilderness, a wish
deeply imbeded within the blood and bones of Israel: Gen
26:22, Abraham blessed the Lord who "has *made room*
[same Hebrew word] for us, and we shall be fruitful"; *cf.,* Pss
4:2; 31:8; 66:12. V. 6, *the Lord on my side: cf.,* Rom 8:31, "if
God is for us, who is against us?" The reference to *all nations*
in v. 10 may designate the king as speaker, but it could
equally apply to individual travelers or merchants harassed
by foreigners on their way to Jerusalem. V. 10, *in the name
of the Lord:* according to the covenant, it was the Lord's

"vocation" or "promise" to bring Israel through difficulties to peace (see Ps 113:1-3). Vv. 14-16 resonate lines in Moses' song of praise and victory: Exod 15:2, "the Lord is my strength and my song"; 15:6, "thy right hand, O Lord, glorious in power"; 15:12, "thou didst stretch out thy right hand." The entire history of Israel converges within this moment of thanksgiving and praise. V. 18, *the Lord has chastened me sorely:* the word "chastened" reflects sapiential piety (Prov 3:11-12) which was given a firm rooting in prophetical preaching and then in popular piety by Deuteronomy (Deut 4:36; 8:5) and by Jeremiah (Jer 2:19; 31:18; in fact, 31 times in Jer). See Pss 7; 50:16-21.

Vv. 22-25, Community Praise and Prayer. The statement (v. 22) about *the stone. . .rejected. . .the head of the corner* sounds like an ancient proverb: that which is precious, can be despised by some persons but given a place of fundamental importance by other persons of faith. Faith is necessary for *this is the Lord's doing* (v. 23), on *the day when the Lord takes action* (a better way to translate v. 24a). V. 24, *save us:* the phrase, spelled out in Hebrew, reads "Hosanna." At first a cry for help (Pss 12:1; 28:9) or for mercy (2 Sam 14:4), it later became a solemn acclamation that the Lord has indeed saved and granted victory. On the feast of Tabernacles it was sung each day as the congregation encircled the altar and on the octave day seven times. That laity could come this close to the altar would point to preexilic times; later only priests were permitted in what became the "court of the priests."

Vv. 26-27, blessing, resonating the "priestly benediction" in Num 6:24-26.

Vv. 28-29, conclusion, sung by the individual (v. 28) and the entire congregation (v. 29).

(IV) Ps 118 occupies an important place in New Testament theology. Two verses are each quoted once: v. 6, *with the Lord on my side. . .*, this phrase enters the final chapter of Hebrews, urging Christ's disciples to fulfill faithfully the laws of hospitality and basic morality, despite the cost. V. 24, *rejoice and be glad* help to describe a vision of heaven,

the marriage feast of the lamb (Rev 19:7). Quoted most
frequently are vv. 22-23 about *the stone...rejected* [yet
becoming] *the head of the corner...the Lord's doing* and
vv. 25-26, *Hosanna... Blessed in the name of the Lord is he
who enters* [or comes — a better way of reading the phrase].

Vv. 22-23 are introduced by the synoptic gospels within
the parable of the vinedressers: quoted at first by Jesus that
the kingdom of God will be taken away from those
unworthy of it and be given to "a nation producing the fruits
of it," which could mean to sincere Israelites who manifested the fruits of the kingdom (Matt 21:42-43). In this case
"stone" indicated the continuity of God's kingdom from
earlier scriptures to the new age (as in Isa 28:16-17) and its
strength to withstand all opposition (as in Dan 2:44). Mark
12:10-12 relates the passage of Ps 118:22-23 more closely
with the death of Jesus, caused by ungrateful, jealous people. Luke 20:16-18 cites the same passage more with the
necessity of making a clear decision for or against Jesus. The
context of the quotation in Acts 4:11 is explicitly "Jesus...
whom you crucified, whom God raised from the dead." Acts
adapts the passage from Ps 118 by speaking of a stone that
was *spurned*, like the Suffering Servant in Isa 53:3 and of the
only *name* in which there is *salvation,* drawing upon Joel
3:5. Each of these citations must be studied in their own
context. We reach the conclusion not only that Ps 118
occupied an important place in teaching about the death
and resurrection of Jesus but also that the Old Testament
psalm was re-read within a new context that presumed faith
in Jesus as Messiah, and was used to delve more deeply into
this mystery.

Vv. 25-26 are introduced into Jesus' triumphal entry into
Jerusalem, again with a slightly different nuance in Mark
11:9; Matt 21:9; Luke 19:38; John 12:13. V. 26 is also cited
when Jesus weeps over Jerusalem (Matt 23:37-39 and Luke
13:34-35).

Both the Eastern and the Western Church appointed Ps
118 to be sung on Easter with the refrain from v. 24.

Psalm 119

This longest psalm of the Psalter meditates upon the "law," externally in a highly structured way, but thematically in a completely unstructured way! As Roderick A. F. MacKenzie remarks: "One could start with the last verse and recite it backwards, and the general effect would be the same." Our comments, therefore, will center around general conclusions and the psalm in its totality.

External details. The eight lines of each stanza (doubled in most English translations) begin with the same letter of the Hebrew alphabet, so that all twenty-two letters have a complete stanza in the order of the alphabet (see Pss 9-10). Only Ronald Knox ever attempted to copy this form in English translation! Each of the 176 lines contains one of eight synonyms for law — with two exceptions. In v. 90 a ninth synonym for law occurs, and no synonym at all is found in v. 122. Perhaps with wry humor the psalmist wanted to inform us that he or she was not too rigid after all! The long psalm blends almost every type or style, again with the exception that the great moments of Israel's history are totally absent. The dominant forms are sapiential (beginning with v. 1) and lament (vv. 22, 23, 25 as examples), but also praise (vv. 7, 164, 171, etc.), confidence (vv. 50, 56, etc.), prayer (vv. 10, 17, etc.), thanksgiving (vv. 44, 71, etc.). Yet we meet none of the excitement and community participation of the hymn, none of the intense agony of the laments. Ps 119 will not rank high among poet laureates, but it deserves honorable mention for perseverance — and for other qualities as we shall see.

Anthological style. As in the case of Ps 96, Ps 119 reveals long meditation upon the treasury of biblical tradition. The favorite book was Deuteronomy, then came Proverbs, Job, Jeremiah and Ezekiel, finally, in a lesser way, Isaiah 40-55. Again the exception! A psalm which inserts a word for "law" in every line but one has no allusions to the most important legal corpus in Israel, the Priestly Tradition or "P" of the Pentateuch. Neither does it refer to the covenant, and draws very little from the historical books of the Deuteronomic tradition (Josh-Judg-Sam-Kgs). We cite a few examples of the anthological style which can be checked against the text of Ps 119:

Ps 119:2 and Deut 4:29, "You will seek the Lord your God; and you will find him, if you search after him with all your heart and with all your soul."

Ps 119:70 and Isa 6:10, "Make the heart of this people fat [or gross]..."

Ps 119:76 and Isa 51:3, "For the Lord will comfort Zion..."

Ps 119:85 and Jer 18:20, "Yet they have dug a pit for my life."

Ps 119:89 and Isa 40:8, "The word of our God will stand for ever."

Ps 119 infused a new character into these allusions. While most of these texts are community oriented — even those of a sapiential nature — Ps 119 is intent upon personal, individual piety. According to a word that occurs within its lines (*siah*, "to meditate," in vv. 15, 23, 27, 48, 78, 148), one ought to go over in thought, muse on, linger upon, even to mumble the sound repeatedly. In this way biblical texts sink deeply into the subconscious and rise again to consciousness with new life and coloration.

Setting. Because of the frequent interaction with the Book of Deuteronomy, the psalm may have originated in the contemplative background of a preacher of the word of God. According to Deut 31:9-13, levites were to preserve the law, read it before the people and explain its impact upon their daily lives, that the peoples and "their children...may hear and learn to fear the Lord your God, as long as you live in the land which you are going over the Jordan to possess." However, because 119 ignores the stipulations of the covenant law and never quotes from it, it is also possible that the poem was composed among the disciples of the sages, in a school similar to the one conducted by Jesus ben Sirach (Sir 51:23). In this case we are dealing with a more private, less temple or sanctuary orientation to religious practice.

Law. If Ps 119 never quotes from the Priestly Tradition, perhaps the most important part of the Mosaic Torah or

Law, we must inquire what the psalmist really meant by "law." It is a way of life, learned and integrated by the law of Moses but not identifiable with it; it is a keen sensitivity to oral traditions as these transmit the ideals, the sorrows, and the struggles of Israel's ordinary folk; it is personal dedication to what one perceives to be the best, not just conformity to a legal code; it is not searching the past but living in the present moment where God is to be found and where ancient traditions take on a new vitality; it is satisfaction even within monotonous daily life, not with a frenetic drive for excitement and wondrous deeds; most of all, as we shall now see, it is seeking God with one's whole heart (v. 2; *cf.,* Deut 6:5, "love the Lord your God with all your heart, and with all your soul, and with all your might").

Spirit of the Psalm. Following the lead for the most part of Maillot-Lelièvre, we find these themes within Ps 119:

1) The spirit of receiving the law from the Lord, not from books or scrolls, as in v. 19, *Hide not thy commandments from me;* vv. 11-12, *I have laid up thy word in my heart . . . Blessed be thou, O Lord; teach me thy statutes.*

2) The study of the law, therefore, leads personally to God. We should note the subtle way by which the psalmist is drawn immediately to the Lord, as in v. 2, *Blessed are those who keep his testimonies, who seek HIM* [not "it," the law] *with their whole heart,"* or v. 10, *"With my whole heart I seek THEE."* There has been a gentle transition from talking about God to addressing *thee, O Lord.*

3) Perseverance and self-control characterize obedience to the Lord. The psalmist confesses in vv. 33-34, *Teach me, O Lord, the way of thy statutes; and I will keep it TO THE END. Give me understanding, that I may keep thy law and observe it WITH MY WHOLE HEART.* Under the control of the alphabetical style, emotions never get out of hand.

4) The law is a source of genuine, lasting joy: vv. 14, 16, *in the way of thy testmonies I delight, as much as in all riches . . . I will delight in thy statutes.*

5) Prayer is addressed to God in order to keep the law: *Let thy steadfast love come to me, O Lord, thy salvation accord-*

ing to thy promise . . . . Remember thy word to thy servant, in which thou hast made me hope (vv. 41, 49). This prayer is to continue through the night (vv. 55, 62, 147) and *seven times a day* (v. 164). This last verse gave rise to the monastic practice of praying the "Divine Office" at seven designated periods of time.

6) The law is an important part of conversion and religious fervor, as we see in v. 67, *Before I was afflicted I went astray; but now I keep thy word,* and v. 167, *I have gone astray like a lost sheep; seek thy servant; for I do not forget thy commandments.*

Ps 119 in our lives. According to the psalm, every "letter," even the slight differences in writing *beth* and *kaph*, or in writing *waw* and *zayin*, are a gift from God and contain an inexhaustible meaning. Our response to God's law, as made known to us in the deepest levels of our conscience, must be obeyed unquestionably; even the most subtle indication of God's will ought to be followed at once. When we realize that God is speaking in the silence of our heart, the only option to obedience is serious damage to our personality. As Ps 119 enables us to perceive the delicate whispering of the spirit, we are led into genuine mystical experience. The repetition of letter by letter, line by line, yet seemingly getting nowhere, quiets our heart in the richness of the present moment, filled with the Lord's presence.

Ps 119 can lead us into hidden depths of meaning, if we substitute an important aspect of our own lives for the word "law" in each line. We can allow the psalm and its multitude of rich observations to interact with such "obligations" as: an inspiration from God to forgive another person; our duties as spouse or parent, teacher, religious or priest, to family, school or church; the decisions of one's superior; resolutions reached within family caucus or church councils; serious temptations that can disrupt God's presence and our own personal peace.

Psalms 120-134

These fifteen psalms are each entitled "A Song of Ascents" in the RSV, "a gradual canticle" in the Douay-Rheims, hence the name in liturgical books, "Gradual Psalms." There are many explanations for the title: 1) because of the progressive rhythm, repeating words or phrases, at times with some expansion; yet this style is not found in all these psalms and also occurs elsewhere as in Ps 29; 2) because of the fifteen steps from the court of the women to the court of Israel, based upon Ezek 40:22, 37 and the Mishnah; here the levites were said to sing these psalms; 3) because of their being sung on the return from Babylon, yet the temple was in ruins at that time while its existence is presumed in Pss 122 and 134; and 4) because of their being chanted by pilgrims, especially from the distant diaspora, on their dangerous journey to and from Jerusalem, or during their stay in the Holy City. This last reason musters the strongest support.

The Psalms of Ascents cannot be categorized by content or style: the series includes: thanksgiving prayers (Pss 120,124); songs of confidence (Pss 121, 125, 129, 131); laments (Pss 123, 126, 130); royal psalm (Ps 132); song of Zion (Ps 122); hymns of praise (Pss 133, 134); wisdom psalms (Pss 127, 128). Therefore, they are best characterized by their liturgical use in the wider context of pilgrimage to and from Jerusalem.

The spirit is generally calm, a bit sombre in most cases, down-to-earth. The images, even when dealing with grievous pain, tend to be taken from a quiet, pastoral setting (*cf.,* Ps 129). It is almost as though the pilgrims were too tired to expend the energy on violent emotions. Even the hymns of praise are subdued and make use of stereotype phrases (*cf.,* Ps 134).

The psalms center upon the temple at Jerusalem, which beckons the pilgrim and then sends the same person back home with renewed blessing and life.

Linguistic features like the occasional Aramaisms, rubrics that reflect a later period, pilgrimages that are difficult and dangerous — these are some of the reasons that date these psalms in the later postexilic age.

Psalm 120
A Song Of Ascents.

I

¹In my distress I cry to the Lord,
that he may answer me:

II

²"Deliver me, O Lord,
from lying lips,
from a deceitful tongue."

³What shall be given to you?
And what more shall be done to you,
you deceitful tongue?
⁴A warrior's sharp arrows,
with glowing coals of the broom tree!

III

⁵Woe is me, that I sojourn in Meshech,
that I dwell among the tents of Kedar!
⁶Too long have I had my dwelling
among those who hate peace.
⁷I am for peace;
but when I speak,
they are for war!

The first Song of Ascents is either a lament, if we judge from vv. 2-7, or else a song of thanksgiving from the Hebrew text of v. 1, "To the Lord in my distress / / I called, and he answered me." Interpreting the psalm within its liturgical setting, we can see it as spoken gratefully after safe arrival at the Jerusalem temple, yet remembering the harsh circumstances at home and in traveling to the Holy City. The vindictive prayer in vv. 2-4 ought to be judged from the circumstances of the psalmist. Living in a foreign land with no legal rights and protection, these Jewish people could take refuge only in the word. At times they may have invested this word with magical powers, yet they might also be speaking with the conviction that God will not tolerate injustice for ever; their word, joined with God's, will speed the day of full righteousness. For interpreting the vindictive psalms, see Ps 69. In vv. 5-7, the reference to Meshech (in the distant north) and to Kedar (close by in the Syro-Arabian desert) may be indicative of any hostile, non-Israelite people.

Psalm 121
A Song Of Ascents.

I
¹I lift up my eyes to the hills.
From whence does my help come?

II
²My help comes from the Lord,
who made heaven and earth.

³He will not let your foot be moved,
he who keeps you will not slumber.
⁴Behold, he who keeps Israel
will neither slumber nor sleep.
⁵The Lord is your keeper;
the Lord is your shade
on your right hand.
⁶The sun shall not smite you by day,
nor the moon by night.

⁷The Lord will keep you from all evil;
he will keep your life.
⁸The Lord will keep
your going out and your coming in
from this time forth and for evermore.

(I-II) A dialogue psalm to evoke confidence in Yahweh. The opening question (v. 1) sets the style or rhythm, yet it is not certain if the reply is found in a priestly oracle and blessing (vv. 2-8), or if there is further dialogue (in which v. 3 is to be formulated as a second question — "will he let your foot be moved?"), or if the conversation is taking place between parent and child. The first option seems in accord with the language of this psalm. If Ps 120 is interpreted as a thanksgiving prayer after safe arrival at the Jerusalem sanctuary, Ps 121 consists of a priestly blessing of confidence as the pilgrim is about to depart on the hazardous journey home.

(III) V, 1, the reference to hills or mountains, in the plural, makes us think of the journey, physically difficult on account of mountainous terrain, but also dangerous because of robbers and strangers (*cf.,* Luke 10:30 for the journey to Jericho; 1 Sam 19:10; 22:15, David flees for his life in the mountains or wilderness areas). V. 2, the priest's blessing is given in the name of *the Lord who made heaven and earth*, a title found more often in postexilic psalms (Pss 115:5; 124:8; 134:2) but also reaching back into Jerusalem's earliest history (Gen 14:19). V. 4, the Lord *will neither slumber nor sleep*, a statement that is almost contradicted by Pss 7:6; 44:23, yet is firmly attested to by Elijah in 1 Kgs 18:27, attributing sleep only to false gods. Because the Scriptures reflect strong human emotions of fear and anxiety as well as of hope and confidence, such opposing statements were not bothersome to the scribes! Vv. 5-8, Yahweh is protecting the people at all times, so that the journey home can be compared to the journey of one's life; there is an inference here that going home is *like* entering the temple where the worshiper lives beneath the wings of the Lord (*cf.,* Ps 17).

(IV) This psalm can be read in the context of Jesus the Good Shepherd (John 10:25-20; 1 Pet 2:25) and of the dying person about to embark on a lonely journey. It is recited in the church's ancient office of the dead.

Psalm 122
A Song Of Ascents. Of David.

I

¹I was glad when they said to me,
"Let us go to the house of the Lord!"
²Our feet have been standing
within your gates, O Jerusalem!

II

³Jerusalem, built as a city
which is bound firmly together,
⁴to which the tribes go up,
the tribes of the Lord,
as was decreed for Israel,
to give thanks to the name of the Lord.
⁵There thrones for judgment were set,
the thrones of the house of David.

III

⁶Pray for the peace of Jerusalem!
"May they prosper who love you!
⁷Peace be within your walls,
and security within your towers!"

⁸For my brethren and companions' sake
I will say, "Peace be within you!"
⁹For the sake of the house of the Lord our God,
I will seek your good.

Praise and confident prayer extend over this Song of Zion, as these psalms are called in Ps 137:3. Ps 122 begins with the first person "I" but immediately the psalmist is drawn into the excitement of the pilgrimage group (vv. 1-2). Praise of the Holy City follows (vv. 3-5); Jerusalem is "the joy of all the earth" (Ps 48:2), which Yahweh has chosen for his dwelling place (Ps 132:13). This city also guards the throne (now vacant) and the traditions of David. The psalm ends with a lovely, rhythmic prayer for peace (vv. 6-9), in which the psalmist regains his own sense of an individual person: *For my brethren and companions' sake I will say*

...Strengthened with inner joy, the psalmist can confidently return home.

The joy of the initial verses is more subdued yet still within the spirit of Jer 31:1-14, which even includes the invitation, "Arise...let us go up to Zion!" The phrase, *as was decreed for Israel* (v. 4), may refer to the regulation that every adult male was to "appear before the Lord God three times in the year" (Exod 23:17). The prayer for peace (v. 6) begins with a haunting paranomasia in the Hebrew: *sha'alu shalom yerushalaim*

We are reminded of Jesus' pilgrimage to Jerusalem with his parents (Luke 2:41-51), the long journey narrative in Luke's gospel as the context for Jesus' ministry (Luke 9:51ff), and Jesus' weeping over the Holy City (Luke 19:41). Our own earthly pilgrimage is seeking "Mount Zion, the city of the living God, the heavenly Jerusalem" (Heb 12:22; *cf.*, Rev 21:22).

Psalm 123
A Song Of Ascents.

> [1]To thee I lift up my eyes,
>   O thou who art enthroned in the heavens!
> [2]Behold, as the eyes of servants
>   look to the hand of their master,
> as the eyes of a maid
>   to the hand of her mistress,
> so our eyes look to the Lord our God,
>   till he have mercy upon us.
> [3]Have mercy upon us, O Lord, have mercy upon us,
>   for we have had more than enough of contempt.
> [4]Too long our soul has been sated
>   with the scorn of those who are at ease,
>   the contempt of the proud.

This pilgrimage psalm was written for times of distress, either for the individual (the psalm begins in the first person singular) or for the community (especially in the postexilic age, as reflected in Hag 1:6-9; Neh 2:17-19; chap. 4). Israel is like a slave (v. 2) beneath *the scorn of those...at ease* (v. 4). Yet the poeple rediscover their dignity and strength when as men and women they look *to the Lord our God* (v. 2).

Psalm 124
A Song Of Ascents. Of David.

I

¹If it has not been the Lord
   who was on our side,
   let Israel now say—
²if it had not been the Lord who was on our side,
   when men rose up against us,
³then they would have swallowed us up alive,
   when their anger was kindled against us;
⁴then the flood would have swept us away,
   the torrent would have gone over us;
⁵then over us would have gone
   the raging waters.

II

⁶Blessed be the Lord,
   who has not given us
   as prey to their teeth!
⁷We have escaped as a bird
   from the snare of the fowlers;
   the snare is broken,
   and we have escaped!

III

⁸Our help is in the name of the Lord,
   who made heaven and earth.

The psalmist calls upon all Israel to join in a song of thanksgiving, after the removal of a serious obstacle which once blocked the return to Jerusalem. Vv. 1-5 declare what might have happened if the Lord had not intervened; vv. 6-7 gratefully bless Yahweh; v. 8 concludes with a confession of faith in God who manifests omnipotent power, such as the creation of heaven and earth, in such a compassionate way as to care for the psalmist. The danger must have been critical, judging from the images of being swallowed up by raging fire (Num 28:16-25), roaring flood waters (Pss 18:4, 16; 69:1-2), wild animals (Pss 57:4; 58:6). Still another image occurs for deliverance, that of a helpless bird (Ps 11; Lam 3:52). Because these images occur frequently in the Scriptures, it is difficult to identify the danger. The opening line clearly associates the psalm with a pilgrimage to the Promised Land, as it repeats Jacob's words to father-in-law Laban as the former began his journey home: Gen 31:42, "If God . . . has not been on my side, surely now you would have sent me away empty-handed. God saw my affliction and the labor of my hands, and rebuked you last night." The text of this psalm, despite some Aramaisms, is exceptionally well preserved; perhaps Ps 124 is the only psalm in which the Stuttgart Hebrew Bible has no footnotes for variant readings, except that the attribution "of David" is missing in the Septuagint.

Psalm 125
A Song Of Ascents.

I

¹Those who trust in the Lord are like Mount Zion,
    which cannot be moved, but abides for ever.
²As the mountains are round about Jerusalem,
    so the Lord is round about his people,
    from this time forth and for evermore.
³For the scepter of wickedness shall not rest
    upon the land allotted to the righteous,
  lest the righteous put forth
    their hands to do wrong.

II

⁴Do good, O Lord, to those who are good,
    and to those who are upright in their hearts!

III

> [5]But those who turn aside upon their crooked ways
> the Lord will lead away with evildoers!
> Peace be in Israel!

A sturdy, calm faith lies beneath the lines of this *psalm of confidence*. The land of Israel is under the control either of hostile foreigners or of religiously indifferent Jews, perhaps apostates (*cf.,* Isa 56:9—57:13). The psalmist looks forward to the pilgrimage that will lead to the symbol of the strong ancestral faith in the towering Mount Zion, itself surrounded by still other mountains. Within the temple at the end of the pilgrimage, the ancient traditions and (it would seem at this point) the courageous stance of the temple priesthood against oppression will inspire still more courage. Maillot-Lelièvre describe this song as "a true chant of subversion!" secretly gathering strength against an oppressive government. Vv. 1-3 express confidence; v. 4, a prayer for the righteous; v. 5, imprecation of the enemy and a final liturgical refrain: *Peace be in Israel!*

Vv. 1-3. The spirit of these lines vibrates well in Isa 57:13b: "The one who takes refuge in me shall possess the land, and shall inherit my holy mountain." By visibly expressing the interior faith of the people, the mountains tend to reinforce that same faith; they stir further reflection as they bring forth a many faceted symbolism: *i.e.,* the Lord is the Rock (Ps 95:1). In v. 3, it is important to note the careful nuancing of the Hebrew structure. It implies that because *the Lord is round about his people, THEN the scepter of the wicked shall not rest upon the land, AND SO the righteous will not put forth their hands to do wrong.* In vv. 4-5, there is a contrast between the true or reliable person (as the Hebrew word for *upright* connotes) and *those who turn aside upon their crooked ways.* In v. 5, *evildoers* (in Hebrew, "those doing *that* evil action") emphasizes a specific form of apostasy: the betrayal of land and people. Despite the dismal situation, the pilgrimage to Jerusalem implants a new *peace.*

Psalm 126
A Song Of Ascents.

¹When the Lord restored the fortunes of Zion,
  we were like those who dream.
²Then our mouth was filled with laughter,
  and our tongue with shouts of joy;
 then they said among the nations,
  "The Lord has done great things for them."
³The Lord has done great things for us;
  we are glad.

⁴Restore our fortunes, O Lord,
  like the watercourses in the Negeb!
⁵May those who sow in tears
  reap with shouts of joy!
⁶He that goes forth weeping,
  bearing the seed for sowing,
 shall come home with shouts of joy,
  bringing his sheaves with him.

A national lament, similar in structure to Ps 85 and in mood to Jer 31, proceeds from a remembrance of the Lord's saving help in bringing the people back from exile (vv. 1-3), follows up with a prayer for the restoration of their desolate land and for protection against the hostility of the local population (v. 4), and concludes with a consoling promise (vv. 5-6). Although the psalm principally reflects the return from the Babylonian exile in 537 B.C. (they had gone forth into exile weeping but returned joyfully — v. 6), still this return became typical of each pilgrimage to the holy city.

In v. 2, Babylon would be the nation, impressed with Israel's redemption. The Babylonians who had dragged Israel into exile were themselves overcome by the Persians who allowed Israel to return. Vv. 5-6 may have been inspired by an old proverb: *cf.,* Prov 22:8; Job 4:8; Hos 8:7.

It is indicative of the secret joy sustained by strong faith that the phrase repeated most often in this lament is *shouts of joy!*

Psalm 127
A Song Of Ascents. Of Solomon.

1Unless the Lord builds the house,
  those who build it labor in vain.
Unless the Lord watches over the city,
  the watchman stays awake in vain.

2It is in vain that you rise up early and go late to rest,
  eating the bread of anxious toil;
  for he gives to his beloved sleep.
3Lo, sons are a heritage from the Lord,
  the fruit of the womb a reward.
4Like arrows in the hand of a warrior
  are the sons of one's youth.
5Happy is the man who has
  his quiver full of them!
He shall not be put to shame
  when he speaks with his enemies in the gate.

A *wisdom psalm* like this one reflects Israel's long tradition that God is ultimately the source of their external strength, visible in cities and homes, and the creator of life internally within city and home, namely their children. No human work can survive if it ignores God and the bonds of the people's covenant with God. Ps 127 is not denying the importance of human effort, without which cities and families would never come into existence, but it is flatly contradicting the assumption that these can exist happily and peacefully, or even simply exist, without consciously looking to God as their creator and sustainer of life.

A psalm like this one can be described as "devotional wisdom," while another passage in wisdom literature about building a house appears to be more instructional or didactic: "By wisdom a house is built and . . . by knowledge the rooms are filled with all precious and pleasant riches"(Prov 24:3-4).

Ps 127 may have been customarily sung for the birth of a new baby; it quickly adapted itself to pilgrimages to Jerusa-

lem, the spiritual parent of life and blessing for all Israel (Ps
46:4-5; *cf.*, Isa 54:1-8).

V. 1. Frequently enough in the Bible to build a house
means to form a family. This may be due to Israel's remembrance of living in the desert, where a "house" was only a
tent, easily erected or dismantled; what really "made" the
house consisted in wife, husband and children. See 2 Sam
7:27; 1 Kgs 11:38; Jer 24:6; 31:4. Continuity of a "house"
meant that parents lived on in their children: Jer 12:16. V. 2,
sleep can be interpreted as the time of reviving energy and
symbolizes the mysterious but energetic action of God
among people of faith; or *sleep* may refer as well to the
moment of procreation.

Ps 127 challenges each family to reconsider its values and
its source of strength and continuity. It asks all of us to
consider the beatitude of faith, proposed by Jesus in Matt
6:25-34, "Do not be anxious about your life..."

Psalm 128
A Song Of Ascents.

I

¹Blessed is every one who fears the Lord,
who walks in his ways!

II

²You shall eat the fruit of the labor of your hands;
you shall be happy, and it shall be well with you.

III

³Your wife will be like a fruitful vine within your house;
your children will be like olive shoots
around your table.
⁴Lo, thus shall the man be blessed who fears the Lord.

IV

⁵The Lord bless you from Zion!
May you see the prosperity of Jerusalem
all the days of your life!

⁶May you see your children's children!
Peace be upon Israel!

Another *wisdom psalm*, Ps 128 begins in the same way as the final verse of Ps 127, *Happy* or *Blessed* (in Hebrew, *'ashre; cf.,* opening word of Pss 1 and 119). After the initial blessing in v. 1, the psalm addresses the godly person in the second person singular and acclaims one's joy in labor (v. 2), in family (vv. 3-4), and in all Israel (v. 5-6). Just as Ps 127 would have been appropriately sung upon the pilgrim's arrival at Jerusalem, Ps 128 is a blessing before returning home. The psalm echoes long biblical tradition:

who fears the Lord: Pss 34:7, 9; 85:9	eat the fruit of labor: Lev 26:4-5; Isa 3:10
walks in his ways: Ps 27:11; 119:37	wife, a fruitful vine: Hos 14:7

Ps 128 remains within earthly retribution; we need to be reminded that not only in the present life but also in the new heaven and new earth (Isa 65:17; Rev 21:1) our good works and loving friendships will blossom around us. Furthermore, true happiness is shared, first within one's family and also within the larger community of Israel.

Psalm 129
A Song Of Ascents.

I

¹"Sorely have they afflicted me from my youth,"
    let Israel now say—
²"Sorely they have afflicted me from my youth,
    yet they have not prevailed against me.
³The plowers plowed upon my back;
    they made long their furrows."
⁴The Lord is righteous;
    he has cut the cords of the wicked.

II

5May all who hate Zion
  be put to shame and turned backward!
6Let them be like the grass on the housetops,
  which withers before it grows up,
7with which the reaper does not fill his hand
  or the binder of sheaves his bosom,
8while those who pass by do not say,
  "The blessing of the Lord be upon you!

III

We bless you in the name of the Lord!"

In this psalm, sorrow and lament are still heard, as it were, between the words or in the background, but confidence prevails. Through the long history of the ancestors, Israel has seen many conquerors and oppressors come and go, yet Israel already reappears purified, envigorated and renewed in dedication to Yahweh. Through the expenditure of life for the sake of the Lord, even at times through severe punishment suffered for sin, Israel always remains God's elect people (*cf.,* Rom 11:25-36). While the imagery of this psalm is drawn from the peaceful and productive scene of planting (what is more relaxing than to watch a farmer plough one row or furrow after another or to see children scramble over an area, picking loose pieces of grass or weeds?), yet when the image is applied to human beings, there is dreadful pain: ploughing the flesh of a person's back or the lives of people (Mic 3:12; Isa 51:23); recklessly uprooting people from their homeland.

Vv. 1-4 quickly and gratefully scan the history of Israel from the days of youth in Egypt and the wilderness (Exod 4:22; Hos 2:15; 11:1; Jer 2:2; 22:21), through periods of foreign oppression from Egyptians, Philistines, Assyrians and Babylonians. All of these hostile people have been *put to shame.* Vv. 5-8a confess confidence in Yahweh. As the pilgrims slowly made their way to Jerusalem, they would also walk through their history. They were tired from the journey and from the dismal situation of their country (Neh

2:10, 19; chaps. 4 and 6). Foreigners along the way refused to bless them. Yet they would bless one another and be blessed upon their arrival at the holy city: *we bless you in the name of the Lord!*

One can read Ps 129 in conjunction with the litany of Israel's martyrs and saints in Heb chap. 11. "Since we are surrounded by so great a cloud of witnesses, let us also lay aside every weight and sin...and let us run with persever-ance the race that is set before us, looking to Jesus, the pioneer and perfecter of our faith, who for the joy set before him, endured the cross...and is seated at the right hand of the throne of God" (Heb 12:1-2).

Psalm 130
A Song Of Ascents.

I

¹Out of the depths I cry to thee, O Lord!
² Lord, hear my voice!
Let thy ears be attentive
to the voice of my supplications!

II

³If thou, O Lord, shouldst mark iniquities,
Lord, who could stand?
⁴But there is forgiveness with thee,
that thou mayest be feared.

III

⁵I wait for the Lord, my soul waits,
and in his word I hope;
⁶my soul waits for the Lord
more than watchmen for the morning,
more than watchmen for the morning.

IV

⁷O Israel, hope in the Lord!
For with the Lord there is steadfast love,
and with him is plenteous redemption.
⁸And he will redeem Israel
from all his iniquities.

Although an individual lament for sin, Ps 130 echoes at once within the heart of each person and at the end appeals to all Israel. Its grammar speaks in the singular, its spirit in the plural! The sixth of the seven penitential psalms (see Ps 6), it is also one of the best known and most widely recited. The psalm opens with a cry for help, actually a statement of firm confidence that God will hear and take merciful action (vv. 1-2); only after such a firm expression of faith does the psalmist admit sinfulness (vv. 3-4). With firm hope the psalmist awaits the word of forgiveness (vv. 5-6) which is then granted in vv. 7-8, possibly spoken by a priest or else as a reflection upon the liturgical action. Just as Pss 15 and 24 present an entrance liturgy that called for purity and right-eousness, Ps 130 responds more interiorly and poignantly. For the pilgrim then Ps 130 would witness not only a journey from the distant homeland to the temple but also a spiritual transition from sin to new grace, solemnized before all Israel at the temple gate.

Ps 130 is exceptionally simple, strong and sincere. We can delve more profoundly into its spirituality by reading from its sources and parallel places:

v. 1, *depths*, not just of the sea (Ps 69:1-2; Isa 51:9-10) but also of sin (Ps 18:16; Hos 5:2; 9:9), possibly near death (Ps 18:5; Jon 2:3);

v. 2, *Lord, hear my prayer* (Ps 28:2); *be attentive* (2 Chron 6:40);

v. 3, *who could stand?* really no one! 1 Jn 1:10; Ezr 9:15;

v. 4, *forgiveness:* Isa 1:18-19 and 43:22-28, where God becomes the servant carrying the burden of our sins;

v. 5, *I wait:* in the completed tense of the verb, therefore totally absorbed, with strong perseverance. Expressed three times! (Ps 40:1);

v. 7, *steadfast love* of the covenant: Exod 34:6-7;

v. 8, *he will redeem:* the Hebrew strongly emphasizes, "he, Yah-weh, and no one else."

Psalm 131
A Song Of Ascents. Of David.

¹O Lord, my heart is not lifted up,
my eyes are not raised too high;
I do not occupy myself with things
too great and too marvelous for me.
²But I have calmed and quieted my soul,
like a child quieted at its mother's breast;
like a child that is quieted is my soul.

³O Israel, hope in the Lord
from this time forth and for evermore.

On first reading, this psalm envelopes us like a warm spring breeze or in its own words, snuggles up to us like a child in the arms and lap of its parent. Yet, the psalmist is not an infant but an adult who has reached this quiet *confidence* after long struggle against false ambitions, as the negatives infer: *my heart is NOT lifted up, my eyes NOT raised...I do NOT occupy myself with things too great.* The language rejects the haughty ways of many people in authority (*cf.,* Ezek 28:2, 17; Prov 16:5) or of others insecure in themselves and therefore autocratic over others (*cf.,* Pss 18:27; 101:5; Prov 21:4). The psalmist rejects the earlier propensity to venture into the mysterious ways of God, as though to understand and control them (*cf.,* Isa 40:12-14; Job 42:3). Unlike Adam and Eve, the psalmist has no ambition to be like God (Gen 3:5). The mystical insights of the poet blend the spirituality of the psalms with that of the sapiential movement, as the previous citations indicate. The poet must have been a very humble person to compare himself or herself with a weaned child, yet biblical humility is not debasing but rather manifests the patient, strong, appreciative and listening stance of an adult who has learned much over the years, most of all learned to esteem the goodness of others (*cf.,* Isa 50:4-9a). Such a person has suffered, as we find in the biblical background of such words as: to be calm (Isa 28:25; 38:12) and to be silent (Lam 3:26; Ps 42:1, 5).

Psalm 132
A Song Of Ascents.

I-a

¹Remember, O Lord, in David's favor,
  all the hardships he endured;
²how he swore to the Lord
  and vowed to the Mighty One of Jacob,
³"I will not enter my house
  or get into my bed;
⁴I will not give sleep to my eyes
  or slumber to my eyelids,
⁵until I find a place for the Lord,
  a dwelling place for the Mighty One of Jacob."

-b-

⁶Lo, we heard of it in Ephrathah,
  we found it in the fields of Jaar.
⁷"Let us go to his dwelling place;
  let us worship at his footstool!"

⁸Arise, O Lord, and go to thy resting place,
  thou and the ark of thy might.
⁹Let thy priests be clothed with righteousness,
  and let thy saints shout for joy.
¹⁰For thy servant David's sake
  do not turn away the face of thy anointed one.

II-a

¹¹The Lord swore to David a sure oath
  from which he will not turn back:
"One of the sons of your body
  I will set on your throne.
¹²If your sons keep my covenant
  and my testimonies which I shall teach them,
their sons also for ever
  shall sit upon your throne."

-b-

¹³For the Lord has chosen Zion;
  he has desired it for his habitation:
¹⁴"This is my resting place for ever;

here I will dwell, for I have desired it.
¹⁵I will abundantly bless her provisions;
I will satisfy her poor with bread.
¹⁶Her priests I will clothe with salvation,
and her saints will shout for joy.

III

¹⁷There I will make a horn to sprout for David;
I have prepared a lamp for my anointed.
¹⁸His enemies I will clothe with shame,
but upon himself his crown will shed its luster."

(I) This psalm was composed originally for political purposes in the preexilic age and then given its full religious meaning in the postexilic age. As in Ps 89, here too the Davidic dynasty is closely linked with the earlier Mosaic covenant and so received an endorsement from Yahweh to make the Canaanite institutions of royalty, city and temple acceptable to the more traditional minded Israelites. In Ps 132 dynasty and covenant (the latter represented by the ark) blend together in sacred liturgy. David is shown, seeking a secure and dignified resting place for the ark; God is portrayed granting royal privileges and power to David and swearing: "One of the sons of your body I will set on your throne" (v. 11).

On the surface the psalm celebrates the happy moment when David and all Jerusalem brought the ark to the Holy City, "making merry before God with all their might, with song and lyres and harps and tambourines and cymbals and trumpets" (1 Chron 18:3; *cf.,* 2 Sam 6). Ps 132:8-10 is quoted in 2 Chron 6:41-42, this time in connection with Solomon's dedication of his magnificent temple. Quite likely the psalm was sung for solemn festivities amid processions and sacrifices. An appropriate time would be the anniversary of the temple's dedication. In the postexilic age, when the Davidic dynasty disappeared and its powers were absorbed by the priesthood (*cf.,* Zech 6:9-14; Pss 117), the psalm was reinterpreted with a focus almost exclusively upon the temple. The psalm was easily adaptable to this new center of attention by the twenty times a synonym for temple or dwelling place occurs. Yet, hopes for a new, messianic heir to David's throne were not abandoned. Ps 132, like other Davidic or royal psalms (see Ps 2), became an important factor in sustaining faith in God's fidelity to his oath to David.

(II) Ps 132 is intricately structured, not only by the twenty key words, each occurring two times or more, besides the twenty allusions to temple, but also by the parallel structure for the two main parts:

Vv. 1-10; *Assembly at Kiriath-jearim*	vv. 11-16, *Assembly at Jerusalem*
vv. 1-5, David	vv. 11-12, David
1-2, Introduction to oath	11a, Introduction to oath
3-5, David's oath for sanctuary	11b-12, Lord's oath for David
vv. 6-10, Sanctuary	vv. 13-16, Sanctuary
6, Introduction	13, Introduction
7-8, Assembly procession	14, Priestly call to rest
9-10, Condition: Justice	15-16, Results: Salvation
9, for priests and people	15, for the poor
10, for king	16, for priests and people

Vv. 17-18, *Conclusion for David*

This division of the psalm presumes a solemn procession, beginning at Kiriath-jearim (= "Town of the Woodlands," 8½ miles WNW of Jerusalem) and proceeding to the capital city. Very near Kiriath-jearim there lived Obededom, a Philistine into whose care the ark had been entrusted (2 Sam 6:10-12) till David had it brought to Jerusalem.

(III) Vv. 1-10, Assembly at Kiriath-jearim. David was prevented from building a sumptuous temple for the ark; such a building would have been too drastic a departure from Mosaic traditions according to which the ark rested in a tent, typical of desert nomads (*cf.*, 2 Sam 7:4-7); only after the dynasty was more firmly established under Solomon could the construction be undertaken. The psalm begins with attention upon David (vv. 1-5). *Remember:* in liturgical ceremonies to remember meant to relive actively the earlier redemptive deeds of God and to experience their impact now. We are to remember David's *hardships,* a difficult word in that the ancient versions have other readings. The Septuagint and the Vulgate even have something akin to "sweetness" or "gentleness." The emphasis is upon David's humble willingness to stop at nothing to secure God's glory in the midst of the people. God is addressed as "Mighty One," reminiscent of very early days (Gen 49:24; Ps 78:25). It is possible that the divine title is actually addressed to the Ark, upon which God was thought to be invisibly yet personally and graciously enthroned (Exod 25:20-22). David's oath in v. 4 includes a popular piece of wisdom, repeated in Prov 6:4.

Vv. 6-10, Sanctuary focus. In v. 6, the references to Ephrathah and Jaar reach in different directions. Several explanations are offered: they are the place of David's birth and youth (Ruth 4:11; Mic 5:2; Gen 35:19); or else they refer to the people of the area around Bethlehem and Kiriath-jearim, descendants from Ephrathah, second wife of Caleb (1 Chron 2:18-19). In any case David professes his devotion to the ark from his earliest days. The people recall this religious loyalty of David, as they gather at Kiriath-jearim to begin the religious services that will include a procession to Jerusalem. First the community (v. 7) and then the priests, carrying the ark (v. 8), are summoned to begin the procession. V. 8, *Arise O Lord,* repeats the marching/processional song of Num 10:35 and Ps 68:1. If military language echoes in the phrase, *ark of thy might,* it is intended to inspire confidence as much in King David as in the sacred ark! The priests particularly are *clothed with righteousness* (v. 9) meaning liturgical garments (Zech 3:4-5) but also connoting personal holiness and their role as mediators within the covenant religion. The word *saints* includes all the people of Israel assembled for worship (*cf.,* Rom 12:13; 1 Cor 16:1).

Vv. 11-16, Assembly in Jerusalem. Just as the gathering at Kiriath-jearim began with an oath by David about the sanctuary, the ceremonies at Jerusalem begin with the Lord's oath in favor of the Davidic dynasty. In the Scriptures we meet three principal oaths by the Lord: to Abraham for many offspring (Gen 22:15-18); to Israel for the possession of the land (Exod 6:8); and to David. The Scriptures give most attention to the last, which in v. 11 would seem irreversible — although v. 12 introduces conditions. Vv. 13-14, *Zion, my resting place:* as Maillot-Lelièvre remark, "the nomadic God of Mosaic times becomes the resident God, *un Dieu installé*," under the protection of David and especially Solomon. Prayer before the ark professes faith in a long tradition and in many divine promises. We recall Solomon's long prayer at the dedication of the temple, reminding God of the promises to David (1 Kgs 8:25-26) and assuring the people of blessing whenever anyone "comes and prays towards this house" (v. 42). This section ends in v. 16, repeating the words of v. 9.

Vv. 17-18, conclusion. Traditional royal promises converge here: *horn to sprout* recalls a long tradition whereby a principal title for the king was "sprout" or "young twig," a symbol of new life, tenderness and hope, as in Isa 11:1; Jer 23:5; Ezek 17:22-24; Zech 3:8; 6:12. *Horn* by itself symbolized power (Ezek 29:21; Ps 18:2). *Lamp* carried the meaning of prosperity, security and divine presence (1 Kgs 11:36; Ps 18:28). The image may have possibly derived from the temple lamp (Exod 27:20, "command the people of Israel that they bring to you pure beaten olive oil for the light, that a lamp may be set up to burn continually").

(IV) This processional psalm itself underwent changes in interpretation as it processed through Old Testament centuries into the New Testament. Like many other biblical passages it helped to sustain faith that a son of David would come to rule God's people in peace, a promise that is still waiting to be fulfilled through the cross and resurrection of Jesus. Just as the dynasty had to be swept away that the psalm return to its full religious meaning of God's resting in our midst, so also the temple had to be destroyed, as we find in Stephen's speech in Acts 7; or it had to be surpassed by "someone greater" (Matt 12:6) and be rebuilt in three days through the glorious resurrection of Jesus' body (John 2:19-22). The same procession from God's enthronement, to destruction and death, to new life in Jesus, must work its way through our lives, our bodies, "like living stones... built into a spiritual house" (1 Pet 2:5).

Psalm 133
A Song Of Ascents.

> ¹Behold, how good and pleasant it is
>   when brothers dwell in unity!
> ²It is like the precious oil upon the head,
>   running down upon the beard,
>   upon the beard of Aaron,
>   running down on the collar of his robes!
> ³It is like the dew of Hermon,
>   which falls on the mountains of Zion!
>   For there the Lord has commanded the blessing,
>   life for evermore.

(I-II) Common experience and universal hope — the happiness of extended families living peacefully together —dictate the opening lines of Ps 133 and draw it closely to the ranks of wisdom psalms. Yet, the focus modulates towards the sanctuary in the references to Aaron the high priest and to the Zion temple, a style untypical of the sapiential literature. The clue to harmonizing these differences lies in the occasion of pilgrimages to the Jerusalem temple, as found within Pss 120-134. People who live at a distance are generally less hieratic in language, more down-to-earth, the creators and possessors of homespun wisdom. They generally appreciate the blessedness of the temple and the happy occasion of meeting friends during the period of the pilgrimage festival.

The imagery in Ps 133 is a bit difficult to imagine! — precious oil, flowing down on the high priest's robe! — the dew of Mount Hermon drifting some two hundred miles south to Jerusalem! Biblical imagery tends towards exaggerated rhetoric; one part of the metaphor or image clashes with other parts. This tendency becomes very pronounced in apocalyptic literature (*cf.,* Ezek 1; Dan 7). The *mystery* of God's wonder, however, is being effectively communicated.

(III) Typical of the pervasively quiet tone of the pilgrimage psalms (Pss 120-134), the two main figures of speech abound with a generous overflow of serenity: *precious* or scented *oil* that was poured upon the high priest during the anointing service of the later postexilic age (*cf.,* Exod 30:23-33; 40:12-15, but not mentioned in Zech 3:1-9 of the early postexilic age); *dew*, often a symbol of God's mysterious, life-giving blessings (*cf.,* Ps 110:3; Gen 27:28; Deut 33:13; Hos 14:5; Job 29:19). Peace within and among families was able to anoint people with priestly grace to share life and joy. The final phrase, *life for evermore*, looks to many future generations.

(IV) We think of the bond of love, rooted in family, strengthened and centered in Eucharist, in Jesus in whom we form one body with many members (*cf.,* 1 Cor 10-12).

Psalm 134
A Song Of Ascents.

I

¹Come, bless the Lord,
   all you servants of the Lord,
   who stand by night in the house of the Lord!
²Lift up your hands to the holy place.
   and bless the Lord!

II

³May the Lord bless you from Zion,
   he who made heaven and earth!

As an appropriate ending to the pilgrimage "Songs of Ascent" (Pss 120-134), this psalm represents the farewell moment of blessing. The pilgrims ask the priests and levites to continue praising the Lord (vv. 1-2) and to call down the Lord's blessing on themselves as they depart for home (v. 3). Or else the psalm belongs to the longer services at the pilgrimage feast of Tabernacles which included extended night vigils — at least in the later postexilic age.

While the phrase, *servants of the Lord,* can refer to all loyal Israelites (2 Kgs 9:7; 10:23), here it probably refers to levites and priests. (Deut 10:8, "At that time the Lord set apart the tribe of Levi to carry the ark of the covenant of the Lord, to stand before the Lord to minister to him and to bless in his name, to this day"; also Judg 20:28; Neh 12:44). References are made to night office or vigils or prayer in the temple: Pss 1:2; 42:3; 119:55; 1 Chron 9:33; 23:30. Those *who stand. . . in the house of the Lord* designates priests and levites; in fact the phrase (*ma'amad,* in Hebrew) came to specify each of the twenty-four orders of priests who took turns in supervising the daily temple services on a weekly rotation (*cf.,* Luke 1:8). The final verse not only begins with the priestly blessing (Num 6:24-26) but includes the familiar phrase, *he who made heaven and earth* (Ps 121:2; 124:8).

Psalm 135
Praise The Lord!

I
¹Praise the name of the Lord,
    give praise, O servants of the Lord,
²you that stand in the house of the Lord,
    in the courts of the house of our God!
³Praise the Lord, for the Lord is good;
    sing to his name, for he is gracious!
⁴For the Lord has chosen Jacob for himself,
    Israel as his own possession.

II-a
⁵For I know that the Lord is great,
    and that our Lord is above all gods.

6Whatever the Lord pleases he does,
  in heaven and on earth,
  in the seas and all deeps.
7He it is who makes the clouds rise at the end of the earth,
  who makes lightnings for the rain
  and brings forth the wind from his storehouses.

-b-

8He it was who smote the first-born of Egypt,
  both of man and of beast;
9who in thy midst, O Egypt,
  sent signs and wonders
  against Pharaoh and all his servants;
10who smote many nations
  and slew mighty kings,
11Sihon, king of the Amorites,
  and Og, king of Bashan,
  and all the kingdoms of Canaan,
12and gave their land as a heritage,
  a heritage to his people Israel.

-c-

13Thy name, O Lord, endures for ever,
  thy renown, O Lord, throughout all ages.
14For the Lord will vindicate his people,
  and have compassion on his servants.

(I) Similar to Ps 96, this psalm is frequently compared to a mosaic in which an artist has pieced together phrases and lines from other psalms and biblical passages. Some of the more important parallels would be:

v. 1, Ps 113:1
vv. 1-2, Ps 134:1
v. 3a, Ps 136:1
v. 4, Exod 18:11; 19:5;
  Deut 7:6
v. 6, Ps 115:3

v. 7, Jer 10:13; 51:16
v. 8, Ps 78:51
vv. 10-12, Ps 136:17-21
v. 13, Exod 3:15
v. 14, Deut 32:36
vv. 15-18, Ps 115:5-8

As such, Ps 135 is a model for hymn-composition. By its own blending of texts and by their orchestration in liturgical action, the psalm acquires its own place in the Psalter and in Israel's corpus of divinely inspired literature. An anthological style such as this points to a date in the late postexilic age, not only to allow time for the source material to acquire canonical status within the Bible but also to accord with a practice of quoting Scripture to establish one's own authority. Even into the exile (589-539 B.C.) the Bible did not yet quote the Bible!

In a few Hebrew manuscripts Ps 135 is joined with Ps 134; the latter seems to be more of an introduction to praise instead of an independent psalm. Another connection of Ps 135 is with Ps 136. Ps 135:4-21 + Ps 136 are sometimes called the "Great Hallel" (distinguishing them from the "Egyptian Hallel," Pss 113-118) and were sung on the Sabbath morning service and on the Pasch.

(II) The structure of Ps 135 is somewhat involved, a problem that would probably disappear if we knew more about the liturgical division and use of the psalm:

vv. 1-4, Invitation to Praise
vv. 5-18, Motivation for praise;

vv. 4-7, creation   vv. 13-14, refrain or mini-hymn
vv. 8-12, sacred history   vv. 15-18, powerlessness of idols
vv. 19-21, Hymnic conclusion

(III) The invitation to praise (vv. 1-4) forms a small hymn by itself: vv. 1-2, the congregation calls out to priests/levites to praise the Lord; vv. 3-4, a dialogue among the priests:

principal celebrant: other priests/levites:
Praise the Lord . . . .*for the Lord is good*
sing to his name . . . . *for he is gracious*
(altogether) *For the Lord has chosen Jacob for himself, Israel for his own possession.*

Before the psalm praises Yahweh as creator and sustainer of the cosmos, it first looks to Yahweh's choice of Israel *as his own possession.* Creation is for the sake of the beloved people, not vice versa. There is also a hint that Israel's election includes a mission to the universe.

Vv. 5-7, Motivation from creation, sung in solo; v. 5 begins very emphatically, in Hebrew, *ki 'ani yada'ti* — "Certainly I myself am that one who indeed knows." The great elements of the universe are the Lord's instruments, almost his toys: *whatever the Lord pleases, he does.* The impression is left that the Lord knows of many more mysteries across the universe, hidden *in all the deeps* and in *his storehouses* (Deut 28:12; Job 38:22-23).

Vv. 8-12, three important moments from Israel's ancient history are mentioned: the plagues in Egypt, the defeat of Sihon and Og in the days of Moses, very early victories, typical of Israel's preeminence over foreigners, and the Lord's gift of the land. Clearly enough, Israel has no history unless it be that one promised and directed by the Lord. History determines the attitude of faith for the future.

(IV) Israel's mission to the nations, only hinted at in Ps 135 or else seen only in its military aspects, becomes a clear invitation or statement of faith in 1 Pet 2:9-10, "You are a chosen race, a royal priesthood, a holy nation, God's own people, that you may declare the wonderful deeds of him who called you out of darkness into his marvelous light. Once you were no people but now you are God's people; once you had not received mercy but now you have received mercy."

Psalm 136

I
¹O give thanks to the Lord, for he is good,
    for his steadfast love endures for ever.
²O give thanks to the God of gods,
    for his steadfast love endures for ever.
³O give thanks to the Lord of lords,
    for his steadfast love endures for ever;

II

⁴to him who along does great wonders,
for his steadfast love endures for ever;
⁵to him who by understanding made the heavens,
for his steadfast love endures for ever;
⁶to him who spread out the earth upon the waters,
for his steadfast love endures for ever;
⁷to him who made the great lights,
for his steadfast love endures for ever;
⁸the sun to rule over the day,
for his steadfast love endures for ever;
⁹the moon and stars to rule over the night,
for his steadfast love endures for ever;

III

¹⁰to him who smote the first-born of Egypt,
for his steadfast love endures for ever;
¹¹and brought Israel out from among them,
for his steadfast love endures for ever;
¹²with a strong hand and an outstretched arm,
for his steadfast love endures for ever;
¹³to him who divided the Red Sea in sunder,
for his steadfast love endures for ever;
¹⁴and made Israel pass through the midst of it,
for his steadfast love endures for ever;
¹⁵but overthrew Pharaoh and his host in the Red Sea,
for his steadfast love endures for ever;
¹⁶to him who led his people through the wilderness,
for his steadfast love endures for ever;

IV

¹⁷to him who smote great kings,
for his steadfast love endures for ever;
¹⁸and slew famous kings,
for his steadfast love endures for ever;
¹⁹Sihon, king of the Amorites,
for his steadfast love endures for ever;
²⁰and Og, king of Bashan,
for his steadfast love endures for ever;

²¹and gave their land as a heritage,
    for his steadfast love endures for ever;
²²a heritage to Israel his servant,
    for his steadfast love endures for ever.

V

²³It is he who remembered us in our low estate,
    for his steadfast love endures for ever;
²⁴and rescued us from our foes,
    for his steadfast love endures for ever;
²⁵he who gives food to all flesh,
    for his steadfast love endures for ever.

²⁶O give thanks to the God of heaven,
    for his steadfast love endures for ever.

(I) The litany style of Ps 136 is unique in the psalter; yet it is found in Ugaritic literature of the 16th-15th centuries B.C. Twenty-six times the eternal steadfast love of the Lord is acclaimed as Ps 136 proceeds through God's actions in creation and in the early history of the people Israel. The one word, *hesed* or *steadfast love*, centers all of God's actions and intentions in this divine attitude, which in turn is directed towards the chosen people Israel and their peaceful settlement in the land. The word *hesed* has a wide usage in the Old Testament, generally understood in terms of blood relationship or at least treaty alliance (*cf.,* Ps 12). A few texts seem to reach beyond this narrower sense of the word, like Isa 40:6; Pss 59:9-10; 143:12, in which the meaning can be "strength." This word implies a pledge or strong sense of loyalty and so is reducible to the former sense of blood kinship. The history of the universe and of the people of Israel develops from a bond of "blood" or kinship between Yahweh and this chosen nation.

The history, as is evident from the Bible, was not always serene; it was marked with violence, as the slaying of the first-born in Egypt or of famous foreign kings (vv. 10, 17-20). When Ps 136:1 was spoken in 2 Chron 20:21 before a military sortie against Moabites and Ammonites, the phrase, *for he is good,* was struck out, as the Rabbis explained in the *midrash:* there would be "no rejoicing before Him on high over the destruction [even] of wicked people." The question of violence was discussed in relation with Ps 69. The refrain, *for his steadfast love endures for ever,* did not become popular till the postexilic age as in Pss 106:1; 107:1; 118:1, 29; only the disputed texts of Jer 33:11 and Ps 118 include it before the exile. Therefore, the composition of Ps 136 would be around 350 B.C., but before the Books of Daniel and Sirach which quote from it (Dan 3:52-90; Sir 51:1ff).

Ps 136, either by itself or with Ps 135:4-21, constitutes the "Great Hallel" or Song of Praise, sung on the morning of every Sabbath and for the feast of Passover. Other "Hallel" collections are found in Pss 113-18 and Pss 146-150.

(II) The "Great Hallel" opens with an invitation to praise and give thanks (vv. 1-3). This is followed by the motivation (vv. 4-28):

vv. 4-9, honoring Yahweh as Creator;	vv. 17-22, Yahweh, securing land for Israel;
vv. 10-16, Yahweh, Israel's protector in Egypt;	vv. 23-26, Yahweh's love for Israel.

The concluding verse (v. 26), succinctly expresses the spirit and theme of the entire hymn of praise.

(III) Vv. 1-3, invitation to praise. Ps 136 is introduced with *O give thanks* and is the last of the psalms introduced this way (Pss 105-107, 118, and 136). Some scholars would classify the psalm as a song of thanksgiving.

Vv. 4-9, Yahweh Creator. Not only the introductory invitation which places Yahweh, the unique God of Israel, above all other gods (these are reduced to powerlessness, as in Ps 115), but also the refrain extolling Yahweh's *steadfast love,* the unique virtue of the covenant (*cf.,* Ps 12), make sure that creation and history are to be attributed to Yahweh, *who ALONE does* [such] *great wonders* (v. 4). He acts, moreover, for Israel's sake. Yahweh creates *by understand-*

ing. Ps 135 is here reflecting a Semitic mentality that emphasized experiential perception, a wholistic approach, an ability to integrate in favor of one's loyalty and love (*cf.*, Prov 3:19; Jer 10:12).

Vv. 10-16, Yahweh, Protector and Deliverer from Egypt. V. 13 emphasizes the Lord's struggle with hostile forces, often symbolized by sea monsters (*cf.*, Ps 89:9-10); in some mysterious way Yahweh contended at the side of Israel and felt the fury of war.

Vv 17-22, Yahweh, securing land for his people. These verses are very close to Ps 135:11-12.

Vv. 23-26, Yahweh's love for Israel. The word "to remember," at the beginning of this stanza, brings the past into the contemporary moment of liturgical celebration (*cf.*, Ps 132). This response of Yahweh mirrors the spirit of the good shepherd in Ps 23.

V. 26, Conclusion, recapturing the entire psalm. The epithet, *God of heaven*, appears only towards the end of the Persian period, somewhat before 330 B.C. (Ezr 1:2; 5:11, 12; Neh 1:4, 5; Jon 1:9), another reason for a late date of this psalm.

(IV) As sung for the feast of Passover — in the Christian calendar Jesus' resurrection but also his death and burial —Ps 135 enables us to acclaim God's love at every moment of our existence. God is there with us, as we suffer and die many times during a lifetime; no matter what may be the circumstances, personal or outside ourselves, the moment can become one by which we appeal to God's covenant with us and therefore one by which we offer new praise and thanksgiving. Each sabbath brings us into the peace of paradise as at the end of our pilgrimage on earth; again we praise God for each and every moment of the way.

Psalm 137

I

¹By the waters of Babylon,
    there we sat down and wept,

when we remembered Zion.
²On the willows there
we hung up our lyres.
³For there our captors
required of us songs,
and our tormentors, mirth, saying,
"Sing us one of the songs of Zion!"
⁴How shall we sing the Lord's song in a foreign land?

II
⁵If I forget you, O Jerusalem,
let my right hand wither!
⁶Let my tongue cleave to the roof of my mouth,
if I do not remember you,
if I do not set Jerusalem
above my highest joy!

III
⁷Remember, O Lord, against the Edomites
the day of Jerusalem,
how they said, "Raze it, raze it!
Down to its foundations!"
⁸O daughter of Babylon, you devastator!
Happy shall he be who requites you
with what you have done to us!
⁹Happy shall be he who takes your little ones
and dashes them against the rock!

(I) During the early years after 537 and the return from Babylonian exile, but before the temple was rebuilt in 515 B.C., a group of temple singers remembered the tragic horror of Jerusalem's destruction and the crushing discouragement of the exile. They were surrounded with the rubble of a looted and devastated homeland. They would gather for prayer and lamentation at the ruined site of the temple (*cf.,* Jer 41:5). Days were set aside for fasting and mourning (*cf.,* Zech 7:1-14; 8:18-23 — the latter citation is more hopeful). The author of Ps 137 could have belonged to the temple singers. We are told in the annals of Sennacherib that male and female singers were taken captive as booty from Jerusalem, to provide entertainment in the Assyrian court (*cf.,* 2 Kgs 18:13-16). These singers are explicitly mentioned among the returnees at the end of the Babylonian exile (Ezr 2:41).

Two key words, especially in the first part of the psalm are "to remember" (vv. 1, 5, 6, 7) and "to sing." Israel was liturgically "remembering," that is, reenacting and reexperiencing the impact of the exile, perhaps as Christians remember the death of Jesus in the Eucharist (*cf.,* Luke 22:19; 1 Cor 11:25-26). The opening lines of Ps 137 are interlaced with alliteration and onomatopoeia, so that consonants and sounds communicate the mournful dirge and despondent spirit.

(II) The communal lament can be subdivided into three distinct sections: vv. 1-4, lament over the heartbreaking scene; vv. 5-6, a solo part and imprecatory oath against the one who forgets Jerusalem; vv. 7-9, curse of the enemy.

(III) Vv. 1-4, Sad remembrance. Jerusalem's destruction, the discouraging exile and the sight of the devastated homeland blanket the psalmist with sorrow. *By the waters* or many canals of Babylon (*cf.,* Ezek 1:1; 3:15), they gathered for prayer or rest. There may be a reference to the pouring of water as ritually performed in times of mourning (1 Sam 7:6; see also 1 Kgs 8:46-53); it symbolized the pouring out of one's soul or spirit (*cf.,* Ps 42:4; 2 Sam 14:14). *Songs of Zion* may refer to happy melodies in honor of Jerusalem (Pss 76; 84; 87) requested by the captors almost in ridicule — or perhaps sincerely by faithful Jews to break the sorrowful tension. To sing such songs in a *foreign land* would be a profanation, for this land was considered unclean (*cf.,* Amos 7:17; Hos 9:3). These lines support the thesis that Ps 137 was composed and sung (exclusively?) in Babylon; we think that it owes its origin in exile but continued to be sung in burnt out Yehud, as the Persians called the small area around Jerusalem where the people returned.

Vv. 5-6, imprecatory oath upon the Jew who betrayed or forgot the Holy City. There may be a play on words; in

Hebrew, *shakaḥ* certainly means "to forget" but in the Ugaritic it can also mean "to wilt" or "wither"; this same word occurs twice in v. 5. For a musician's right hand to wither would be a terrible curse, like the 80% death of one's body.

Vv. 7-9, curse of enemy. The law of the talion, "eye for eye, tooth for tooth..." (Exod 21:23-25), adds no new punishment but expresses a law of reality: we are punished by our sins, "Your wickedness will chasten you, and your apostasy will reprove you" (Jer 2:18). The Bible adds a prayer of hope that the punishment will be purifying and strengthening, as the Hebrew word *yasar* indicates (*cf.,* Pss 7; 30). Edom was an archetypal enemy of Israel (Isa 34; 63:1-6; Ezek 25:12-14; Obd 10-16).

After the Babylonians destroyed Jerusalem and carted most of the inhabitants into exile, the Edomites moved in to loot and kill. The dreadful curse, "to dash little ones against the city wall," represents what happened at times in the cruelty of war, but how can a twentieth century, nuclear war seem less benign? The word, *little ones* or children, can equally indicate all the inhabitants, especially the adults; and the entire phrase becomes a conventional curse-motif for conquering a city. Examples of this style are given by L. Sabourin, *The Psalms,* 319.

(IV) Revenge and cruelty are never defensible and will inflict their own rage upon the angry person. Yet, we also need words to get the anger out of our system, in the presence of community and particularly before God. Perhaps by expressing it as it really is, clearly before us, we will reject it for ever. Must we actually see a nuclear war before we can reject it? Hopefully, words and pictures of its horror, like the words of Ps 137, may move our world to reject nuclear holocaust. See also Ps 68 for further discussion of the imprecatory or curse psalms.

Psalm 138
A Psalm Of David.

I

¹I give thee thanks, O Lord, with my whole heart;
  before the gods I sing thy praise;
²I bow down toward thy holy temple
  and give thanks to thy name for thy steadfast love
   and thy faithfulness;
 for thou hast exalted above everything
  thy name and thy word.
³On the day I called thou didst answer me,
  my strength of soul thou didst increase.

II

⁴All the kings of the earth shall praise thee, O Lord,
  for they have heard the words of thy mouth;
⁵and they shall sing of the ways of the Lord,
  for great is the glory of the Lord.
⁶For though the Lord is high, he regards the lowly;
  but the haughty he knows from afar.

III

⁷Though I walk in the midst of trouble,
  thou dost preserve my life;
 thou dost stretch out thy hand against the wrath of my
   enemies,
  and thy right hand delivers me.
⁸The Lord will fulfil his purpose for me;
  thy steadfast love, O Lord, endures for ever.
  Do not forsake the work of thy hands.

(I) The Hebrew text presents serious problems; the context remains vague. Ps 138, therefore, is difficult to situate within its proper setting. A spirit of gratitude extends throughout the psalm, possibly from a person after being healed of sickness (vv. 3b and 7). While appreciation is expressed in the singular first person "I," nonetheless, we detect a community at prayer, not only because of the refrain in v. 8b, *thy steadfast love, O Lord, endures for ever,* very similar to the congregational response in Ps 136, but also because of the reference to *all the kings of the earth.* This language would appear somewhat pompous for a private, individual prayer of thanksgiving, unless this person be a king or priest, representative of the nation. The impact of Isaiah, chaps. 40-66, is felt in reading the psalm, even if there are no direct quotations from this prophetic scroll. These facts leave us with a date in the postexilic age, and with the speaker a priest. Kings have disappeared from Israel's government. Even though gratitude pervades the psalm, we also detect problems, as was said above, not only sickness, but also affliction from haughty persons (v. 6b). *In the midst of trouble* the psalmist was preserved from *the wrath of my enemies* (v. 7). If the psalmist was a priest (our position), he may have lived at a distance, for there are few if any allusions to ritual actions. The *spirit* of Ps 138, therefore, is close to Pss 42-43.

(II) The psalm opens with praise and thanksgiving (vv. 1-3), rhetorically shared with *all the kings of the earth* (vv. 4-6), and concludes with confidence (vv. 7-8).

(III) We comment upon several phrases: v. 1, *with my whole heart,* a phrase reminiscent of Deut 6:5, a fact which places Ps 138 within the spirituality of the North, as shared by Hosea, Jeremiah and Isa 40-66, and was to be noticeable in the ministry of Jesus (*cf.,* Mark 12:28-30). V. 1, *before the gods,* a phrase that was theologically difficult for the rabbis and translated as angels (Greek Septuagint), kings (Syriac) and judges (Aramaic Targum). If the phrase comes from the influence of Second Isaiah (Isa 41:23; 42:17; etc.), then these gods are standing by helplessly, a very ungodly posture like that in Ps 115. The RSV text of v. 2c, *thou hast exalted...thy name and thy word,* is itself a grammatical correction; the Hebrew text seems disturbed and artificially lengthened, literally, "thou hast exalted thy word above all thy name." One explanation (A. A. Anderson) understands *word* in the active sense of Yahweh's actions which always exceed what we *understand* them to be in the Lord's *name.* V. 4, *All the kings of the earth:* they praise Yahweh to the extent that

Israel, the Lord's herald, shares the message with them (*cf.,* Isa 49:7). The refrain in v. 8, along with the reference in v. 2b to the Lord's *steadfast love* and *faithfulness* echoes the Mosaic covenant (*cf.,* Exod 34:6-7) and places Israel's confidence and world salvation within the purpose and mission of the Lord's elect people. Most of all, Israel is *the work of thy hands* (Isa 60:21; 64:7); in submitting to the Lord, Israel finds its purpose and confidence.

(IV) From a literary and a theological viewpoint, Ps 138 may not be a great poem. For Israel it may have served the very practical purpose of bringing the exalted poetry of Second Isaiah down into the realm of a monotonous and even discouraging routine. Ps 138 thus shared in the spirit of postexilic Israel and spoke its language. After all, even if Second Isaiah's glorious promises were not fulfilled, still the people were back in their beloved land. We too may stand in need of second rate poetry for our dreary days!

Psalm 139
To The Choirmaster. A Psalm Of David.

I-a

¹O Lord, thou hast searched me and known me!
²Thou knowest when I sit down and when I rise up;
   thou discernest my thoughts from afar.
³Thou searchest out my path and my lying down,
   and art acquainted with all my ways.
⁴Even before a word is on my tongue,
   lo, O Lord, thou knowest it altogether.
⁵Thou dost beset me behind and before,
   and layest thy hand upon me.
⁶Such knowledge is too wonderful for me;
   it is high; I cannot attain it.

-b-

⁷Whither shall I go from thy Spirit?
   Or whither shall I flee from thy presence?
⁸If I ascend to heaven, thou art there!
   If I make my bed in Sheol, thou art there!

⁹If I take the wings of the morning
   and dwell in the uttermost parts of the sea,
¹⁰even there thy hand shall lead me,
   and thy right hand shall hold me.
¹¹If I say, "Let only darkness cover me,
   and the light about me be night,"
¹²even the darkness is not dark to thee,
   the night is bright as the day;
   for darkness is as light with thee.

-c-

¹³For thou didst form my inward parts,
   thou didst knit me together in my mother's womb.
¹⁴I praise thee, for thou art fearful and wonderful.
   Wonderful are thy works!
 Thou knowest me right well;
¹⁵ my frame was not hidden from thee,
   when I was being made in secret,
   intricately wrought in the depths of the earth.
¹⁶Thy eyes beheld my unformed substance;
   in thy book were written, every one of them,
 the days that were formed for me,
   when as yet there were none of them.
¹⁷How precious to me are thy thoughts, O God!
   How vast is the sum of them!
¹⁸If I would count them, they are more than the sand.
 When I awake, I am still with thee.

II-a

¹⁹O that thou wouldst slay the wicked, O God,
   and that men of blood would depart from me,
²⁰men who maliciously defy thee,
   who lift themselves up against thee for evil!
²¹Do I not hate them that hate thee, O Lord?
   And do I not loathe them that rise up against thee?
²²I hate them with perfect hatred;
   I count them my enemies.

-b-

²³Search me, O God, and know my heart!

Try me and know my thoughts!
24And see if there be any wicked way in me,
   and lead me in the way everlasting!

(I) Religiously one of the most appealing, prayerful
poems of the entire Old Testament, Ps 139 is also one of its
most complicated and disturbed poems grammatically and
textually. The copy found among the Dead Sea Scrolls, like
the Greek Septuagint and Latin Vulgate, intensifies the
problem. For instance, the latter two ancient versions read
v. 17 as: "Your friends, O God, have been greatly honored
by me, their rule has been greatly strengthened." The Latin
liturgy called upon this passage for celebrating the feast of
the apostles. St. Jerome's Latin translation directly from the
Hebrew reads v. 17b still differently: "How vast are their
poor." The Dead Sea Scroll from cave XI provides an
improved reading for v. 11b, "and night has imprisoned
me."

We proceed on the assumption, to be discussed later, that
Ps 139 is a single composition. The author was a faithful
Jew, lost somewhere in the diaspora, seemingly *at the uttermost parts of the sea* (v. 9), appalled by the idolatry of the
gentiles and even Jews who had apostatized and passed over
into the ranks of the gentiles. This latter situation had been
faced by Second Isaiah (Isa 40-55) during the Babylonian
exile. Like the author of Ps 139, this prophet reveals a mind
that swept ecstatically across the universe, peered into the
wondrous mystery of God's concern for Israel, argued
against idolatry and apostasy and eventually while writing
the Servant Songs (Isa 42:1-4; 49:1-9a; 50:4-9a; 52:13-53:12)
found himself isolated, lonely and even persecuted. These
same circumstances are found again in the Book of Job, and
much more poignantly still in the prophecy of Jeremiah. A
kinship of spirit and at times of vocabulary and motif
extend from Jeremiah into Second Isaiah, Job and Ps 22,
and eventually into Ps 139. Important differences show up
as well. Ps 139 lacks the strong element of prayer in Jeremiah (12:1-5; 20:7-18) and in Ps 22. It does not relive and
actualize great moments of Israelite history like the new

exodus in Isa 40-55. It totally lacks the dialogue style of Job
and the explicit interaction with temple worship in Jeremiah. Nor does any intense persecution close in upon the
psalmist.

The psalmist, however, takes personally the affrontery of
those who *maliciously defy thee. . .and hate thee, O Lord*
(vv. 20-21). If this explanation is accurate, then the "curse of
the enemy" in vv. 19-24, does not come from personal
vendetta but from outrage at the blasphemy against Yahweh from former Jews. Most of all, the psalmist is amazed at
the inexplicable wonder of Yahweh, present across the universe, still in control even when rejected by sinners. This
explanation still allows the later use of the psalm in temple
worship as proposed by H.-J. Kraus and others. According
to these authors, when a dispute or suspicion of crime could
not be solved locally, it was deferred to the central sanctuary
(Deut 17:8-13). One of the rituals stipulated that the defend-
ant abjure the crime, solemnly declare innocence, spend the
night within the temple (*cf.,* Ps 7), and await an oracle or
exoneration in the morning. Against this position, however,
is the fact that the psalmist does not seem to be condemned,
nor even under suspicion, but rather is suffering from insults
heaped by idolators upon Yahweh.

(II) Upon close scrutiny the unity of the psalm becomes
ever more apparent. The stylistic device of "inclusion" ver-
bally unites beginning and end, vv. 1-3 with vv. 23-24. The
words, *search* and *know*, are repeated in vv. 1-2 and v. 23,
the word, *way*, in v. 3 and v. 24. It is possible that we have
here, according to Hebrew stylistic norms, a summary or at
least an allusion to the first major section (vv. 1-18) in vv. 1-2
and 23, and to the second major section (vv. 19-24) in vv. 3
and 24. No one can search to the end of the wondrous
knowledge of Yahweh in vv. 1-18; each one is horrified at
the wicked in vv. 19-24 who reject good ways (v. 3) and
follow a wicked one (v. 24). Jan Holman, whose explanation we are following here, indicates other structural parallels and interlacing: for instance, in section one, v. 1 and v.
18, v. 2 and v. 17 parallel each other, with a central point in

this juxtaposition found with vv. 6 and 14, where praise is more intense. As for section two, we discover that vv. 19 and 24, vv. 20 and 23, vv. 21 and 22 present very similar motifs. Structurally, there are several chiasms here (*cf.,* Ps 19:1). These intricacies of style lead us to conclude: 1) that vv. 19-24 are very important for interpreting the entire poem; and 2) that Ps 139 is basically a lament over widespread apostasy; it was influenced by Second Isaiah and Job to reach ecstatically towards Yahweh, wondrously present in the darkness of pregnancy as in the sweep of the sun across the universe, in the depths of the earth and still more profoundly and sadly in the depths of apostasy. Yet as v. 12 declares, despite all its textual confusion, such "night is bright as the day" with the Lord. Viewing the psalm as a personal lament, we look upon the splendor of Yahweh in close, personal relationship with our sorrow and trials.

The psalm can be subdivided for reflective reading:

Vv. 1-18, with hymnic element:
    vv. 1-6, Yahweh's
        omniscience, with intro-
        duction (vv. 1-3)
    vv. 7-12, Yahweh's omni-
        presence
    vv. 13-18, wonders of one's
        birth

Vv. 19-24, with curse and lament
    vv. 19-22, curse
    vv. 23-24, prayer and
        conclusion.

The psalm dates quite late in the postexilic period, on account of: many Aramaisms and words/phrases foreign to normal biblical Hebrew; the influence of Job, especially in the rare terms; the lack of liturgical phrases and actions.

(III) Vv. 1-6, Omniscience of Yahweh. The focus seems exclusively upon Yahweh, very clearly so in v. 2 which begins emphatically, "You are that [only] one who knowest..." Yet Yahweh is viewed as reflected from the psalmist's life in all its aspects and steps. An example of Aramaism occurs here, not only in grammatical structure but also in the phrase, a single word in Hebrew, *my lying down.* In biblical Hebrew this verb refers to bestiality (Lev 18:23; 30:16) or the crossbreeding of animals (Lev 19:19), but in the Aramaic language it lost this crude denotation and signified simply "bed" or "rest." Vv. 1-6 echo again in Rom 11:33, "O the depth of the riches and wisdom and knowledge of God! How unsearchable are his judgments and how inscrutable his ways!" Paul then quotes from Isa 40:13-14, also one of the favorite biblical sources of the psalmist.

Vv. 7-12, Omnipresence of God. These lines resonate Job 11:7-8, "Can you find out the deep things of God? [They are] higher than heaven. . .deeper than Sheol." Amos 9:2-3 also refers, in God's name, to those who presume to "dig into Sheol [and] climb up to heaven [as though they can] hide from my sight at the bottom of the sea." A similar phrase occurs in a letter from Palestine to an Egyptian Pharaoh of the fourteenth century B.C. The phrase, therefore, was in popular use for a long time. Yet, the idea was also denied by official or orthodox Judaism who claimed that Yahweh could not be contacted in Sheol (Pss 6:5; 30:9; 88:5-6, 11-12). The psalm, it seems, does not belong to the Jerusalem ritual but to popular religiosity and to Jews in the distant diaspora.

Vv. 13-18. The wonders of conception, pregnancy and birth are seen within this and other classic texts of the Old Testament: Pss 22:9-10; 71:5-6; Job 10:8-11; Isa 49:2; Jer 1:5. Some of these deal with the mystery of prophetic vocation when people find themselves under fire; others with life's meaningless tragedies, in any case with the heroic confession of faith that the Lord's tender care and strong sense of purpose reach back to conception. At each stage of one's life we remain within a dark womb with continuous need to look to Yahweh for our mission, purpose, protection and fulfillment. All through life we are enclosed within the darkness of mother earth where the Lord's tender hands are intricately forming us into the ideal man and woman, like Adam and Eve's birth in paradise (Gen 2:7, 18-22). Each one's personal existence belongs *in thy book* (v. 16), where the names of all the elect are written and where the loneliness of each one is absorbed within the happiness of the Lord's family (Ps 69:28; Exod 32:33; Dan 7:10; 12:1).

Vv. 19-24. The enemy here is not threatening the psalmist's life or security. These hypocrites are enemies of Yahweh, and the devout person should have no contact with them (*cf.,* Ps 101:3b-5). The psalm ends with the wish that Yahweh will *lead me in the way everlasting.* The identical phrase is not found elsewhere in the Old Testament and we are tempted to see here an allusion to life after death. Such a religious doctrine began to appear in the late postexilic age. If Ps 139 emerged from popular piety, particularly in Egypt or somewhere else in the diaspora where theological developments came more easily than in Jerusalem, then the psalmist would have eventually plunged beyond the dark boundaries of life into the full light of eternity, from the womb of earth to paradise. Another possibility, more in accord with Jerusalem's orthodox theology would see here a reference back to the ancient ways of the ancestors (*cf.,* Jer 6:16; 18:15).

(IV) If Ps 139 originated in a tradition that included Jeremiah, Second Isaiah, Ps 22 and Job, then we are reminded of the necessity of long-suffering perseverance, of absolute trust in God, of seeing by faith the strong love of God particularly in life's darkest moments, within the mother's womb, within earthly trials, within ecstatic prayer, within disappointment and collapse round about us, beyond the borders of serious sickness and death. Within each of these "wombs" the Lord is knitting each one of us together. "Wonderful are thy works!"

The Latin Vulgate has come up with a translation quite different in many places; this tradition continually surfaced in the liturgy of the early church: *i.e.,* for the feast of the Lord's resurrection, v. 18b, "I rose up and am still with thee," + vv. 5-6, "thou hast laid thy hand upon me...thy knowledge is become wonderful." A psalm, intensely personal as this one, has led into the personal mystery of Jesus, his resurrection to new life. Jesus was knit into a new heavenly being while lying within the womb of his tomb. In the ancient liturgy the psalm was sung or recited on late Friday afternoon (Vespers), again uniting our prayers with the peaceful sleep of Jesus when "night [was about to become] bright as the day"(v. 12) in the Lord's resurrection.

Ps 139 speaks eloquently to the modern tragedy of widespread abortion and to the neglect of disabled people, both of whom are lost within a dark womb.

Psalm 140
To The Choirmaster. A Psalm Of David.

This individual lament is plagued with many textual problems, particularly in the central section (vv. 6-11). In the Hebrew the lines are laborious; there are more than the average number of rare words. The psalmist seems victimized by calumny and prays to the Lord to set the record straight. In fact, those who reject a person's covenantal right to the land themselves have no place in that land (vv. 11 and 13). The psalm is subdivided: vv. 1-5, prayer and lament; vv. 6-11, appeal to the Lord and curse against the enemy; vv. 12-13, confidence that *the Lord maintains the cause of the afflicted.* We are reminded of James' epistle and its description of the evils of the tongue: "The tongue is a little member and boasts of great things. How great a forest is set ablaze by a small fire!..." (3:5).

Psalm 141
A Psalm Of David.

A psalm of individual lament, this poem belonged to a circle or school of piety, strongly influenced by the wisdom movement. In this way it is close to Pss 1 and 119. The author may have lived in the diaspora and asked that his prayers be accepted like the evening sacrifices at the Jerusalem temple (v. 2). There comes to mind the prayer of the three young men in the fiery furnace: "Yet with a contrite heart and a humble spirit may we be accepted, as though it

were with burnt offerings of rams and bulls...such may our
sacrifice be in thy sight this day, and may we wholly follow
thee..." (Dan 3:39-40 in the NAB; vv. 16-17 in other editions). If the psalm originated in the diaspora (this is only an
hypothesis), it found its way firmly into the Jerusalem temple where it was chanted each evening with the lighting of
the lamps (*cf.,* Exod 30:7-8; Dan 9:21). The early Church
continued this practice. St. John Chrysostom wrote bluntly
and tersely: "The psalm is more obscure than the darkness"
of night when it is recited; and again, "Obscure psalm, which
all the world chants without comprehending it." The difficulties of the psalm reach beyond textual reconstruction in
vv. 5-7; some scholars refuse to translate them; the Jerusalem Bible (French edition) has changed its text four times in
four different editions. Despite these textual problems,
many pieces of good advice and strong piety still come
through in the psalm.

For our convenience we divide the psalm between: vv.
1-2, a call for help; vv. 3-5, a prayer for strength and wisdom
not to sin; vv. 6-7, incomprehensible, perhaps a curse
against sinners; vv. 8-10, refuge in the Lord.

Psalm 142
A Maskil Of David, When He Was In The Cave. A
Prayer.

I

¹I cry with my voice to the Lord,
  with my voice I make supplication to the Lord,
²I pour out my complaint before him,
  I tell my trouble before him.
³When my spirit is faint,
  thou knowest my way!

II

In the path where I walk
  they have hidden a trap for me.
⁴I look to the right and watch,

but there is none who takes notice of me;   no refuge
remains to me,
    no man cares for me.

III

⁵I cry to thee, O Lord;
    I say, Thou art my refuge,
    my portion in the land of the living.
⁶Give heed to my cry;
    for I am brought very low!

Deliver me from my persecutors;
    for they are too strong for me!
⁷Bring me out of prison,
    that I may give thanks to thy name!
The righteous will surround me;
    for thou wilt deal bountifully with me.

(I-II) Humble strength and obvious sincerity characterize
this individual lament. Even though the psalmist has drawn
heavily from other laments and prayers, the words and
phrases have been thoroughly absorbed and presented anew
with a creative, heartfelt anguish. If we interpret v. 7 literally, *Bring me out of prison*, then the psalmist is being
detained till the time of trial (Lev 24:12; Num 15:34); Israel
did not have prisons to punish criminals or to isolate them
from society. Yet, already the psalmist is experiencing a
living death, abandoned even by friends. No one brings food
and comfort (*cf.,* Ps 22; Jer 38). In view of the strong
individual tone of Ps 142, this explanation seems preferable
to interpreting *prison* metaphorically of persecution and
disgrace, as in Lam 3:7, "He [Yahweh] has walled me about
so that I cannot escape; he has put heavy chains on me."
Contrary to the preceding psalm, the Hebrew text is well
preserved, but the poetic rhythm is very uneven — due to the
psalmist's distress (?). After a descriptive invocation (vv.
1-3ab), there follows a lament (vv. 3cd-4) and a prayer for
assistance (vv. 5-7).
    (III) The *title* refers to David's shelter in a cave while

fleeing from Saul, either at Adullam (1 Sam 22:1-2) or at En-gedi (1 Sam 24:1-7). A later editor who added the title attempted to show how the psalms can be associated with one's daily life as well as with Israel's tradition. While the cave protected David from the enemy, the prison, on the contrary, turned into a severe danger and crisis for the psalmist. These contradictions did not disturb the editor. His purpose was not historical exegesis but practical application and hope.

Vv. 1-3ab, invocation. The psalm begins energetically, even dramatically: *my voice,* in Hebrew *qol,* the same word for thunder in Ps 29. By contrast the introduction closes with attention riveted upon Yahweh, as in v. 3b, "On the contrary, you are that one who knows my way," a translation to reflect the force of the Hebrew grammar. There is still another contrast between the "thunderous" or "roaring" cry of the psalmist in the opening phrase and the Hebrew word in v. 1 for *supplication, siaḥ,* which implies quiet mumbling and continuous interior meditation (*cf.,* Ps 119).

Vv. 3cd-4. The lament bemoans the loss of every human comfort and aid, like Jer 25:34-5, "Wail, you shepherds... and roll in ashes.... No refuge will remain for the shepherds, nor escape... "

Vv. 5-7, Prayer for help. The psalmist has one last refuge, the Lord, like Jer 17:17, again emphatically, "Thou art my only refuge in the day of evil." The Lord is *refuge* (Ps 91:2, 9) and *portion* (Ps 16:5) *in the land of the living* (Ps 27:13) —this line of v. 5bc is not only a good example of the psalmist's absorption of tradition, but it also makes us think of the levite who composed Ps 16. He had lost respectability and health, essential for priests who stood in behalf of the people before the living glorious God, but thereby discovered in the Lord one's only refuge, life and honor (*cf.,* Num 18:20; Deut 10:9). In v. 6b the psalmist slips back into the interior dungeon of fear and emotional isolation; quickly, however, faith brings this imprisoned person into the liturgical assembly (v. 7cd) to participate in a ceremony of thanksgiving (Ps 22:22-31, "in the midst of the congregation I will praise thee...").

(IV) St. Francis recited this psalm while dying, waiting to be released from brother flesh and reunited with all brothers and sisters in the heavenly assembly, there to be dealt with bountifully by the Lord. We are reminded too of Jesus' imprisonment on Holy Thursday evening, or the Lord's silence on the cross. Sooner or later each person shall be cast into the prison of powerlessness and darkness and walk the fearful steps through the door of death. Ps 142 enables us to walk confidently as we say, *Thou art my refuge, my portion in the land of the living.*

Psalm 143
A Psalm Of David.

I

¹Hear my prayer, O Lord;
  give ear to my supplications!
  In thy faithfulness answer me, in thy righteousness!
²Enter not into judgment with thy servant;
  for no man living is righteous before thee.

II

³For the enemy has pursued me;
  he has crushed my life to the ground;
  he has made me sit in darkness like those long dead.
⁴Therefore my spirit faints within me;
  my heart within me is appalled.

⁵I remember the days of old,
  I meditate on all that thou hast done;
  I muse on what thy hands have wrought.
⁶I stretch out my hands to thee;
  my soul thirsts for thee like a parched land.   *Selah*

III

⁷Make haste to answer me, O Lord!
  My spirit fails!
  Hide not thy face from me,

lest I be like those who go down to the Pit.
8Let me hear in the morning of thy steadfast love,
  for in thee I put my trust.
Teach me the way I should go,
  for to thee I lift up my soul.

9Deliver me, O Lord, from my enemies!
  I have fled to thee for refuge!
10Teach me to do thy will,
  for thou art my God!
Let thy good spirit lead me
  on a level path!

11For thy name's sake, O Lord, preserve my life!
  In thy righteousness bring me out of trouble!
12And in thy steadfast love cut off my enemies,
  and destroy all my adversaries,
  for I am thy servant.

(I-II) The last of the seven penitential psalms (Pss 6, 32, 38, 51, 102, 130, 143), this individual lament according to E. Beaucamp "is a *pot-pourri* of all the lamentations of the psalter." From an indication in v. 8, where the psalmist asks God to allow the petitioner to *hear in the morning of thy steadfast love*, some conclude that the psalm was chanted at night as a prayer for relief in the ensuing day. The Greek church, however, links it with Pss 3, 37, 62, 87 and 102 as a daily morning prayer. After an opening request that the Lord *give ear* [and] *answer* (vv. 1-2), a lament follows with the final *selah* or pause in the psalter (vv. 3-6). The psalm concludes with petitionary prayer (vv. 7-12). We cannot determine the occasion of its composition; the date is most probably the late postexilic age, principally for the citation of or allusion to many earlier psalms.

(III) For commentary we cite the many references to other biblical passages; by studying these passages we learn how the Bible quotes the Bible!
Vv. 1-2, Opening request
  hear my prayer: Pss 28:2; 39:13; 54:2
  give ear: Pss 5:1; 17:1

in thy faithfulness, classic covenant formula: Pss 4:2;
39:13; 102:2.
no one is righteous before thee: important theme in Job —
4:17; 9:2; 3; 15:14; 25:4. Quoted also in Rom 3:20, "For
no human being will be justified in his [God's] sight by
works of the law since through the law comes knowledge
of sin."
Vv. 3-6, lament
enemy has pursued me: Ps 7:1
crushed my life: Ps 94:5
like those long dead, whose impact on later generations is
lost from memory: Ps 88:10; Lam 3:6
my spirit faints: Ps 142:3
remember, meditate, muse: Pss 77:5-6, 11-12; 119:52
my soul thirsts for thee like dry land: Ps 63:1
Vv. 7-12, New series of petitions
make haste: Pss 69:17; 102:2
my spirit fails: Ps 84:2
hide not thy face: Pss 27:9; 102:2
like those who go down to the Pit: Ps 28:1; 88:4
in the morning, always a favorable time: Ps 46:5
steadfast love: Ps 26:3
I put my trust: Ps 78:22
teach me thy way: Pss 25:9-10; 86:11
I lift up my soul: Pss 25:1; 86:4
teach me to do thy will: Pss 25:4-5; 40:9
good spirit: Neh 9:20, "Thou gavest thy good spirit to
instruct them"
on a level path (Hebrew, level earth): Isa 40:3; 42:16
for thy name's sake: Ps 106:8
preserve my life: Pss 30:3; 119:25
(IV) Ps 143 shows the advantage of memorization of
biblical texts. These come spontaneously to our assistance.
They enlighten moments of distress, not only with the presence of God but also with God's wisdom and strength. This
attitude is shown at the heart of Ps 143 (v. 5), where we are
encouraged to *remember* (in Hebrew, *zakar*, to re-live and
experience anew), to *meditate* (in Hebrew, *hagah*, to mum-

ble, quietly repeat and absorb like gentle spring rain), and *muse* (*siah*) synonym of *hagah* and the origin of the word normally translated "to meditate" in the Latin Vulgate and as such has come into Christian spirituality.

Psalm 144
A Psalm Of David.

In many ways Ps 144 strikes us as a combination of parts that were not adequately blended together. Perhaps if we knew more of postexilic life, then we would appreciate how the changes were not so abrupt as we imagine, in the ritual acts of the temple or in the instructional method of the sages. Vv. 1-11 incorporates lines and phrases from Ps 18:2, 4, 9, 14, 16. Because Ps 18 is closely related to the royal psalms, some scholars, like A. Deissler, refer Ps 144 to the messianic hopes of the postexilic period for a new Davidic king. The eschatological language of vv. 5-8 — smoking mountains, lightning like flashing arrows — does not so much remind us of Mount Sinai as of divine intervention in the new age (*cf.*, Isa 64:1-4). Another Davidic allusion may be found in vv. 3-4, about the lowliness of humankind that is elevated on high (see Ps 8). The anthological style of borrowing elsewhere from the Bible disappears in vv. 12-15, where we find ourselves closer to sapiential literature and the blessings upon the upright person. This sapiential influence already appeared in vv. 3-4 (Job 7:17; 8:9; Eccles 6:12; Pss 127-128). The second part (vv. 12-15) contains expressions seldom found elsewhere in the Hebrew Bible yet common enough in the postexilic Aramaic language.

In view of this somewhat awkward combination of parts, it is difficult to categorize Ps 144 within any single literary form: communal lament seems to dominate the first section (vv. 1-11), yet this sorrow is mitigated by messianic Davidic hopes; the second section (vv. 12-15) is mostly sapiential in character, a type of spirituality that is generally not interested in messianic hopes and directs attention to the responsibilities and possibilities of the present moment.

Psalm 145
A Song Of Praise. Of David.

I

¹I will extol thee, my God and King,
and bless thy name for ever and ever.
²Every day I will bless thee,
and praise thy name for ever and ever.

II

³Great is the Lord, and greatly to be praised,
and his greatness is unsearchable.

⁴One generation shall laud thy works to another,
and shall declare thy mighty acts.
⁵On the glorious splendor of thy majesty,
and on thy wondrous works, I will meditate.
⁶Men shall proclaim the might of thy terrible acts,
and I will declare thy greatness.

III

⁷They shall pour forth the fame of thy abundant
goodness.
and shall sing aloud of thy righteousness.

⁸The Lord is gracious and merciful,
slow to anger and abounding in steadfast love.
⁹The Lord is good to all,
and his compassion is over all that he has made.
¹⁰All thy works shall give thanks to thee, O Lord,
and all thy saints shall bless thee!

IV

¹¹They shall speak of the glory of thy kingdom,
and tell of thy power,
¹²to make known to the sons of men thy mighty deeds,
and the glorious splendor of thy kingdom.
¹³Thy kingdom is an everlasting kingdom,
and thy dominion endures throughout all generations.
The Lord is faithful in all his words,
and gracious in all his deeds.

V

¹⁴The Lord upholds all who are falling,
   and raises up all who are bowed down.
¹⁵The eyes of all look to thee,
   and thou givest them their food in due season.
¹⁶Thou openest thy hand,
   thou satisfiest the desire of every living thing.
¹⁷The Lord is just in all his ways,
   and kind in all his doings.
¹⁸The Lord is near to all who call upon him,
   to all who call upon him in truth
¹⁹He fulfils the desire of all who fear him,
   he also hears their cry, and saves them.
²⁰The Lord preserves all who love him;
   but all the wicked he will destroy.

VI

²¹My mouth will speak the praise of the Lord,
   and let all flesh bless his holy name for ever and ever.

(I) An acrostic or alphabetical psalm in which each line or series of lines begins with the succeeding letter of the alphabet (*cf.,* Pss 9-10; 119), Ps 145 is not a poetic masterpiece. The style is too rigid for creative brilliance. Yet Ps 145 has been recognized by the early rabbis and by Christian tradition as one of the most inspiring pieces of religious literature in the psalter. It has been recited three times daily in the synagogues, morning, noon and night, and according to the Babylonian Talmud (Berakoth, 4b), whoever recited this psalm three times daily was assured a place in the world to come. The Dead Sea scroll from cave II placed a refrain after each verse: "Blessed be Yahweh, and blessed be his name for ever and ever." V. 2 was incorporated into the ancient Christian hymn of praise, the *Te Deum;* vv. 10, 15-16 into the traditional prayers before eating. Ps 145, therefore, is a fitting conclusion to the final, small collection of Davidic Psalms (Pss 138-145).

By reason of the acrostic arrangement Ps 145 may come under the umbrella of a sapiential psalm, but its principal spirit is one of praise. As such, it manifests a strong universal sweep: v. 9, *Lord is good to all;* v. 10, *all thy saints,* the Hebrew word means fidelity to the covenant; v. 15, *eyes of all;* v. 16, *every living thing;* v. 18, *all who call upon him in truth;* v. 21, *all flesh.* The acrostic arrangement means that *all* the letters of the alphabet are involved in this hymn. Ps 145 emphasizes the Lord's royal power and kingly position that sweep across time and space.

(II) The acrostic arrangement usually makes it difficult to perceive logical development and strophic arrangement. A. Deissler recognizes these clusters of praise:

vv. 1-2, introductory song	vv. 11-13, Kingdom of Yahweh
vv. 3-6, grandeur of Yahweh	vv. 14-20, Providential care
vv. 7-10, goodness of Yahweh	from Yahweh
	v. 21, Conclusion

In accord with ancient versions, the RSV adds an extra line at v. 13, where the Hebrew text is missing an entry for the letter *nun.* This addition, a refrain, is very similar to v. 17. The Qumran scroll from cave eleven places a refrain after each line: "Blessed be Yahweh, and blessed be his holy name, for ever and ever." This type of confusion and correction comes easily from liturgical or congregational use. The psalm is placed late in the postexilic age, not only because of the acrostic arrangement but also because the vocabulary is late Hebrew and there is a notable dependence on other psalms: *i.e.,* v. 1 on Pss 30:1; 25:1; v. 2b on Ps 34:2; v. 3a on Pss 48:1; 96:4; etc.

Psalm 146

I

¹Praise the Lord!
   Praise the Lord, O my soul!
²I will praise the Lord as long as I live;
   I will sing praises to my God while I have being.

II

3Put not your trust in princes,
in a son of man, in whom there is no help.
4When his breath departs he returns to his earth;
on that very day his plans perish.

III

5Happy is he whose help is the God of Jacob,
whose hope is in the Lord his God,

IV

6who made heaven and earth,
the sea, and all that is in them;
who keeps the faith for ever;
7 who executes justice for the oppressed;
who gives food to the hungry.

The Lord sets the prisoners free;
8 the Lord opens the eyes of the blind.
The Lord lifts up those who are bowed down;
the Lord loves the righteous.
9The Lord watches over the sojourners,
he upholds the widow and the fatherless;
but the way of the wicked he brings to ruin.

V

10The Lord will reign for ever,
thy God, O Zion, to all generations.
Praise the Lord!

We come to the final mini-collection within the Book of Psalms, a series of "Hallel" or praise psalms (Pss 146-150), similar to the "Egyptian Hallel" (Pss 113-118) and the "Great Hallel" (Ps 136). Pss 146-150 each begin and end with *Praise the Lord — Hallelujah!* This ensemble was to be sung in the daily morning service of the synagogue after Ps 145. Praise dominates these psalms. Ps 146, however, contains still other aspects, not only of thanksgiving but also of the more sober tradition of the sapiential movement (*i.e., do not put your trust in princes*, v. 3). As is commonly the case

in psalms composed in the late postexilic age, the anthological style of quoting and/or alluding to earlier psalms prevails here: v. 2 and Ps 104:33; v. 3 and Ps 118:9; v. 7 and Ps 103:6; v. 8b and Ps 145:14.
The psalm can be divided liturgically between:

vv. 1-2, the congregational call
   to praise
vv. 3-4, priestly exhortation

v. 5, Priestly blessing
vv. 6-9, Congregational Confession of faith
v. 10, Hymnic conclusion

Ps 146 breathes an elegant yet humble style. These adjectives do not cancel out each other. The psalm reaches majestically towards the one *who made heaven and earth* and introspectively into the depths of *my soul;* it praises the Lord generously *as long as I live...while I have being.* Ps 146 projects a pageant of divine action across this grandiose, four-dimensional panorama. At this point princes are put aside and attention is focused upon the oppressed and the hungry, prisoners and the blind, resident aliens (sojourners), widows and the orphan. In their company *the Lord reigns for ever.*

Psalm 147

I

¹Praise the Lord!
   For it is good to sing praises to our God;
   for he is gracious, and a song of praise is seemly.
²The Lord builds up Jerusalem;
   he gathers the outcasts of Israel.
³He heals the brokenhearted,
   and binds up their wounds.
⁴He determines the number of the stars,
   he gives to all of them their names.
⁵Great is our Lord, and abundant in power;
   his understanding is beyond measure.
⁶The Lord lifts up the downtrodden,
   he casts the wicked to the ground.

II

7Sing to the Lord with thanksgiving;
  make melody to our God upon the lyre!
8He covers the heavens with clouds,
  he prepares rain for the earth,
  he makes grass grow upon the hills.
9He gives to the beasts their food,
  and to the young ravens which cry.
10His delight is not in the strength of the horse,
  nor his pleasure in the legs of a man;
11but the Lord takes pleasure in those who fear him,
  in those who hope in his steadfast love.

III

12Praise the Lord, O Jerusalem!
  Praise your God, O Zion!
13For he strengthens the bars of your gates;
  he blesses your sons within you.
14He makes peace in your borders;
  he fills you with the finest of the wheat.
15He sends forth his command to the earth;
  his word runs swiftly.
16He gives snow like wool;
  he scatters hoarfrost like ashes.
17He casts forth his ice like morsels;
  who can stand before his cold?
18He sends forth his word, and melts them;
  he makes his wind blow, and the waters flow.
19He declares his word to Jacob,
  his statutes and ordinances to Israel.
20He has not dealt thus with any other nation;
  they do not know his ordinances.
  Praise the Lord!

(I-II) Within the Greek Septuagint, the Latin Vulgate and the early liturgical books, Ps 147 was divided into two psalms, called Ps 146 (= vv. 1-11) and Ps 147 (= vv. 12-20). It will be recalled that since Pss 9-10, which were considered a single psalm in the Greek and Latin traditions the Hebrew tended to be one ahead of the Greek-Latin in the enumeration of the psalms. With Ps 147 the three major ancient traditions finally harmonize again, so that Pss 148-150 are counted the same way in all traditions. See the introduction to Pss 9-10.

As a matter of fact, we detect *three*, quasi-independent hymns in Ps 147:

vv. 1-6, Yahweh, Lord of History for the redeemed people Israel;
vv. 7-11, Yahweh, Lord and Provider of Nature;
vv. 12-20, Yahweh, Lord of Zion through the creative word.

It is best to think of the three sections of Ps 147 as originally united in authorship and purpose. Throughout, the poet was influenced by Pss 33 and 104 and by Isa 40-55. The centering upon Zion in the third section locates the psalm within temple ritual. Because of attention to snow and water in the second and third parts, Ps 147 may belong to the feast of Tabernacles in Sept-Oct, almost at the end of the dry season when Israel prayed for rain and prepared for the winter months ahead. References to rebuilding Jerusalem occur in vv. 2 and 13; only here in the psalm the verbs are in the perfect or completed tense of the verb, indicating the work already completed. We are thinking, therefore, of a date sometime after 445 B.C. when Nehemiah dedicated the city walls (Neh 12:27-43).

(III) Vv. 1-6. In the first hymn, Yahweh gathers the outcasts and brokenhearted of Israel into the rebuilt city. The Lord who numbers, controls and directs the course of the stars (Isa 40:26; Bar 3:34) is also the Healer of Israel, as we read in Hos 6:1, "Come, let us return to the Lord; for he has torn, that he may heal us; he has stricken, and he will bind us up." This traditional prayer in Hosea was not to be said lightly or flippantly, for such "I have slain...by the words of my mouth" (Hos 6:4-6), but nonetheless Hosea was convinced that Yahweh was truly Israel's healer (Hos 11:3; 14:4). To number the stars not only meant that Yahweh was supreme over the gods worshipped by other nations, but also that Yahweh directed the seasons of the year.

Vv. 7-11. The second hymn extends our gaze across the universe still more enthusiastically, to the *heavens with clouds,* to wild animals whose *cry* for food is itself considered a prayer. Yet the Lord's major concern again narrows to the elect people Israel *who hope in his steadfast love* (Ps 71:14).

Vv. 12-20. The final hymn weaves together the life-giving force of water and the Lord's word. This heavenly nourishment is abundantly but also carefully bestowed at the proper time of season of the year. Yahweh's word, like rain and snow that come from the heavens, never returns empty but accomplishes the Lord's will (Isa 55:10-11). God's word, similar to the rain, does not remain in mid-sky to be admired but soaks the earth and reaches again towards heaven in very earthy forms of life. This fertile, powerful word has been entrusted to Israel, the Lord's chosen people. As Maillot-Lelièvre remark, the effects of the word, like rain, are universal, but the secret of love within the word is confided to Israel.

(IV) The same cycle of the word is seen again in Jesus, the Word Incarnate who dwells among us. This divine word comes from the heavenly throne and manifests among us the glory of the godhead (John 1:14), and shows us the way to return along the same path to the eternal bosom of God's love (John 14:6).

Psalm 148

I

¹Praise the Lord!
  Praise the Lord from the heavens,
  praise him in the heights!
²Praise him, all his angels,
  praise him, all his host!

³Praise him, sun and moon,
  praise him, all you shining stars!

⁴Praise him, you highest heavens,
and you waters above the heavens!

⁵Let them praise the name of the Lord!
For he commanded and they were created.
⁶And he established them for ever and ever;
he fixed their bounds which cannot be passed.

II

⁷Praise the Lord from the earth,
you sea monsters and all deeps,
⁸fire and hail, snow and frost,
stormy wind fulfilling his command!

⁹Mountains and all hills,
fruit trees and all cedars!
¹⁰Beasts and all cattle,
creeping things and flying birds!

¹¹Kings of the earth and all peoples,
princes and all rulers of the earth!
¹²Young men and maidens together,
old men and children!

¹³Let them praise the name of the Lord,
for his name alone is exalted;
his glory is above earth and heaven.

III

¹⁴He has raised up a horn for his people,
praise for all his saints,
for the people of Israel who are near to him.
Praise the Lord!

(I-II) As in Ps 19, the liturgical action of praise is first orchestrated in the heavenly world (vv. 1-6) and then in the earthly sphere (vv. 7-13). The conclusion promises strength and peace (v. 14). The universe constitutes the sacred place for worshipping the Lord. Almost the entire psalm is a call to praise. Motivation is quickly provided in vv. 5b and 13b, introduced in each case by the particle *ki* or "indeed!" Ps 148 remains within a long tradition. Its earliest roots reach back into the hymns of ancient Egypt and Mesopotamia; these, in turn, were continued in such biblical passages as Pss 33, 103, and 104; Job 38; Jer 5:22; 31:13. Ps 148 itself influenced the Song of the Three Young Men in the fiery furnace (Dan 3:52-90; RSV vv. 28-68). We must date Ps 148 at least before the composition of Daniel (167-164 B.C.). A date around 350 would seem closest to the truth.

(III) Vv. 1-6 remind us of the heavenly council as depicted in such places as Pss 2; 8; 29; 82. Various levels of the heavenly sphere were described more carefully in later Jewish literature, but already three were distinguished in Babylon, seven or nine in Greece. St. Paul in 2 Cor 12:2 speaks of being "caught up to the third heaven." The power of the creative word rings out in v. 5. Israel's and our own obedience to this word will produce the lavish prosperity which God provides across the heavens.

Vv. 7-13 direct our gaze to planet earth. Even sea monsters, the object of fearful battles in Pss 74:13; 89:9-10; Isa 51:9-10, are now tamed into Yahweh's obedient and worshipping creatures.

V. 14, the conclusion, announces strength and continuity for the people Israel (*cf.,* Ps 89:24; 132:17). The imagery, once reserved for royalty, is now bestowed upon priest and people in the postexilic age (*cf.,* Zech 6:9-14; Isa 55:3).

(IV) We live in a world, highly charged with wonder and praise. Before we awaken each day, the universe is already calling us to worship. God like the father of the prodigal son is already seeking us from afar (Luke 15:20). Enthroned above the universe is Jesus; "in him all things were created, in heaven and on earth, visible and invisible, whether thrones or dominions or principalities or authorities." He has come "to reconcile to himself all things, whether on earth or in heaven, making peace by the blood of his cross" (Col 1:16, 20). Like the seer of Patmos who composed the Book of Revelation (Rev 1:9) we too hear "every creature in heaven and on earth and under the earth and in the sea, and all therein, saying, 'To him who sits upon the throne and to

the Lamb be blessing and honor and glory and might for
ever and ever!'" (Rev 5:13).

Psalm 149

I-a

¹Praise the Lord!
 Sing to the Lord a new song,
 his praise in the assembly of the faithful!
²Let Israel be glad in his Maker,
 let the sons of Zion rejoice in their King!
³Let them praise his name with dancing,
 making melody to him with timbrel and lyre!

-b-

⁴For the Lord takes pleasure in his people;
 he adorns the humble with victory.

II-a

⁵Let the faithful exult in glory;
 let them sing for joy on their couches.
⁶Let the high praises of God be in their throats
 and two-edged swords in their hands,

-b-

⁷to wreak vengeance on the nations
 and chastisement on the peoples,
⁸to bind their kings with chains
 and their nobles with fetters of iron,
⁹to execute on them the judgment written!
 This is glory for all his faithful ones.
 Praise the Lord!

(I) A magnificent victory song, Ps 149 may be understood
by attending to its canonical place in the Psalter. Ps 149 is
sandwiched between a hymn of cosmic wonder (Ps 148) and
a hymn of liturgical glory (Ps 150), with "ritual" action
either across the universe (Ps 148) or within the temple (Ps
150). Ps 148 announces the wonder of the Lord's presence
across the heaven and earth for the sake of Israel, the Lord's

chosen people. Ps 149 realistically recognizes, again in praise, that such wonder is possible only after strenuous battle. This dark side of the cloud, lowering over the earth, reverses the glorious pageant of light on the other side facing the sun; such is the case with Gen 3's story of rebellion after Gen 2's account of the first, peaceful paradise, or with Ps 19B's recognition of sin after the glorious paean of praise in Ps 19A. Perhaps closer to our situation here, Deut 7 combines the most tender expressions of God's election of Israel ("because the Lord loves you," v. 8) with the harshest terms of the *herem* or extermination war ("you must utterly destroy them," the nations, v. 2). The military summons in Ps 149 may represent a rhetorical, exaggerated (albeit, dangerous and at times realistic) song of victory. It partakes of the eschatological wars announced in Ezek 38-39, of the collapse of heaven and earth in preparation for the new age in Isaiah, chaps. 24-27 or 65-66. It draws upon early memories of Israel's victories in the days of Moses and David, only to transform these into a prophetic scene of victory for the poor and needy (*cf.,* Isa chap. 1). Rather than attempt to explain or justify these military odes, it is better to hear them in the context of ancient times, especially when those times were sustained in hope only by eschatological dreams of the final victory. Unfortunately victory songs like Ps 149 were sung by Christians as they marched against other Christians (see Ps 68, section IV of commentary).

Because the psalm draws upon Isa 40-55 of the time of the exile and upon Isa 56-66 of the postexilic period and because it resonates the spirit of such literature as Zech 9-14 and Obadiah, Ps 149 is to be dated in the postexilic age, perhaps around 300 B.C.

(II) Ps 149 is divided into two sections:

vv. 1-4, a call to praise (vv. 1-3) with motivation from the Lord's care for the needy (v. 4);
vv. 5-9, a new call to praise in the sound of battle (vv. 5-6) with motivation in the victorious results (vv. 7-9).

(III) One of the strongest arguments for a Maccabean date of any psalm (that is, after 164 B.C.) occurs in vv. 1-2. The references to *the assembly of the faithful* does not occur elsewhere in the Hebrew Bible, yet its Greek equivalent is found in 1 Macc 2:42, "company of Hasideans," who united themselves temporarily with the Maccabean guerrilla band. The word, "Hasideans," is a transliteration of the word, "faithful," in Ps 149. Yet we need not conclude that the phrase never existed before the Maccabean period. The *new song* in v. 1 recalls Isa 42:10 or the more theological expression in Isa 48:6-7, "From this time forth I make you hear *new* things, *hidden* things which you have not known. They are created *now,* not long ago . . . " This song is intoned *on their couches*, perhaps referring to prayer mats (A. A. Anderson) that were taken into the temple for all night vigils (*cf.,* Amos 2:8; Pss 7 and 17), or an allusion to the position taken for eating a sacred meal at which songs were sung (Matt 26:30). The *two-edged sword* in v. 6 is difficult to explain: literally, "sword or double mouths," with a similar expression in Isa 41:15 where the word, "double mouths," refers to the sharp biting teeth of the threshing sledge. Metaphorically the word is picked up in Prov 5:4 (?); Sir 21:3; Heb 4:12; Rev 1:16; 2:12. Thus it has a firm place in the New Testament, for the fierce justice of God's word. In its final verse, Ps 149 refers to the heavenly book: *cf.,* Pss 69:28; 139:16.

(IV) The vindictive or war psalms were discussed in connection with Pss 68 and 69; other aspects, in association with the Davidic psalms (*i.e.,* Ps 2) and the Zion psalms (*i.e.,* Ps 46).

Psalm 150

[1]Praise the Lord!
   Praise him in his sanctuary;
   praise him in his mighty firmament!
[2]Praise him for his mighty deeds;
   praise him according to his exceeding greatness!

[3]Praise him with trumpet sound;

praise him with lute and harp!
4Praise him with timbrel and dance;
praise him with strings and pipe!
5Praise him with sounding cymbals;
praise him with loud clashing cymbals!
6Let everything that breaths praise the Lord!
Praise the Lord!

(I-II) The Book of Psalms was introduced by a greeting and warning from the sapiential movement in Ps 1, by a greeting and enthronement for Davidic kings in Ps 2. Immediately afterwards, there occurs the first and major collection of Psalms of David (Pss 3-41), marked principally by anguish and prayer for help. Now at the end the Psalter concludes with overwhelming praise. The final word of the entire Psalter is Hallelujah! Just as the other four books within the Psalter concluded with a solemn doxology (Pss 41:13; 72:18-19[20]; 89:52; 106:48), the curtain is rung down on the entire Book of Psalms with a super-solemn call to praise, an entire Ps 150. It is even possible that Pss 146-150 were intended as the majestic closing (see the introduction to Ps 146). Counting the number of Hallelujah's in Ps 150 tempts rabbis and scholars to intriguing parallels. There are ten Hallelujah's within the body of the psalm (vv. 2-5), honoring the ten words of creation in Gen 1 or the ten words of the decalogue in Exod 20 and Deut 5; if we include v. 6 plus the opening and concluding *Praise the Lord,* we arrive at the number thirteen, corresponding to the thirteen titles or attributes for Yahweh in the great revelation to Moses on Mount Sinai (Exod 34:6-7). Different from other hymns of praise, Ps 150 consists entirely of a call to adoration; no lines are reserved for motivation. In this regard it is close to Ps 148. The psalm was composed around 300 B.C.

(III) In v. 1 the two magnificent temples of the Lord's presence become the center of our praise: the one above the celestial waters, the other at Jerusalem. Heaven and earth reflect one another. The Lord's throne room above the celestial waters is seen in Pss 29 and 148:4. When Israel responds obediently and lovingly to the will of God, these heavenly waters remain in place, but if Israel disobeys, they come roaring down upon earth in chaotic floods and mammoth destruction (Gen 7:11; Ps 107: 23-28). Such dangers, however, are distant from the mind of the psalmist at this point. Heaven and earth joyously unite in the temple and therefore in the people Israel. The *mighty deeds* in v. 2 refer to the extraordinary way by which Yahweh directs world history and the cosmic family of animate and inanimate beings to the benefit of the chosen people (*cf.,* Deut 3:24). Within vv. 3-5 all the "eager longing" and "inward groaning" of the universe (*cf.,* Rom 8:19, 23) are orchestrated in harmonious temple praise by means of all sorts of musical instruments: trumpet (Pss 47:5; 98:6), lute (Ps 33:2), harp (Ps 98:5), strings (Ps 45:8) and pipe (Gen 4:21; Job 21:12; 30:31), resounding and clashing cymbals (2 Sam 6:5; 1 Chron 13:8). It is interesting to note that strings and especially pipes were not normally found in temple celebrations; in fact, the pipe was invented by Jubal of the corrupt line of Cain (Gen 4:17-24). We suspect that Ps 150 glories in a redeemed universe where everything and everyone are again rejoicing innocently and exultantly within a new paradise. Such seems to be the thought of v. 6 where *everything that breathes,* that pulses with the rhythm of life in the universe, is resonating the glorious presence of the Lord.

(IV) We are called upon to echo the same innocent joy and wondrous praise. We are to address "one another in psalms and hymns and spiritual songs, singing and making melody to the Lord with all your heart, always and for everything giving thanks in the name of our Lord Jesus Christ to God the Father" (Eph 5:19-20).

The Stuttgart edition of the Hebrew Bible, following the tradition of a Theodulphian manuscript and Jerome, add at the end: "The Psalter is complete; there are 2,527 verses." Every verse, indeed as we realized with Ps 119, every word and every letter of each word, possesses a sacred character which can transform our lives into songs of praise and gratitude, eternally, for God.

BIBLIOGRAPHY

I) Recommended Popular Commentaries

Anderson, A. A., *The Book of Psalms.* New Century Bible, 2 vols. (London: Oliphants, 1972; Grand Rapids: Eerdmans, 1981). Particularly valuable for meaning and impact of important Hebrew words. Knowledge of Hebrew not required.

Botz P., *Runways to God. The Psalms as Prayer* (Collegeville, Minn: Liturgical Press, 1979). Written from the viewpoint of the New Testament, liturgical readings and a strong spirituality for today.

MacKenzie, R. A. F., *The Psalms.* Old Testament Reading Guide, n. 23 (Collegeville, Minn.: Liturgical Press, 1967). Short commentary on select psalms. Excellent insights.

Murphy, R. E., "Psalms," *Jerome Biblical Commentary* (Englewood Cliffs, N.J.: Prentice-Hall, 1968) ch. 35. After quick orientation to each psalm for literary form and structure, key words or ideas are explained.

Rogerson, J. W., & McKay, J. W., *Psalms.* The Cambridge Bible Commentary on the New English Bible. 3 vols. (London, New York, Melbourne: Cambridge University Press, 1977). An introduction to the ancient setting and literary form precedes the text of each psalm; then important words or phrases are clarified.

223

Sabourin, L., *The Psalms. Their Origin and Meaning.* 2 ed. (New York: Alba House, 1974). First a long introduction on the external features, original setting and theology of the psalms; then, each psalm is presented according to literary form and scholarly consensus of opinion.

Weiser, A., *The Psalms. A Commentary* (Philadelphia: Westminster Press, & London: SCM Press, 1962). Perhaps the fullest English language commentary, with a new translation and an exposition that weaves together the ancient meaning with contemporary impact.

II) Principal Sources for this Commentary

Beaucamp, E., *Le Psautier.* Sources Bibliques. 2 vols. (Paris: Gabalta, 1976, '79). Exceptionally valuable for the canonical structure of the psalms and for key words frequently repeated in the psalter.

Briggs, C. A., & Briggs, E. G., *A Critical and Exegetical Commentary on the Book of Psalms.* 2 vols. (Edinburgh: Clark, 1906). An older classic, written before the stress upon literary form, stressing philology and textual scholarship.

Dahood, M., *Psalms.* Anchor Bible. 3 vols. (Garden City, N.J.: Doubleday, 1966, '68, '70). A commentary for scholars, exclusively from the background of the Ugaritic or ancient North West Semitic language. Brilliant insights.

Deissler, A., *Die Psalmen.* 2 vols. (Dusseldorf: 1963, '64; 2 ed., 1977); French translation, *Le Livre des Psaumes.* 2 vols. (Paris: 1966, '68). Each psalm is divided in this study according to a fourfold system similar to our own; New Testament parallels & implications.

Jacquet, L., *Les Psaumes et le Coeur de l'homme.* 2 vols. Pss 1-41, 42-100 (Duculot: 1975, '77). Best all-round commentary in any language, a lifelong undertaking, exceptionally rich and comprehensive. Includes translation, general presentation, textual notes, exegesis, Christian and liturgical utilization, appendices for modern writers.

Kraus, H.-J., *Psalmen.* Biblischer Kommentar AT, I5, 2 vols., 4 ed. (Neukirchen: 1971). Second best all-round commmentary, presenting each psalm according to text & translation, literary form, role in Israel's life & worship, principal words, religious application.

Maillot, A., et Lelièvre, A., *Les Psaumes.* 3 vols.(Genieve: Labor et Fides: 1961, '66, '69). Rich insights into the religious meaning of the psalms. Includes a new translation and clear critical notes.

Mowinckel, S., *The Psalms in Israel's Worship* (Nashville: Abingdon, 1967; Oxford: Blackwell, 1962). Classic work on the relation of the psalms with Israel's ancient forms of worship.

Tournay, R., et Schwab, R., *Les Psaumes* (ed. 2; Paris: 1955) — remains one of the most comprehensive and enduring introductions; excellent scholarly and religious perceptions.

III) Other References

Alonso, Schokel, L., "The Poetic Structure of Psalm 42-43," *Journal for the Study of the Old Testament* 1 (1976) 4-11.

Brillet, Gaston, *Meditations on the Old Testament.* The Psalms. New York: Desclee, 1960.

Clifford, R. J., "Psalm 89: A Lament over the Davidic Ruler's Continued Failure," *Harvard Theological Review* 73 (1980).

_____, "In Zion and David a New Beginning: An Interpretation of Psalm 78," *Traditions in Transformation,* Festschrift F. M. Cross, Winona Lake, In.: Eisenbrauns, 1981.

Dalglish, E. R., *Psalm Fifty-One in the Light of Ancient Near Eastern Patternism.* Leiden: Brill, 1962.

Delitzsch, F., *Biblical Commentary on the Psalms.* London: 1887.

Desnoyers, L., *Les Psaumes. Traduction rythmée d'apres l'Hebreu.* Paris: 1935.

Dumortier, J. B., "Un Rituel D'Intronisation: Le Ps. LXXXIX 2-38," *Vetus Testamentum* 22 (1972) 176-196.

Fishbane, M., *Text and Texture.* New York: Schocken Books, 1979.

Holman, J., "The Structure of Psalm CXXXIX," *Vetus Testamentum* 21 (1971) 298-310.

Kenik, H. A., "Code of Conduct for a King: Psalm 101," *Journal of Biblical Literature* 95 (1976) 391-403.

Roberts, J. J., *The Old Testament Text and Versions.* Cardiff: University of Wales Press, 1951.

Sanders, J. A., *The Dead Sea Psalms Scroll.* Ithaca, N.Y.: Cornell University Press, 1967.

Shepherd, Jr., Massey H., *The Psalms in Christian Worship.* Collegeville, Minn.: Liturgical Press, 1976.

Tsevat, Matitiahu, *A Study of the Language of the Biblical Psalms.* Journal of Biblical Literature Monograph Series, IX. Philadelphia: 1955.